Chris Hu..9 at sixteen. He was commissioned from Sandhurst at twenty-one and later qualified as a counter-terrorist bomb-disposal operator. He served with a number of specialist counter-terrorism units and during his career deployed to numerous operational theatres.

For his actions during his Iraq tour he was awarded the Queen's Gallantry Medal by HM Queen Elizabeth II.

Also by Chris Hunter

EIGHT LIVES DOWN

and published by Corgi Books

EXTREME RISK

A Life Fighting the Bombmakers

CHRIS HUNTER

CORGI BOOKS

TRANSWORLD PUBLISHERS
61–63 Uxbridge Road, London W5 5SA
A Random House Group Company
www.rbooks.co.uk

EXTREME RISK
A CORGI BOOK: 9780552157599

First published in Great Britain
in 2010 by Bantam Press
an imprint of Transworld Publishers
Corgi edition published 2011

Addresses for Random House Group Ltd companies outside the UK
can be found at: www.randomhouse.co.uk
The Random House Group Ltd Reg. No. 954009

The Random House Group Limited supports The Forest Stewardship Council
(FSC), the leading international forest certification organisation. All our titles
that are printed on Greenpeace approved FSC certified paper carry the FSC
logo. Our paper procurement policy can be found at
www.rbooks.co.uk/environment

Mixed Sources
Product group from well-managed
forests and other controlled sources
www.fsc.org Cert no. TT-COC-2139
© 1996 Forest Stewardship Council

Typeset in 11.75/16.25pt Electra by Falcon Oast Graphic Art Ltd.
Printed in the UK by CPI Cox & Wyman, Reading, RG1 8EX.

2 4 6 8 10 9 7 5 3 1

For Jimmy, Galeano, Chris, Gaz, Daniel, Oz and Dan,
whose time and luck ran out

Acknowledgements

I am indebted to my editor, Bill Scott-Kerr, for his friendship, patience and saint-like perseverance, and to all the staff at Transworld, without whom this book would not have been possible. There are so many of you to whom I owe a huge debt of gratitude, but I would like to thank the following in particular for their unstinting support: Katrina Whone, Stephen Mulcahey, Phil Lord, Patsy Irwin, Madeline Toy, Sheila Lee, Kate Tolley, Sophie Holmes, Janine Giovanni and Larry Finlay. Once again, your encouragement and enthusiasm has been truly inspirational and I am grateful to you all.

My special thanks go to Mark Lucas, my friend and literary agent. For the long nights you spent working with me on *Extreme Risk*, and for your guidance, wisdom and dogged perseverance, I am truly grateful. Without your encouragement and support I know this book would not have made it to print. You are a very special person, as is Mindy, and from the bottom of my heart I thank you both; you've been an inspiration to me on so many levels.

I am also indebted to Mark's colleagues at LAW, especially to Alice Saunders for her characteristically stoic support, and to my children's fiction agent, Philippa Milnes-Smith. Thanks also to Richard Foreman for the brilliant work you continue to do, and also to Olga Tramontin and Geoff Thatcher for the months of painstaking research you put into this book. My thanks go to a select group of authors who never cease to amaze and enthuse me with their inspirational writing and authorial mastership: Steve Cole, Gerald Seymour, Colonel Richard Kemp CBE, and Patrick Mercer OBE MP; working with you all continues to be an inimitably enjoyable experience.

I would also like to thank the Ministry of Defence for its invaluable advice and assistance, particularly the team at the Public Relations (Army) Directorate as well as my former colleagues at the Defence Intelligence Staff and across the Ammunition Technical Officer community. I am truly grateful for your judicious advice and for your provision of the necessary checks and balances to ensure I didn't inadvertently write something that could compromise the safety of our servicemen and women.

Finally, my very special thanks must go to the soldiers with whom I worked, for allowing me to tell their stories. Many of you cannot be named for obvious reasons, but you know who you are. For the sacrifices you've made, your devotion to duty and your enduring professionalism I have nothing but respect and admiration, for you and your wonderful families. Serving with you has been an honour and a privilege and was without doubt the most enjoyable part of a very special career.

I have described the events in this book as I experienced them at the time, but for reasons of security, certain names, places, tactics, techniques, equipment and procedures have been changed. In all cases, the views expressed are mine alone and may not necessarily reflect official British Ministry of Defence or government policy, or that of foreign countries.

CROATIA, BOSNIA & HERZEGOVINA

Europe

CROATIA,
BOSNIA &
HERZEGOVINA

Africa

Varazdin   Cakovec
Krapina   Koprivnica
ZAGREB   Bjelovar
            Virovitica

CROATIA

Rijeka   Karlovac   Sisak   Pozega   Osijek
                                Slavonski
                                Brod   Vukovar

                Prijedor
Bihac   Lipak
            Banja Luka
        Republika Srpska   Tuzla
BOSNIA   SERBIA
AND   Srebrenica
Zadar # HERZEGOVINA
                SARAJEVO
        Rumboci   Mt Igman △   Gorazde
Sibenik   Lipa   *Lake*
                   Prozor
Split

                        Republika
                        Srpska

A d r i a t i c   MONTENEGRO

              S e a

                Dubrovnik

ITALY

MAP KEY

⊡ National capital

○ Other cities

N

0   miles   50

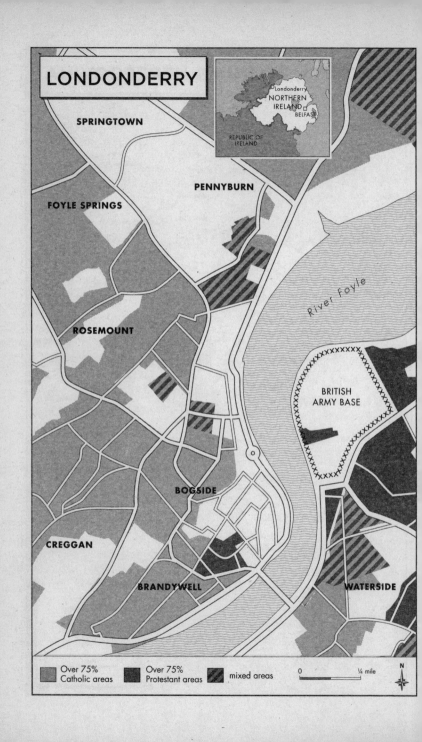

LONDONDERRY

SPRINGTOWN

PENNYBURN

FOYLE SPRINGS

ROSEMOUNT

River Foyle

BRITISH ARMY BASE

BOGSIDE

CREGGAN

BRANDYWELL

WATERSIDE

Londonderry
NORTHERN IRELAND
BELFAST
REPUBLIC OF IRELAND

Over 75% Catholic areas
Over 75% Protestant areas
mixed areas

0   ¼ mile

N

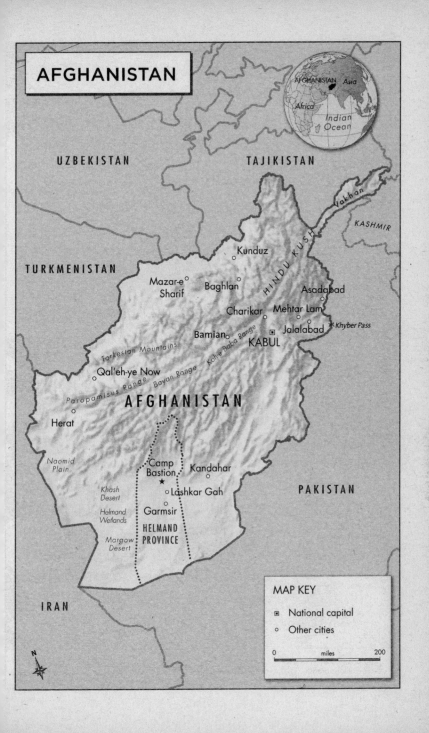

AFGHANISTAN

UZBEKISTAN

TAJIKISTAN

AFGHANISTAN Asia

Africa

Indian
Ocean

TURKMENISTAN

Yakhan

KASHMIR

Kunduz

Mazar-e
Sharif

Baghlan

Asadabad

HINDU KUSH

Charikar

Mehtar Lam

Bamian

Koh-e Baba Range

Jalalabad

Khyber Pass

KABUL

Torkestan Mountains

Qal'eh-ye Now

Paropamisus Range

Bayan Range

AFGHANISTAN

Herat

Naomid
Plain

Camp
Bastion

Kandahar

Khash
Desert

Lashkar Gah

Helmand
Wetlands

Garmsir

Margow
Desert

HELMAND
PROVINCE

PAKISTAN

IRAN

N

MAP KEY

▣ National capital

○ Other cities

0   miles   200

Prologue

When you gaze long into the abyss, the abyss also gazes into you.

Friedrich Nietzsche

23 February 1993

'We're here.'

I open the door and step out onto a glistening river of glass, a trail of broken bottles and smashed windscreens from the row of burnt-out cars that line the road.

'Don't look at anybody, and don't speak to anybody.' Tim removes a cosh from the dashboard. 'You might think you can handle yourself, but you won't last five minutes here. Keep your mouth shut and don't fuck about.'

The last time I saw my brother was a little over two years ago – the night he excommunicated himself from our family and broke my mother's heart. I'm shocked by how much he's changed: we're strangers now.

The drab grey tower blocks that surround us are

identical to the ones I've seen on the news reports from Sarajevo. Most look empty, their windows boarded up or broken, and street gangs congregate outside them in what were once children's play areas. The hopscotch marks have long since been obscured by dog shit and hypodermic needles.

There's a grocery on the far side of the road, the only shop that's still trading on the estate. Steel bars and a metal roller-shutter are poised to greet any ram-raider who gets beyond the concrete bollards. Spots of chewing gum pepper the pavement around its entrance like acne.

We pass a group of teenage girls drinking White Lightning in the dull glow of the street lamps. It must be the only thing that stops them dying of exposure.

'What you lookin' at, you fuckin' spastic?'

For some reason Tim has left his calliper and brace behind, emphasizing his curious crab-like limp, caused by the brain injury he sustained in a needless car accident some years ago. It must have seemed like a good idea at the time: the whole crew had been out for lunchtime drinks and on the way back he'd seen one of his mates mooning out of the leading car. He'd decided to copy him – which was fine, until the driver hit a bump in the road and Tim was flung out, smashing the back of his head as he landed. He stopped breathing for three minutes.

He avoids eye contact and limps on, but I know he's raging inside; we both are.

We reach the entrance to the flats. The inhabitants have chucked their rubbish into the communal garden. There's not a bin or a black bag in sight. The garden is a foot deep in used condoms, glue bags, lighter-gas canisters, and raw, untreated shit.

The stench turns my stomach.

I make for the lift.

Tim shakes his head. 'It doesn't work.'

Rave music blasts out of a flat at the top of the stair-well. The whole place reeks of stale piss. The cream paint on the walls has turned several shades of brown and rust peels off the railings. Used tin-foil wraps, discarded bongs and yet more hypodermic needles carpet almost every step.

As we make our way onto the fourth floor, another group of mutants emerges from the shadows. One of them starts to wheel his arms and scream obscenities at us. 'What you lookin' at, you fucking wang'a?'

I remember Tim's advice and break eye contact. As I do so, I notice him reach inside his jacket for the cosh.

The hairs on the back of my neck stand on end – the feeling you get just before things are about to kick off. But the yobs continue past us and head down the stairs in search of easier prey.

As we enter the flat, we're assaulted by the sickly

sweet smell of cannabis, cigarette smoke and White Lightning. A glass coffee-table loaded with ashtrays and drug-making paraphernalia stands between the settee and an empty television cabinet. A pair of plastic garden chairs sits on the left-hand side of the fireplace. Bob Marley blasts out from a stereo system behind them.

The walls are covered with graffiti, but the place is bare. There are no pictures, no books and no television; the only ornaments are the myriad used needles and burnt spoons. Two boys – neither of them a day older than sixteen – sit on a sideboard, drinking cider from old Pot Noodle containers, and half a dozen starry-eyed junkies stir from various stages of intoxication and begin mauling Tim like zoo animals at feeding time.

A rough-looking female emerges from the kitchen, wearing faded jeans and a black bomber-jacket. She flashes us a smile like a witch-doctor's necklace. 'Hello, darlin'.' She stumbles forward and throws her arms around my brother. She's one of his dealers, and she's absolutely banged off her tits.

She grabs me by the hand. 'Come with me, handsome . . . Let's get you a nice drink.'

The kitchen is just like the rest. There's no cooker, no fridge, no washing-machine; just a kettle and a shit-load of rubbish.

In the minute or so it takes me to escape back to the lounge, Tim has cleared a space on the coffee-table and stuck three king-size Rizlas together. He sprinkles the tobacco from two Marlboro Reds and crumbles some dope onto the paper cradle. He lights the spliff and inhales deeply. 'Wanna shot?'

'No thanks.' I excuse myself and head for the toilet, where the two kids from the sideboard are now hitting the gas big-time. One cradles the canister in his hands and sprays pure butane into his mouth. Moments later, he's lying on the floor, fucked out of his head.

Back in the living room, Tim's dealer and several of her junkie mates are preparing foil and a tooting tube. It's what smackheads call 'chasing the dragon'.

The tension crackles between us on the way back to Lewes. He tells me he doesn't want to see me again after today. I can't believe his life has come to this.

To avoid further conversation, he switches on the radio. The newsreader announces that a massive bomb, concealed inside a rented van, has exploded in a car park directly beneath New York's World Trade Center. More than a thousand people have been injured in the blast.

I look into his sensitive, intelligent, fucked-up face and see his eyes start to fill with tears.

1

9 February 1994

The ice-cold water freezes me to the core. I grip my rifle tightly, but I can't feel a thing. I've lost all sensation in my hands and feet. We've been lying in this shallow grave for three hours, paralysed by the freezing rain and remorseless wind. My body's beginning to cramp up and my tongue's starting to swell. Pretty soon my hearing and sight will go, and then the hallucinations will kick in. After that I'm proper-fucked.

'This place is colder than a mother-in-law's kiss.' Duncan slurs his words and tries to force a smile as he lies shivering beside me. Our platoon has spent all night, shoulder to shoulder, in this ambush position on Sandhurst's 900-acre training area. Duncan's attempts at humour are all that's kept me going. Yesterday he even brought a smile to the face of our instructor.

21

'Hurry up, Mr Stone,' Colour Sergeant Maclaren bellowed. 'My dead mother could dig that hole faster than you!'

Quick as a flash, Duncan replied, 'Only 'cos she's got a six-foot start, Colour Sergeant.'

Anybody else would have had his head ripped off, but Duncan, with his cut-glass accent and Oxford education, could charm the knickers off a nun.

I try to think of something funny to say back to him, but I'm no comedian at the best of times and right now my face is frozen solid.

I shake my head and, not for the first time, ask myself why I'm putting myself through forty-four weeks of gruelling hardship, humiliation and pain. As we lie here on this barren hillside, barely able to keep our eyes open, I feel myself falling deeper and deeper into a zombie-like trance. I don't know how much longer I'm going to last.

Then, in the gully beneath us, a dozen or so moonlit targets rise up from the undergrowth, each one illuminated just enough for us to make out the image of a Soviet soldier. It's our signal to initiate the ambush.

I feel a surge of adrenalin course through my veins. I feel my body coming back to life. This is it. We're on.

But my excitement is short-lived. Instead of a hail of gunfire, there's total silence.

Rich Burrows has landed tonight's 'platoon

commander' appointment, but he's not reacted. And his acting platoon sergeant, Ben Pierce, hasn't uttered a word either. They must both have fallen asleep.

There's the dull thud of a boot connecting with a helmet. 'Mr Fucking Burrows,' Colour Sergeant Maclaren rasps, 'feel free to start shooting whenever you're ready.'

Within seconds the air is pulsating with gunfire – a few loud pops and cracks, then a roaring barrage.

I disengage the safety catch of my SA80 assault rifle, thrust it tightly into my shoulder and position the leaf of my sight on the central mass of a target. As I squeeze the trigger, the force of the bullet coming out of the muzzle pulls me forward, then kicks me back with every shot.

Tracer rounds are punching through the Soviets and ricocheting off the rocky ground behind them. The volume of fire is awesome. The air fills with soil and smoke.

To my left, a light support weapon unleashes a deadly burst of automatic fire into the killing area. I change magazines and carry on, thinking of the damage that each round must do to a body as it comes to the end of its 900-metre-per-second flight. I wonder what it must be like to be on the receiving end. We're told the only way to repel an ambush is to defy logic and face fire with fire . . . to fight back, with complete and total aggression. Jesus . . .

Minutes later, Rich Burrows gives three long blasts on his whistle. The firing subsides, and he begins barking instructions. The clearance parties are ordered down into the gully to search the enemy 'bodies' as the cut-off teams watch out for 'squirters' – enemy survivors attempting to escape the ambush site.

Even if they were a real enemy, they'd never have survived. The scene beneath us is truly apocalyptic. The bottom of the gully has been completely decimated.

Moments later the platoon has lifted off. Now we're moving at speed, through a wood and along one of the hundreds of muddy dirt-tracks that cross the windswept landscape. Each of us runs in silence, resolute and dogged, locked in our own thoughts as we head towards the extraction point – a small clearing on the edge of a lake.

I look at the other members of my platoon and see the pain and fatigue etched on their faces. Each of us is carrying webbing, a rifle and a forty-five-pound pack loaded with combat equipment, rations and ammunition. And we're in tatters.

Soldiering is dirty, unpleasant and brutal work, and training exercises are no exception. We're cold, wet, tired and miserable and yet there's not a single man who'd contemplate jacking it in.

Except me.

We've been constantly reminded that as officers in the British Army we'll be deploying on dangerous operations and giving orders that will put all our lives at risk. That we'll need to lead our men fearlessly and from the front. There's a great deal expected of us. But to operate like this, for long periods of time under such extreme conditions, takes a certain type of person – and I still question whether I'm up to the task. Eighty-five per cent of the cadets here hold a university degree and half have a public-school education. I have neither. I went to a flick-knife comprehensive and joined the Army as an enlisted soldier at sixteen with few hopes and limited prospects. Fortunately, we've got one of the best platoons in the Academy – where every man pulls his weight and attacks whatever's thrown at him with absolute professionalism and determination. It certainly makes leadership a whole lot easier when you're working with motivated people, and these guys are the real deal.

Unfortunately Colour Sergeant Maclaren doesn't appear to share my sentiments. He's the archetypal Sandhurst instructor: a consummate professional, sharp, immaculately turned out, with masses of operational experience. But, like generations of instructors before him, on first appearance he comes across as a complete megalomaniac with a not particularly mild form of Tourette's. I remember the apocryphal tale of the young cadet forgetting to remove his beret as he entered the hallowed memorial chapel at his first families' 'church parade'. His sergeant major is said to have flashed him an icy death-stare and bellowed, 'Take your hat off in the house of the Lord, you cunt.'

As we move into the extraction point and begin taking up fire positions, the colour sergeant calls Rich Burrows and Ben Pierce over for a debrief. 'What happened back there, gentlemen? You took so long to initiate that ambush I thought you were waiting for the fucking UN to sort it out.'

His tone sounds jovial enough, but Rich gets defensive and dredges up some crap excuse about waiting for the optimum moment to strike.

The colour sergeant's face darkens. 'You were fast-a-fucking-sleep, Mr Burrows. That was the worst ambush I've ever seen. And as for a stealthy extraction, you made more noise than a skeleton wanking in a biscuit tin. You need to start thinking like men of action and acting like men of thought.' He goes on to mutter something about the two of them belonging in a 'fucking brassière' – presumably because he thinks they're a pair of tits.

To our amazement, Rich decides to gob off again instead of taking it on the chin. 'I'm sorry, Colour Sergeant, but I disagree. You're wrong!'

The colour sergeant's expression turns chillier than

the prevailing wind. Rich's outburst is a mistake that we're all now going to pay for. 'I've only ever been wrong once, Mr Burrows,' he says, 'and that's when I thought I was wrong but was actually mistaken. So don't question me, and definitely don't cross me. Because if you do, I'll fucking nail you to it.'

He then announces that the helicopter due to extract us has suffered a mysterious mechanical failure, and we're going to have to do a ten-mile forced march back to base – another of the long line of tests designed to push us over the edge.

Hungry and wet, our platoon closes into Rich, who briefs us on the route we're going to be taking back to camp. The blokes are half listening as they desperately try to strip away any unnecessary layers of clothing. It's going to be at least a ten-miler.

'This weather's outrageous,' Al Murray says – and he's one of the most resilient blokes I've ever met.

'Stop whingeing, Mr Murray,' Colour Sergeant Maclaren retorts. 'Rain is merely sunshine . . . in liquid form.' And with that he sets off at full racing-pace across the training area.

We've covered less than a mile and my lungs feel like they're going to explode. My soles and heels are starting to blister as they rub against my sodden boots and every inch of my body is in shreds. I'm praying for the moment the adrenalin and endorphins start to kick in . . . for anything that will numb the pain.

As we emerge from another coniferous wood at the edge of a row of electricity pylons, Colour Sergeant Maclaren points to a nearby hill. 'OK, gentlemen, dump your Bergens. To the top and back. Go!'

We shrug off our packs and begin a half-hour beasting session.

Fifteen minutes in, the colour sergeant decides to offer us some words of encouragement. 'The secret to running up hills, gentlemen, is that it's just like running on the flat . . . but with a bit of an incline.'

Unbelievable! Yesterday I heard him telling a cadet there's no such thing as bad weather – just 'inappropriate choice of clothing'.

Finally the punishment stops; we pick up our packs and continue the forced march back to camp. The lack of sleep and relentless physical exertion is now taking its toll. I can feel myself starting to hallucinate and some of the platoon is falling behind. I try to focus as I attempt to keep up with the man in front.

I've been a soldier for five years but I've never felt pain like this. My body is telling me to give up, and right now I'd love nothing more. But I can't. I'd get so much stick from my brothers back home if I rapped it at this point. And, besides, I've always wanted to be a British Army officer. Failure is simply not an option.

'Better to sweat on the training ground than bleed on the battleground, eh, fellas?' the colour sergeant quips, as he runs up and down the line.

The mud and gravel crunch rhythmically beneath my feet. We carry on for another couple of miles and the colour sergeant starts to pick up the pace again. Sweat's pouring off me now and a thick film of mud coats my body. My head is pounding and I can feel my legs begin to go.

'Mr Hunter, I know people who set up charities for men like you. Stop fucking monging it!'

I'm in shit state, but Maclaren's words of wisdom are exactly what I need. I've been told that the physical-fitness sessions at Sandhurst are far harsher than those experienced by enlisted recruits, but never actually believed it until now.

Ten-mile speed-marches are followed by a session of command tasks. Then there's the weekly ritual of the three-mile log race (where a thirty-foot log has to be carried by eight cadets over undulating, arduous terrain and through streams, mud and thick forests). But the real killer is lack of sleep. Even when we're back in camp our day never starts later than 6 a.m. and doesn't end until gone midnight. The morning rush for the hot shower and shaving mirror is normally followed by a two-minute breakfast and a block inspection, after which we spend the rest of the day 'doubling' from one lecture to another.

The range of subjects is phenomenal: war studies, law, the Geneva Convention, tactics and military history, interspersed with frequent kit inspections, gym-beastings, initiative tests, weapons training, drill, night navigation and battle-craft exercises . . .

A few days ago we were sent into a chamber filled with CS gas. Dressed in protective nuclear, biological and chemical (NBC) warfare suits, we had to walk around the chamber, then remove our respirators and shout out our name, number, rank and date of birth. The deep breath that followed brought on the world's worst coughing fit, streaming eyes and a burning sensation in our noses, throats and mouths – all so we could gain confidence in our respirators.

After a gruelling two-and-a-half-hour march, we finally make it back to the Academy. The palatial college build-ings, trout lake, sports pavilions and perfectly manicured lawns seem a world away from where we've just been, but within minutes we're wading through streams and throwing ourselves over scramble nets and ten-foot water jumps, sliding down wet ropes, scaling six- and twelve-foot walls, shuffling along parallel bars, and crawling through barbed-wire entanglements and water-filled tunnels.

'The only way you're going to get through this course, gentlemen, is through teamwork. No one can be a lone Jack here and succeed.'

He's absolutely right. The assault course is the perfect place to identify people who are 'Jack'. At university, where most of these guys have spent the last three years, many of them were encouraged to concentrate on their own academic development, but here at Sandhurst it's a completely different dynamic. The focus is on the team and achieving the mission. Nothing else matters.

The colour sergeant makes us complete the 800-metre course three times – in full kit – and each time we have to run it faster than the last.

Our platoon stands at the finish, doubled over, shaking, coughing but jubilant as we watch another hapless bunch – covered with cuts and bruises – throw themselves over the twelve-foot wall.

'Well done, gentlemen. That's the end of that little outing. Now form three ranks and I'll march you back to the accommodation. It'll save you having to walk . . .'

2

We never understand how little we need in this world until we know the loss of it.

James Matthew Barrie

10 February 1994

'Two minutes!' Duncan shouts.

It's 5.58 a.m. and we've been up all night, cleaning and preparing our equipment for this morning's inspection. The corridor is filled with the aromas of pine air-freshener and freshly ironed starch, and members of the platoon career from one room to another, switching and borrowing kit.

Stripped of any creature comforts, our locker layouts are identical: toiletries on one shelf, socks on another, each shirt, pullover and combat jacket meticulously positioned with the left sleeve draped over the right. We've even been taught how to make a bed correctly: sheets and blankets tucked in with eight-inch hospital corners, pillows ironed and counterpanes draped precisely six inches from the floor. This is military bull-shit at its finest.

'Stand by your beds.'

Maclaren enters the corridor in his immaculate Highland dress uniform and is greeted by Duncan, today's duty cadet. He calls us to attention and informs the colour sergeant that 8 Platoon Gaza Company is awaiting his inspection.

The colour sergeant makes his way along the corridor. The first room he enters belongs to Bikram, one of three foreign students on our platoon. Almost immediately, he notices dust on the window-sill. His face turns to stone. 'Mr Bikram, if you'd done a shit on the table it wouldn't be the first filthy thing I noticed. Reshow at 1900 hours this evening.'

He storms into Henry Arden's room. Henry's an international polo player who's hoping to become a cavalry officer but he's struggled more than most with the transition to military life. 'Mr Arden, you look like a sack of shit with a belt round its middle. When you use the iron you're actually supposed to switch it *on*.'

As Maclaren works his way through Henry's locker, he notices something that's definitely not part of the official layout. A bottle of Rémy Martin is hidden in a combat boot. Predictably, he goes ballistic. 'What the fuck is this doing in your locker, Mr Arden?'

Henry panics. 'I like cognac, Colour Sergeant.'

'And I like shagging women,' replies our instructor, 'but you don't find them in my locker. Reshow 1900 hours, you fucking creature!'

Maclaren makes his way from room to room, scrutinizing every detail with forensic precision and reprimanding virtually every cadet for one crime or another.

By the time he gets to me, he's on a roll. Having listened to him conjure up a string of devastating one-liners to highlight my companions' uselessness, I know he'll make no exception for me. He walks into my room and, amazingly, straight out again. For a brief moment, I think I've actually managed to pull it off. But just as I begin to crack a smile he turns to me and says, 'Mr Hunter, you've got a twisted bootlace, and you know what they say: "Twisted lace, twisted mind." Reshow at 1900 hours.' Then for good measure as he disappears next door: 'And stop grinning. You've got a face like a wanking monkey.'

When he's finished his inspection, he parades us in the corridor.

'When I walked in this morning,' he says, 'I initially thought you'd used your uniforms to clean your rifles. But now that I've seen your rifles, I realize I was mistaken!' He then goes into a semi-humorous rant, telling us that our best turnout falls somewhere between refugee and Oxfam. He has a point: our rifles, uniforms and accommodation are supposed to be spotless, but having returned from the exercise, and spent all day in lessons, then tried to get everything squared away during yet another night without sleep – it's proved an impossible task.

The debrief is going OK until Ahmed, another of our foreign cadets, yawns in front of the colour sergeant.

It's a mistake none of us will repeat.

'What's the matter, Mr Khalifa?' Maclaren yells. 'You tired? Well, you shouldn't be. You people get more sleep than the Unknown fucking Soldier.'

Cue another merciless beasting.

'Push-ups, gentlemen, aren't they great?'

'YES, COLOUR SERGEANT!'

'Think push-ups are great? Wait till I get you into the half push-up position . . .'

And so it continues . . .

As I strain to hold the position, my arms burning and filling with lactic acid, I think of the card my eldest brother sent me before I left for Sandhurst:

HOW TO PREPARE YOURSELF FOR SANDHURST

- *Have somebody shout at you the entire time. Have this same person criticize you incessantly and then fine you two weeks' salary for no apparent reason.*

- *Run. Run a lot. Once in the morning, once at noon and once before supper. Run at least five miles each time, and do loads of press-ups too. Pretend you enjoy it because you want to appear 'hard'.*
- *Stand to attention in a car park in the rain for five hours, or until you pass out and fall face first into the tarmac.*
- *Have somebody shout at you every time you're foolish enough to go outside without a hat on, slouch, or put your hands in your pockets. Do some more press-ups.*
- *Cut your hair weekly, making it shorter each time, until you look bald.*
- *Give yourself thirty minutes less than you need for lunch and eat so quickly you don't taste the food.*
- *Clean and shine everything to perfection. Have somebody shout at you and call you a 'creature' regularly. Pretend to clean and shine everything to perfection again later that evening (changing nothing); then have the same person inspect it and say 'good turnout'.*
- *Do more press-ups.*

The platoon forms up on the parade square a short while later. We're arranged into a line from tallest to shortest, and told to number-off. Each number is cracked out like a rifle round: 'One, two, three, four . . .

sixteen, seventeen . . .' Nerves jangling, some cadets try to anticipate their number, only to stammer and fail; the punishment is fifty press-ups and the whole process is repeated again.

The colour sergeant barks: 'Odd numbers one pace forward, even numbers one pace back . . . March!'

The line disintegrates into a disorderly rabble as both odds and evens stand arguing over who is in the wrong.

'You lot give spastics a bad name,' he says despairingly.

Eventually we get it right and form up into three ranks. One of the cadets asks the colour sergeant when we're going to progress to sword drill.

'Fucking sword drill?' he exclaims. 'I wouldn't even trust you with a knife and fork!'

For the next hour, he hammers us back and forth across the length and breadth of the Academy's sacred parade square. As we practise marching up and down, turning left and right, swinging our arms front to rear, shoulder-high, our instructor informs us that we are to drill what Genghis Khan was to human rights.

Having already jailed two of the platoon for making mistakes, he eventually calls the lesson to a halt, threatening to kill us all twice unless we sort our act out.

Duncan can't help himself. 'How can you kill us twice?' he asks.

As quick as a flash, the colour sergeant points to an

ambulance parked outside the guardroom. 'See those medics over there? Well, after I've killed you, I'm going to get them to resuscitate you . . . and then I'm going to kill you all over again.'

The drill lesson finally ends and we're told to make our way to the Defence Studies Department for a lesson on 'conflict management'.

Maclaren is busy speaking with Sergeant Major Evans, a Welsh Guardsman and veteran of the Falklands War. As I attempt to pass them, carefully avoiding eye contact, he collars me. Major Hudson wants to speak to me 'immediately'.

I make my way into Old College and hurry along its oak-panelled corridors, past portraits of famous generals and royalty. I rack my brain for reasons why I've been summoned by the OC.

I knock warily on his office door and, after a brief pause, he calls me in. I march into his spacious office, stand to attention and snap out a razor-sharp salute. The major sits behind a large oak desk, phone in hand. I feel slightly awkward, as if I'm intruding, but he motions me to take a seat and quickly ends his call.

'Please sit down, Chris,' he says. He looks pained. 'There's . . . there's no easy way to say this . . . I'm afraid I've got some very bad news . . .'

His eyes dart around the room. You can normally see

a lot in someone's eyes but nothing can prepare me for
what he's about to say.

'It's your brother, Tim . . .'

3

One ceases to recognize the significance of mountain peaks if they are not viewed occasionally from the deepest valleys.

Dr Al Lorin

27 February 1994

The wind roars and the freezing rain slices relentlessly into the mountain. I force one foot in front of the other, focusing on each laboured step as I try in vain not to slip on the icy rocks.

The climb seems to go on for ever; the path has disappeared and I'm soaked to the skin, but I have to keep going. I raise my head and look once more at the ridge-line above me. I've come here to search for an answer. Maybe I'll find it at the summit; perhaps I'll find it within me. I clench my fists and force myself to take a long, deep breath before beginning the final ascent.

I'm crawling on my hands and knees, scrambling

furiously up the scree-covered slope. For every three metres of height I gain, I slide back two. The rain is pelting my face. I'm in turmoil, and yet I'm somehow revelling in this mountain storm. Snowdon is one of those solitary places where I come to take stock of my life; it's the place that sustains me.

I press on, head down, forcing myself upwards until I reach the ridge. I pause for a moment and prepare myself to tackle Crib Goch, the hazardous knife-edge arête.

I've been climbing for two hours now and the fatigue is kicking in big-time. I work my way up the first of the three pinnacles, trying to steady myself against the driving wind, then the next two. I know I can't look down: there's a sheer thousand-foot drop to my right, where the cloud has swallowed the ground.

Moments later, there's a deafening roar and a barrage of lightning blasts into the side of the mountain. By the time I reach the summit of Garnedd Ugain, Snowdonia's second highest mountain, the cold, wind, rain and fatigue have sapped my last reserves of strength. My knees are buckling; my vision has become blurred and every part of me aches. I'm starting to stagnate, I'm shutting down. This is madness, but I've got to keep going. It's the only way I'm going to sort my head out. I'm so close now.

I trudge on, my feet squelching as I take the final

steps up the gravel path to the summit. I've never felt so mentally and physically drained.

The wind howls across the summit, driving huge pillars of cloud before it. I close my eyes and slump back against a solitary rock, allowing myself – perhaps for the first time – a moment of respite. I try to make sense of the thoughts spiralling around inside my head.

I'm still unable to shake off the details of Tim's death. I'm in crisis; I feel empty. I want to scream out loud.

But I don't. Instead I sit, cold and forlorn, lonely and yet somehow not alone, looking out across the water-logged peaks of the Snowdon Horseshoe as bolts of lightning flash through the angry sky.

I think back to the last time I saw Tim. He'd done with living. His dead eyes no longer saw a future. I was too wrapped up in my own life to hear his cry for help. I'd let him down; it feels like a burden I'll carry to my grave.

I picture him limping, alone, through the icy, moonlit streets. I try to imagine what was going through his mind as he left the sleeping town behind him, the abseil rope coiled over his shoulder. I see him trekking across the winter fields towards the bridge that spans the bypass. The pain in his leg must have been excruciating; according to the coroner's report, he'd discarded his calliper and brace.

I wonder what they must have been like, those last

few steps to the centre of the bridge; the last few steps to the iron railing where he tethered the rope, slid the noose over his head and jumped.

Anger and regret flow through me and tears fill my eyes. I'd managed to remain composed when Major Hudson told me of Tim's death, but now I'm sobbing like a child. My big brother was always there for me when I was growing up, but when he really needed me, I was somewhere else . . .

I feel the tears freeze against my face. My body is numb with cold and the release of pent-up emotion. I take a deep breath and finally resign myself to the fact that it's over. There's nothing I can do to bring him back.

But maybe I can do something to stop others meeting the same fate.

I sit there in silence as lightning splits the sky. I need to make amends. I want to assuage my guilt. I want to make a difference.

I pull on my pack and begin the slow descent. As the last of the daylight slips beyond the distant mountains, all I can think about is where I'm going to go from here. Soldiering is all I ever wanted to do; I thought that by joining the Army I could somehow make the world a better place. But the voice inside my head is telling me – screaming at me – to take a different path.

By the time I reach the empty car park the storm has finally abated. And so has the one that's been raging inside my head.

4

We are what we pretend to be, so we must be careful what we pretend to be.

Kurt Vonnegut

28 February 1994

The OC looks up as I come through the door. He doesn't miss a trick. 'So this is the scene where Dirty Harry hands in his badge, right?'

I take a deep breath. 'I've always wanted to serve, sir. I've always wanted to be an army officer. But after everything that's happened . . .'

I talk about the events leading up to Tim's death – his car accident, the drug-dealing, the journey to the tower block and the effect his suicide has had on me. Major Hudson sits back in his chair, saying nothing, but listening intently and compassionately to every word.

'It's not that I dislike being in the Army,' I say awkwardly. 'I absolutely love it. It's just that my gut instinct's telling me I've got to do something different. I know it probably sounds a bit corny, but I need to do something where I feel I'm making a genuine difference . . .'

'And you don't think the Army can give you that. So, tell me, what do you think will?'

'I was thinking maybe something along the lines of fighting global drug-trafficking, sir.'

The major steps away from his desk and moves over to the window. He stares out over the tree-lined parade square and the glimmering lake beyond it, saying nothing.

Eventually he turns back to me and says, 'During my time here dozens of cadets have stood where you are and told me they want to leave, and without exception I've encouraged them to do so. I've done so for two reasons: first, because from the moment a cadet decides to leave, mentally he's already left, and more importantly, because for every cadet who doesn't want to be here there are hundreds who'd do anything to take his place.'

His brow furrows. For a moment I think he's going to start tearing strips off me for wasting his time. But he doesn't. Instead he opens his drawer and hands me a piece of paper. It reads:

Go as a pilgrim and seek out danger far from the comfort and the well lit avenues of life. Pit your every soul against the unknown and seek stimulation in the comfort of the brave. Experience cold, hunger, heat and thirst and survive to see another challenge and another dawn. Only then will you be at peace with yourself and be able to know and to say: I look down the farthest side of the mountain fulfilled and understanding all, and truly content that I lived a full life and one that was my own choice.

It's from the play *Hassan*.

'I sense you're cut from a very different cloth. You don't want to leave because you're some duffer who can't hack it. You want to leave because you're one of those wonderfully idealistic young men who feel the need to right the wrongs of the world . . .'

I try to tell him there's some truth in that, but it was a rhetorical question, and he's on a roll.

'You know what, Chris?' He looks me straight in the eye. 'I totally respect your decision. But if you really want to make a difference, if you genuinely want to have an impact on the global drugs trade, then stay in the Army and fight terrorism.'

For the next ten minutes or so he goes into full-on transmit-mode. He begins explaining how terrorist groups use the sale of illegal drugs to fund their global terror operations. He talks about some of the key players and the methods employed to identify and interdict them. He describes the job of the military intelligence services and explains the role they and the Special Forces play in counter-terrorism operations.

'And there are people like this guy here . . .' He points to a photo on the wall. An operator in a protective EOD suit, laden with equipment, makes the long walk towards a vehicle bomb in Northern Ireland. He's walking past a placard hanging on the side of a Methodist church that reads: *Prepare to meet thy God*.

'The destruction and the loss of life caused by terrorist bombs are well documented and will never be forgotten,' he continues, 'but the number of lives that those men and women have saved, and the damage prevented by their courage and devotion to duty, is impossible to quantify.'

He tells me they're called ATOs – ammunition technical officers. 'They're the Army's bomb-disposal experts; they do their work without any fuss and their successes are rarely publicized. Theirs is a quiet war, a war without fanfare. It would take you a few years to get there – and you'd have to prove yourself as an officer first – but you've got exactly the right temperament, and if you wanted it badly enough, I've no doubt at all that you could be one of them.'

I take another look at the photo. I don't need any

more convincing. Suddenly everything's clear. I'm going to stay in the Army and do whatever it takes to be a bomb-disposal specialist.

5

Never part without loving words to think of during your absence. It may be that you will not meet again in this life.

Jean Paul Richter

10 February 1995

'No man can wander without a base,' I once read. 'You have to have a sort of magic circle to which you belong . . . somewhere you identify with, to which you always happen to go back.' For me, that place is Hay-on-Wye.

Straddling the Anglo-Welsh border on the northern tip of the Brecon Beacons, the sleepy town is known to most people for one thing. There are only about nineteen hundred inhabitants but dozens of bookshops. The town has become a Mecca for Bohemians and bibliophiles. Its cosmopolitan flavour, quirky little streets and spectacular backdrop of the Black Mountains make it a very special place to live.

I've not been home for months and as I drop down

the hill from Clyro and drive over the bridge spanning the river Wye, I'm filled with a heady mixture of excitement and trepidation. I'm massively looking forward to seeing my civvy mates again, but not to telling my mother I'm deploying to Bosnia.

Mum has been extremely fragile since Tim's death, and I remember how worried she was when my eldest brother, Jamie, went to fight in the Falklands. His ship was hit by an Argentinian 500-pounder. The huge bomb crashed through the decks above him and came to rest only a few feet from where he was working. It was only by sheer luck that it failed to explode. The enemy pilot had been flying so low that its fuse didn't have time to arm.

I slow at the T-junction on Bridge Street. Groups of bikers have gathered outside the Three Tuns – Wales's oldest pub – smoking cannabis and drinking real ale. The sweet smell wafts through my car window as I pull up outside my parents' restaurant.

Frank, my stepfather, is busy in the open kitchen rustling up his legendary Italian cuisine – the intoxicating scent of garlic and basil makes my mouth water. My mother holds court at the centre of the room. The customers love her: her warm smile and friendly nature make everybody feel instantly at ease.

One of the locals sees me standing in the doorway and taps her on the shoulder. She rushes over and throws her arms around me. 'Daaaarling, what a lovely surprise!'

Frank drops what he's doing and raises a bottle of Peroni in my direction. 'Here you go, Tosh,' he says, in his Cockney-Italian accent. 'Welcome home.'

It's good to be back. I dump my bags and take a seat at the only empty table. My parents' ever-popular restaurant is packed with locals as well as tourists today, so I decide to neck my Peroni and make the five-minute journey through town to the Blue Boar to catch up with my third brother Adam and the rest of our mates.

A couple of hours later, I head back. Frank is preparing more culinary delights before they reopen for dinner. 'Fancy a cappuccino, Tosh?' he asks.

We shoot the breeze for a while; I'm doing the talking while he's busy chopping fresh garlic for the Bolognese sauce bubbling away on the stove.

'How's Mum?' I ask him.

'Not great, son,' he replies. 'She's putting on a brave face in front of the customers but, to be honest with you, I don't think she'll ever get over it.'

He tells me how she cried herself to sleep every night for the first few months after Tim died; she cried until she had no more tears. And now all that remains is a feeling of incurable grief.

'I mean, how do you ever get over the loss of a child?'

Later, I get a chance to sit down with Mum and have a proper one-on-one. We're having a light-hearted chat about who's doing what to whom in the town, and then she wants to hear about my army buddies. But the talk soon turns to Tim; his death is like an open wound.

She revisits some of the happier memories from his childhood and painfully compares them with the turbulence of his adult life. She's searching for answers but, of course, there are none.

'The coroner told me it would have been all over very quickly.' Fighting back the tears, she searches for some crumbs of comfort. When Tim leapt from the bridge the rope decapitated him. His head was found some distance away from his lifeless corpse by an ill-fated lorry driver. The poor guy said the vision of Tim's eyes staring into the bitterly cold night would stay with him for ever.

As the sun disappears beneath a grey mantle of cloud we jump into the car and make our way along the winding country lanes that lead up into the Black Mountains. We park at the foot of Hay Bluff and climb through the veils of mist until we reach the summit from which Tim's ashes were scattered.

As we sit in silence, staring out over the Golden Valley, I take a deep breath. 'Mum, I've got something to—'

She squeezes my hand and places a finger tenderly

on my lips. She already knows about my Bosnia deployment. 'Sending a child to war is the most counter-intuitive thing a parent can ever do,' she says. 'Promise me you'll stay safe, darling. I'll be holding my breath until you return.'

6

The tragedy of war is that it uses man's best to do man's worst.

Harry Emerson Fosdick

5 May 1995

The mist rolls across the valley floor. Sounds lose their echo and the wisps of cloud beneath my feet glitter like snow. I want this moment never to end. Bosnia is a land of extremes. From its war-torn streets to its breathtaking rural landscapes, it's a place where sound meets stillness, where darkness collides with light. And between them lies a population ravaged by civil war.

There's something intensely poignant about the way the beauty of this magical mountain is etched against the canvas of devastation that surrounds it. I can't quite make up my mind whether nature remains sublimely indifferent to human tragedy, or touchingly optimistic.

I take a mouthful of water, pick up my rifle, throw my pack onto my back and begin the steep climb down the tree-covered mountain towards our camp in Lipa. I'm told it means 'Lime Tree' but I'm fucked if I know why; I doubt there's one within a hundred miles of here. The village is about ten Ks from the nearest point where Croatian troops regularly battle against the Serbian militia.

I knew that joining a bunch of people who've known each other for years would be a daunting experience, but trying to lead a tight-knit group of blokes, most of whom are older than me, is proving far harder than I thought. It seemed much easier to gain acceptance as a young NCO; now that I'm an officer, I really have to work at it. Earning – and keeping – their respect is the key. Field Marshal Slim – of Second World War Burma fame – would tell young officers that they should resist the temptation to try to make their place overnight. His words still ring in my ears: 'Respect will be given as of right, but will soon be lost if you fail to live up to the standards that will be expected of you by your soldiers. The byword for all you do is "example".' I know I've still got a long way to go.

I drop down onto the mist-covered plateau and head through our barbed-wire perimeter fence. The sky-blue UN flag cracks in the wind above the HQ building as the men and women who protect this camp – the Multinational Division's Supply Area – begin to rise from their beds.

I enter the twelve-foot-square tent I share with my troop sergeant. He's already washed and dressed and looks immaculate in his neatly pressed combat fatigues.

'Morning, Boss. Like a brew?'

I've definitely struck gold with Brummie Lees. He's in his late thirties, good-humoured, shaved hair, stocky and tanned from the ten days we've just spent 'acclimatizing' on Croatia's Dalmatian coast.

I've only been with the troop for a matter of weeks and, if I'm honest, I'm still trying to find my way with Brummie. He's as much under the spotlight as I am because he's also judged on how I perform over the next two years. And because my success is so important to him, he has the unenviable task of bringing me to the point at which I can start to add some value to the proceedings and we can begin working together as a coherent team. My job is to lead the troop and take care of personnel issues. His is to administer it; that's what troop sergeants do. He doesn't want my job, he wants the sergeant major's – but I'm sensitive to the fact he commanded the troop before my arrival and as my 2i/c he'll continue to do so in my absence. He was hand-picked for this role by our commanding officer, and with good reason.

From what I can make out, his judgement is flawless – so no worries there. But he's still a bit of a closed book, and all I've established about him so far is that his journey here hasn't been easy. He spent the majority of his teen years incarcerated in a young offenders' institution and the moment he was free he joined the French Foreign Legion. When I asked him why, he told me people join the Legion for one reason: to forget. When I asked him what he was trying to forget he promptly replied, 'I can't remember.' It's the oldest gag in the world, but I know it conceals a world of pain.

Bang on cue, Private Hook, one of the youngest members of our troop, enters the tent with a fistful of paperwork.

'Ah, Private Hook, the boss and I were just chatting about golfers . . . What's that plastic thing they put in the ground and then put the ball on?'

'Tee, Sergeant?'

'Good lad,' Lees says. 'You'll go far. Milk and three sugars for me and a coffee for the boss.'

I know we're going to get on famously. There's something reassuringly solid about Sergeant Lees. His stout frame and sharp wit inspire confidence; his genial expression and clear gaze tell me he's a man I can trust.

After breakfast, we head out to visit our guys on sangar duty. Two of our sections are manning the sand-bagged structures that protect the entrances to the camp, while our third section is busy constructing another fortification near the HQ building.

We leave the tented accommodation and make our

way a half-mile or so east to the sangar at the inter-
section of the main road to Sarajevo. A soldier trains his
general-purpose machine-gun on the Bosnian-Croat
militia (HVO) checkpoint some fifty metres away, while
another scans the ground between them with his
binoculars. They've been on stag for much of the night,
and it's reassuring to see they're still completely
switched on.

'Hello, fellas, how's tricks?' I ask.

'Couldn't be better, sir,' Private Dougan replies
cheerily. 'Which is more than I can say for those losers
over there.'

Dougie Dougan is one of the senior privates in the
troop and doubles as my driver and radio operator on
convoy-escort tasks. He's also the spitting image of Chris
Evans, the ginger-haired television presenter.

'Why's that, then, Dougie?'

'Because up until about two o'clock this morning the
spanking new floor you see beneath our feet belonged
to them. You snooze, you lose!'

This boy's priceless. The HVO had got so pissed last
night that they fell asleep and failed to man their sangar.
Our lads, fed up with having to stand in puddles of
water, sneaked over to their position and ripped up all
the flooring.

Brummie and I are still chuckling as we walk into the
admin tent where Corporal Clarke is preparing a patrol

trace. Nobby is the slightest and most softly spoken of the three section commanders, but he's a lion of a man and his section love him. The boys are resting up, shooting the shit about their basic training. One of them is in full flow about the time his recruit-troop sergeant threw his boots out of the window because they didn't meet his exacting standards. 'Pity the window was shut!' he says, to a chorus of laughter. 'And to cap it all, the cheeky bastard made me pay for the glass. Said I should have anticipated he was going to throw them out!'

One of the slower members of the section proudly recounts the time he was pulled up on parade for looking 'like a dog fucking a bag of nails'.

'Nice one, Brains,' Nobby says. 'And I see you've continued to maintain the same low standards ever since.'

'What about you, Rob?' one of the others asks the section's 2i/c, a big, bullet-headed monster of a man. 'What's your funniest memory from training?'

'How the fuck am I supposed to remember that far back?' Lance Corporal Benson grunts. 'I was filling magazines when you were still colouring them in!'

'Fucking A, Rob,' Brummie says. 'And when did you start cracking into books without pictures?'

Benson gives him a huge grin. 'If you want to change the world, Sergeant Lees, then you must get an education. He who reads, leads.'

I'm beginning to love this eclectic mix of Jocks, Taffs, Brummies and Mancs as if they were my own family. They've all been through the mill, but they're devoted and loyal and I can't think of a group of blokes I'd rather be in a war-zone with.

They're seriously switched on and, unlike the average university graduate, who probably hasn't had a fight since primary school, these lads have lived on the street and survived to tell the tale. As Brummie says, 'Once a man's nose has been broken two or three times in a bar fight, he'll risk it all again without giving it a second thought.'

Brummie and I share some more banter over a brew, then head back to see how work's progressing on the new sangar. He asks me how I'm settling in. I tell him I love the job, but am still feeling a bit overwhelmed. I feel like a dick admitting it to him, but the truth is, I'm worried I'll fuck up.

He offers me some advice I know I'll never forget. 'Never have a wishbone where your backbone should be, and always follow the three Rs: respect for yourself, respect for others and responsibility for your actions. And, Boss, you're new to this game, so we expect you to fuck up from time to time.' He pauses. 'Just don't abuse the privilege, OK?'

As we near the other end of camp, we hear Corporal Lawrence tearing a strip off one of his boys: 'You're about as useful as a one-legged cat trying to bury a shit. I bet your village was beside itself when you joined up, you fucking idiot!'

It turns out that while the rest of the lads were digging and filling sandbags, Private Allen was failing the 'simple' task of ensuring they were laid correctly. Now, because the sangar is considered structurally unsound, the section has to dismantle it and start again.

'I see you've not lost your inspirational leadership qualities, Jim,' Brummie says. They've been friends ever since he left the Legion and joined the British Army.

'As I'm sure the boss will be the first to agree, Brum, the best leaders inspire by example. But when that's not an option, brute intimidation works a treat.'

Tall, quick-witted and with a streak of old-fashioned gallantry, Jim's a brilliant NCO and, by all accounts, has made more than one conquest over the years.

Conscious that time's against him, he gets straight back into work mode. 'Right, lads, lesson number one: if at first you don't succeed, do it like you were fucking taught!' He tasks two of the lads to reconstruct the sangar under the supervision of Nick Wolstein, his 2i/c, and points another two in the direction of the admin tent. 'See that twelve by twelve? I want you to take it down and turn it into a fuck-all by fuck-all.'

The rest of the lads are told to keep filling sandbags. When de Souza – one of the more seasoned privates –

asks Jim why he's not lending them a hand, he replies, 'Do you think I was born a corporal?' But he chucks me and Brummie a shovel and the three of us get stuck in.

Brummie and I peel off a few hours later, as the sangar nears completion, leaving the blokes to admire the fruits of their day's labour. Bathed in a warm sense of accomplishment, the two of us walk back through the trees that line the northern perimeter road. Their leaves shimmer and dance in the breeze.

An elderly couple shuffles up the road towards us. We stop briefly and greet them in German, but they introduce themselves in perfect English as guests of the farmer whose land we're renting. They seem a little taciturn at first, but then start to open up about the country and its customs. Brummie and I are like sponges. Our thirst for local knowledge is unquenchable.

We're having a pleasant natter under a cloudless sky and it feels good to enjoy a bit of normality. But when I ask how long they've lived here, there's an awkward silence. They look at one another and, after a nod from her husband, the elderly lady begins to share one of the most heartbreaking stories I've ever heard.

They'd lived in the ancient Croatian city of Mostar until April 1992. 'That's when the war started for us. A truck exploded in the city, outside the barracks, demolishing it completely. Soon afterwards, Muslim and Croat troops entered our village. One of the villagers dared to stand up to them. He was in his car, arguing with them, so they set it on fire. He tried to clamber out and a Croatian soldier slit his throat there and then. He burnt to death in that car.'

Brummie and I are rooted to the spot.

They tell us about the fateful night that the Ustashi came to their flat in Mostar, beat them and took away their gold bracelets, watches and wedding rings – a lifetime of memories. 'They took it all before our eyes.' As he recounts the terrible events of that day the old man starts to cry. They'd beaten him with a stick until he fainted from the blows. Then they'd beaten his wife. She'd recently had surgery and when she showed them the wound, they took the bandage from her and stuffed it into her mouth.

'They tried to choke me,' she says. 'Then they put a knife to my throat and cursed my Serb mother. They tied us and put us aboard a truck and took us to a concentration camp. They stripped us naked and forced us to salute the Fatherland. Then they beat us with sticks, rubber hammers; they kicked us with their boots and pounded our bodies with their fists.

'They brought grass and forced us to eat it. They forced the YPA soldiers captured with us to have intercourse with one another. Those who refused were beaten until they did.

'Then they took turns torturing us. They hit my husband mostly on the arms with a metal cable and broke them both above the wrists. He fainted from the pain. He was covered with blood.'

She turns to her husband and cradles his pained face in her gentle old hands. 'Before the war, there were thirty thousand Serbs in Mostar. After the ethnic cleansing, there were only three hundred.'

I feel numb. When the Allied troops reached the Nazi death camps at the end of the Second World War, General Eisenhower ordered them to get everything on record: films, photographs, documents and the statements of the survivors. He knew that somewhere down the track somebody would say it never happened.

Barely fifty years have passed and it's happening all over again.

7

The first thing a young officer must do when he joins the Army is to fight a battle, and that battle is for the hearts of his men. If he wins that battle and subsequent similar ones, his men will follow him anywhere; if he loses it, he will never do any real good.

Field Marshal Viscount Montgomery of Alamein

21 July 1995

'How do I know you're lying? 'Cos your fucking lips are moving. Now tell me again, what else have you two little pricks been thieving?'

I've just stepped into the tent I share with Brummie and have to walk straight out again because he's in the middle of disciplining two young privates. Yesterday they'd decided to help themselves to several boxes of electrical equipment and were caught trying to mail them back to the UK. Unfortunately the lunatics stole the stores from the supply area we've been sent here to protect and now a shit-storm has erupted in the

Regimental HQ. The incident has done us no favours at all.

'Listen, you pair of fucking clowns, I was in uniform before you were in liquid form, so don't even think about trying to pull the wool. If you don't start furnishing me with some answers, this hard shiny thing at the end of my foot is going to connect sharply with the soft dangly objects in each of your trousers.'

Brummie's inimitable interrogation technique brings a smile to my face and works a treat on the boys: they're soon singing like canaries.

I leave our tented village and head out along the metal trackway past rows of diesel generators and ISO shipping containers to the eastern sangar where Corporal Macintyre and the rest of his section are staging-on. Discipline isn't usually a problem on ops as soldiers don't have the time, freedom or alcohol to mess up, but because our primary task here is static sentry duty the boredom is really starting to cause us problems. The OC's fuming about the thieving incident – so much so that he gave me a massive bollocking this morning in full view of the rest of the regiment.

As I near the end of the dusty plain and approach the admin tent, I can hear the lads chatting inside.

'I think he's a complete cock,' one of them says.

'Yeah, well, he's only got himself to blame for being shit . . .'

I'm frozen to the spot.

'I mean, what sort of OC bollocks a young troop commander in front of his own troop?'

'Sir!'

Corporal Macintyre's stealthy approach makes me jump. A former regimental boxing champion, Mac's as hard as nails – a powerhouse of a man who also happens to be the spitting image of Mike Tyson.

I feel like a child who's just been caught with his hand in the sweetie jar. 'Er . . . hi, Corporal Macintyre . . . how's it going?'

I can now see from his expression that he's got more important things on his mind than junior troop commanders ear-wigging outside admin tents.

'Just been up to Regimental Ops, sir. Have you heard the news?'

'What news?'

He holds up a briefing document. 'The massacre . . . at Srebrenica . . .'

As a veteran of previous Balkans tours, Mac speaks with compelling gravity. He explains how during his last tour of Bosnia – two years ago – the commander of the UN mission declared Srebrenica the first of the country's 'safe areas'. But about a week ago Serb forces began stripping the town's Bosnian Muslim males of their personal belongings and identification. Then on 13 July seventeen of them were bussed to the Jadar river, lined up and executed. Immediately afterwards, three more truckloads of men aged between fourteen and fifty were driven to the river Cerska and shot.

Apparently the Serbs had told them that the Geneva Convention would be observed if they gave themselves up. A hundred and fifty more were killed and buried in a ditch. Others were simply buried alive.

Clearly distressed, Mac tells me how between a thousand and fifteen hundred Muslims were captured in fields near Sandiçi later that afternoon and taken to a warehouse in Kravica. The Serbs threw in hand grenades and opened fire on them with everything they had, including an anti-tank weapon.

As he details these horrific events, I realize the noise inside the tent has subsided. The members of his section have come outside and are completely absorbed by what he's saying.

'That was just day one,' he says grimly. 'The following day, over two and a half thousand Muslims who'd been held prisoner in the Grbavci school in Orahovac were taken in trucks to nearby fields and stabbed, beaten and shot. Then the Serbs managed to persuade another three hundred and fifty to surrender this morning. A hundred and fifty of them were forced to dig their own graves before being topped.'

The Dutch UN troops stationed in Srebrenica made no attempt whatsoever to resist the advancing Serbs –

effectively giving them a green light to carry out the largest mass-murder in Europe since the Second World War. More than seven thousand Bosnian Muslims have been massacred in the past ten days.

I can see my own sense of powerlessness and frustration etched on the faces of the young men around us.

I walk back to our tent, rage and frustration boiling up inside me. I'm ashamed to call myself a UN peace-keeper. And yet I can't bring myself to blame the Dutch soldiers: I know they'd have wanted to intervene – what decent human being wouldn't? My real resentment is towards the UN hierarchy for ordering them to stand by while thousands of men perished and hundreds of women and children were tortured, raped and killed.

Moments later, Private Foster appears, nose bleeding, face bruised and grazed.

'Sir, I want to make a formal complaint.' He spits out a broken tooth. Lance Corporal Benson, Nobby's 2i/c, has just assaulted him.

'Are you absolutely sure?'

'Absolutely.' He insists that he'll take it all the way to court martial if necessary.

I sit him down and begin trying to establish the facts. It quickly emerges that Lance Corporal Benson chinned Private Foster for insubordination. I think back to my time as an NCO: if a private had gobbed off to me, I'd probably have done exactly the same. But the military has moved on since then: it now has a zero-tolerance policy on assault.

I send for Lance Corporal Benson. He's seething. I'm going to have to tread really carefully. I've always been able to hold my own in a punch-up, but Rob Benson is well out of my league. I know that if I say the wrong thing he's likely to take a swing at me, and that'll be the end of his career. I also don't fancy being on the receiving end of one of his right hooks. He wears a skinhead like he means it and could knock me out as easily as I could beat him in a spelling test.

'Corporal B, I've received a formal complaint from Private Foster regarding an alleged assault. I need you to tell me your side of the story.'

He immediately admits hitting Foster. I can't help admiring his honesty and integrity. When I ask him why, he tells me that our wonder-boy has been undermining him continually and disobeying his commands.

'I'm sorry, Boss. Private Foster may be Mr Goldenbollocks in the eyes of the officers, but to the rest of us he's a lazy little shit who seems to be under the impression that army life consists of one long NAAFI break punctuated by frequent rest periods. He's not a team player, and if you don't believe me, ask yourself why he came crying to you instead of taking it like a man.'

Private Foster bows his head, face now bright red.

'I hear what you're saying, Corporal B, but why the fuck didn't you just talk to him?'

'I could have said a thousand words, Boss, but why go through all that rigmarole when a punch in the mouth told him exactly what was on my mind?'

It's a cracking line, but as it stands, he's likely to be charged with assault. And if he's charged, he'll almost certainly insist that Foster's charged too. Then I'll have lost two good men.

'Right, here's what I'm going to do . . .'

I tell Private Foster that, in spite of what Corporal Benson may think, he's an outstanding soldier with a promising career ahead of him. But if he decides to take this further, he'll be charged with insubordination and will also be responsible for wrecking the career of a talented NCO. 'There's an old Irish proverb,' I tell him. '"Many a man's mouth has broken his nose." If you gob off, then you need to be prepared for the consequences.'

I then rip into Corporal B big-time. He's supposed to be setting an example to the men in his section, not beating the crap out of them.

'So, gentlemen, I'm giving you a choice: either you both accept my award or you can both go to court martial.'

They reply in unison. 'Your award, sir.'

For the next three weeks, they're going to be joining

me for my daily phys sessions: a forced march in the morning, circuits at lunchtime and a ten-mile run every evening. If they haven't learnt to tolerate each other by the end of that, they never will.

Nobby, Mac and Jim, the three section commanders, arrive in our tent later that morning. Brummie and I are busy writing reports and discussing how best to keep the guys motivated.

'Can we have a word, Boss?' Jim asks.

The endless stream of sangar duties and patrols is beginning to have a detrimental effect on their men. The news about Srebrenica hasn't helped. To make matters worse, we've been told that as of tomorrow we'll be providing escorts for the aid convoys going into Sarajevo. The boys have been working their tits off and they badly need a break.

'So, what do you recommend, fellas?'

Mac tells us about a place called Rumboci on the shores of Lake Prozor, halfway between our camp and Sarajevo. It's about a two-hour drive. 'During my last tour we used to go there all the time. The chef would give us meat for the BBQ and we'd take a couple of cases of beer and sign out the adventure training gear from the stores. It was cracking, Boss. The boys would love it.'

At Sandhurst we were taught to punish failure and

reward success, and there have been some serious fuck-ups in the troop recently. The last thing I want is to be seen as some pushover who rewards the boys for pissing about. But the fact is, they do need a break and, as of tomorrow, the pace of life is going to be ramping up massively.

I glance over to Brummie, who knows exactly what I'm thinking. He nods his head. I ask the boys to give me five.

8

Maybe this world is another planet's hell.

Aldous Huxley

21 July 1995

'What do you mean "time off"? Those fuckers get more time off than Clint Eastwood's safety catch!'

'But, Jake—'

'Mate, chill. I'm only joshing with you. Of course they can have the afternoon off.'

I'm still finding my feet with Jake Garside, but I can already see he's one of the best captains in our corps. He's the sort of bloke soldiers naturally warm to, a man's man who lives by two solid principles: the honour of his country and the safety of his men. His own wellbeing always comes last. True to his word, within an hour he's persuaded virtually every officer and senior NCO in camp to stag-on so that the lads can enjoy some downtime.

We pull out of the main gate in our three-vehicle

convoy and wind our way up the dusty mountain track, through rocky outcrops and coniferous woods to the Bosnian-Croat town of Mandino Selo. From there, we continue along the main supply route – known as Route Triangle – and on to Rumboci. We turn off the MSR at the north-west corner of Lake Prozor and drop down through what appears to be a deserted village, though the houses look incredibly modern.

We park up alongside the shore.

In the few minutes it takes Brummie, Dougie and me to shut down the radios and debus from our Land Rover, the food, canoes and crates of beer have all been unloaded with military precision and the boys have centralized their weapons and stripped down to their shorts, revealing their milky white bodies and perfect 'squaddie tans' – sunburnt forearms and matching Vs at the base of their necks.

Jim oversees the setting up of the BBQ while Nobby distributes the beer and Mac constructs a death-slide from the edge of a cliff onto an island about a hundred metres away. Most of the lads huddle around the BBQ, offering Jim uninvited advice on how best to get it lit. The rest swim or lie at the water's edge, soaking up the warm summer rays.

'This is the life.' Barney Watts, the only member of the troop still fully clothed, turns towards the lake and gives us his favourite Billy Connolly line: 'A well-balanced person has a beer in each hand.' As he takes a slurp from each can, one of the lads runs up behind him and executes a perfect rugby tackle, launching him straight into the water. Unfortunately Mac's good-natured 2i/c isn't the slimmest of blokes and he hits the water with a massive splash, extinguishing the freshly lit BBQ.

'Right, Barney, that's fucking it,' Jim yells. 'I'm going to kick your arse so hard the only thing you'll be brushing before bedtime is my size ten.'

Barney only manages a few gargling sounds as he spits out a mouthful of sooty water.

'Nice one, Boss,' Brummie says. 'This is exactly what the boys needed.'

We've become more like friends than colleagues in recent weeks, but it still feels good to get his tacit approval.

I give him a grin and tell him I'm going for a quick mooch around the village.

'Fucking hell, Boss, can't you sit still for five minutes?' He mutters something under his breath, then grabs his weapon and body-armour.

I tell him to stay where he is, but he's having none of it. 'You don't need to hold my hand everywhere I go.'

'Yes, I do,' he says. 'I promised your mum.'

That knocks me sideways. 'Did you just say . . .?'

'She'd never forgive me if something happened to you.'

He explains that my mother wrote to him shortly before we deployed – specifically asking him to watch out for me.

I don't know whether to be grateful or to die of shame.

The trees sway gently in the warm summer breeze as we make our way into the village. The crunch of our boots resonates against the eerie silence. To our right stands a burnt-out mosque. There's a huge hole in its minaret, from a tank shell by the look of it. We're surrounded by empty, white-washed three-storey houses. Every window has scorched frames and no glass. The silence is making my short hair stand on end. It has a ghostly quality that I can't quite identify. I pull my SA80 assault rifle firmly into my shoulder and glance across the street. Brummie has done the same.

'Why don't they have any windows, Brum?'

He points to the scorch marks. 'Looks like whoever cleared the houses used blast incendiaries.' The attackers pour petrol on each floor of a building, leave it to vaporize, then return and ignite the fumes. The blast blows out the windows and burns the contents, but still leaves the superstructure intact. 'That way, the building can be reoccupied.'

As we move on, I realize what's been bugging me about the quality of the silence. It reminds me of Auschwitz. I visited the Nazi death camp a few years ago. I never saw or heard a single bird; it's exactly the same here.

'I'm going to take a look inside one of these houses, Brummie. I want to get a better idea of what happened here.'

He mumbles something disapproving, but follows me anyway.

We climb the concrete steps and enter the empty hallway through the door-less front porch.

'I don't think we should be doing this, Boss. This place is screaming out for a booby-trap.'

He's right. Every instinct tells me this is a bad idea, but the need to understand what happened is enough to lure me up three flights of stairs.

'Boss, look!'

As our eyes adjust to the darkness of the attic, we see a mass of clothing and dozens of pairs of damp-smelling shoes in untidy piles, stacks of personal documents and several hundred family photographs. It's like the scene from *Schindler's List* when the Jews are forced out of their homes and ordered to leave all their personal belongings.

I stand there, dry-mouthed, imagining the horrors experienced by the poor family who were evicted from this home.

We edge our way back down the stairs. Brummie heads for the master bedroom and I find myself drawn to another partially open door. Inside is a baby's cot under a huge mural of Minnie Mouse. There are two large holes in the cot, and both the mattress and the wall beneath the mural are covered with dark patches of blood.

My stomach cramps and I begin vomiting uncontrollably.

The baby was executed with a shotgun at point-blank range.

'Boss? You OK?'

Brummie runs into the room, glances at the cot and throws up violently as well.

Gradually he straightens, and gives me a look of infinite sadness. 'Come on, Boss,' he says quietly. 'Let's get out of here.'

As we emerge into the street a black-clad, silver-haired lady shuffles towards us, frantically waving her arms. 'You must leave. Please . . . go now!'

We calm her down and plead with her to tell us what happened.

Haltingly, she tells us of the night the Croat militia entered Rumboci and announced that the villagers had twenty-four hours to leave or be killed. Some heeded the warning and did as they were told, but most of the Muslims who'd built a life there weren't prepared to go without a fight.

They didn't stand a chance.

The militia began shooting anybody they deemed to be a threat, then looted the houses and demanded that all gold, jewellery and money be handed over to them.

'They stripped me and my husband naked and pounded us with their rifles. They took our money, then one of them ordered me to give him my wedding ring.'

I look into the old woman's long-dead eyes and feel the most intense rage welling up inside me.

She tells us how the militia took some male prisoners to the basement of one of the houses and began torturing them. The younger women were taken to the basement of a separate building, stripped naked and raped. Afterwards, the survivors, bloody and disfigured, were led outside and shot.

She turns and points at the house behind us.

'The house you were in a moment ago . . . They were all killed. The baby was shot; the parents and their other child were hanged outside. I saw them . . .' She's now sobbing uncontrollably. 'The two adults were dead. But the third rope . . . the third rope was still moving . . .'

Being so light, the child lived for another twenty minutes while the old woman and the other villagers looked on helplessly.

I am shaking uncontrollably.

She suddenly stops sobbing and claws at my arm. 'Are you here alone?'

I shake my head. 'The rest of our troop are swimming—'

'*Dear God, no!*' she cries. 'Get them out . . . *now!*'

There's a final twist in her awful tale. Knowing what lay ahead of them, some of the young mothers tied their car batteries to their necks, cradled their babies in their arms and plunged into the lake.

Brummie turns and sprints back to the lads, yelling at them to get out of the water.

'Why, Brum?' one asks.

'Because it's full of dead fucking bodies!'

In the cookhouse at Lipa, we eat our dinner in silence. Tonight even the soup tastes of death.

9

Beware of extremism in religion; for it was extremism in religion that destroyed those who went before you.

The Prophet Mohammed

25 August 1995

I grab my kit and head for the team vehicles. The atmosphere is electric. The lads are busy shrugging on their body armour and Kevlar helmets. Weapons are being loaded, radios checked, goggles fitted, engines fired. Everyone is running through their last-minute mental lists, triple-checking weapons, rehearsing actions-on.

'Dougie, where's Sergeant Lees?'

We're supposed to be on the road. Last night we were given the mother of all fast-balls: after the Serbs' killing spree in Srebrenica, they switched their attention to the streets of Sarajevo. Three weeks ago they blew up the marketplace, killing scores of civilians, and they've been shelling the shit out of it ever since. Our orders are to RV with a huge ammunition convoy on the outskirts of the city, and escort it safely through Sarajevo airport and up to the UN gun lines on Mount Igman. After months of doing nothing, we're finally going to give those fuckers a good pasting. It's definitely not before time.

'I don't know, Boss – I've not seen him all morning.' Dougie flashes me a look of concern. 'That said, you've still got time to find him. I'm afraid the Rover's fucked. We're not going anywhere in a hurry.'

You couldn't make this shit up.

When I ask him why, he looks at me deadpan. 'Shit happens, Boss. The journey of a thousand miles begins with a broken fan-belt and a flat tyre. But don't worry – I'm all over it like a seagull on a sick prawn!'

He's right. There's no point in getting excited about it. I make my way across to the operations room to see if Jake Garside has any info on Brummie's whereabouts.

He offers me a forlorn look. 'Yes, mate, and I'm sorry for not telling you sooner, but I've literally only just found out myself . . .'

This isn't sounding good.

'Sergeant Lees was involved in a road traffic accident last night and has been casevaced back to the UK.'

When I ask if he's OK, Jake's brow furrows. 'It's too early to say.'

For the next few minutes he tells me what he does

know. Brummie and Sergeant Major Durrant – one of our regiment's most legendary soldiers – were on their way back from a task when they hit a crater in the road and lost control of the vehicle. Brummie's got spinal injuries, but the medics don't yet know the extent of the damage.

'I know you two are close. He's a good friend of mine too. But for now you're going to have to focus on the Mount Igman task. I'll let you know the minute we have any more news.'

By the time I get back to the boys, Dougie has repaired our Land Rover and Sergeant 'Shak' Khan, the orderly room senior NCO, has assumed the role of troop sergeant. He's busy briefing the lads on the route we're going to be taking.

'Good morning, sir,' he says, in his perfect English accent. 'It appears Route Triangle is blocked due to an overturned water-bowser, so I've suggested to the men that we take an alternative route.'

Minutes later we're on our way. At Sergeant Khan's suggestion, Dougie, Cleggy and Corporal Wolstein man the rear Land Rover, while he, Lance Corporal Benson and I are in the lead vehicle. That way, the sergeant and I can get to know one another over the course of the journey.

As we meander along the winding, dusty roads, dwarfed by the snow-capped mountains either side of us, we do what all new acquaintances in the Army do: swap life stories.

I tell him about turning my back on my family's restaurant business. 'I was robbed of my youth, joined up at the tender age of sixteen . . .' I mention that I'd originally trained in the Army as a Russian linguist and then found myself working in the murky world of intelligence, but having realized I was the world's worst Russian speaker, decided to go to Sandhurst. 'That's how I ended up here in the Royal Logistic Corps – it's the only route for officers to becoming an ATO.'

I discover that Sergeant Khan is the youngest of six and moved to Bradford from Islamabad as a boy. His life in Pakistan was a stark contrast to his current home. One of his brothers is in prison, and the others are all doctors or lawyers. He laughs ruefully as he tells me about the outrage that met his announcement that he was joining the British Army. To this day, his father refuses to acknowledge his son's chosen career – but Shak clearly remains a devoted family man and a devout Muslim.

We continue chewing the fat as we cross a series of mountain passes and begin a steep climb. We've been travelling for about two hours when Rob – who's manning the radio in the back of the Rover – announces that he needs to stop for a piss.

'No worries. We'll pull over when we reach the top of this summit.'

But as we reach the top of the saddle, instead of a rolling mountain plateau, we're met by a group of Kalashnikov-wielding militiamen manning an illegal vehicle checkpoint.

Before I can get a word out, Rob is sending a sitrep back to HQ: 'Zero, this is Alpha Three Zero. India-Victor-Charlie-Papa at grid Tango Sierra 4953 2545, over.'

We'd normally reverse out of the potential contact area, but Dougie has just drawn up behind us and because we're blocking his view and don't have comms with him, he's completely oblivious to the threat ahead. A wave of adrenalin courses through my veins. This isn't good. We're sitting ducks.

The *shemagh*-clad militiamen are shouting and screaming at us, motioning us with their rifles to get out of the vehicle. A roll of razor wire is coiled out across the road in front of us. Behind it they've laid a selection of anti-tank mines.

Shak slowly raises his SA80 to just below window level. He flashes me a sideways glance. 'Mujahideen.'

I can sense Rob push the muzzle of his rifle through the gap between the seats behind me. He levels his weapon and takes aim at one of the militiamen.

'OK.' I focus dead ahead. 'I'll go and speak to them and when I exit the vehicle I'm going to move off to the flank and make a big song and dance about removing the magazine from my rifle. That way, those lunatics with the AKs might just think I'm non-threatening, and Dougie and Woolly will hopefully see what I'm doing and be in a position to react. If things start to go noisy, make sure you brass up as many of those fuckers as you can.'

I pull on the door lever and step gingerly out of the vehicle. The shouting immediately grows louder and more aggressive and every one of the mujahideen swings the barrel of his rifle in my direction.

I keep my weapon pointed up in the air, slowly remove my magazine and place it in my pocket. I've got a round chambered – just in case – along with a cocked Browning 9mm pistol inside my chest webbing, but I still feel massively vulnerable.

The muj are still shouting and screaming. They seem to be speaking a mixture of Arabic and Serbo-Croat, but I can't make out a word.

'We're BRI-TISH SOL-DIERS . . .' I hope that at least one of them speaks English. 'PEACE-KEEPERS . . . FROM THE UN . . .'

One of them seems to have been watching and listening rather than shouting. He replies, in a broad Yorkshire accent, 'Oh, you're Brits. Nice one, mate!'

Surreal.

They're not going to let us through the checkpoint yet, but the situation has taken several steps back from a full-on firefight to one we might be able to blag our way out of. Things are definitely looking up.

The muj invite us into their shack, and before long Omar the Yorkshireman is telling us his story. By the age of twelve he was carrying a knife and doing drugs. He joined a gang and adopted a life of crime – fuelled by women and alcohol. It was only in his late teens, he tells us, that a cousin took him to a mosque and his life took a turn for the better. He'd discovered Islam. Unfortunately, though, it was the radical version, and since finding his new faith, he'd also developed a deep hatred for the immorality and decadence of Western society.

When I ask him why he became a jihadist, he tells me that back in 1993 – in a North London mosque – he'd been shown a thirty-minute video about the ethnic cleansing of Muslims in the Balkans. 'The Bosnian Muslims were white, blond and blue-eyed and had co-existed with Serbs for centuries, but those Christian scum massacred them in their thousands.'

He goes into a rant about the international community refusing to arm the Bosnian Muslims and about some crazy Anglo-American conspiracy to reduce the number of Muslims in Europe.

'Do you honestly think you're making a difference here?' I ask him. I can't help myself.

'Of course we are!' He gives a detailed account of the

successful operations conducted by the four thousand mujahideen he claims are operating in the country. He explains that they're supported by highly trained Iranian Special Forces who've been intensifying their activities in central Bosnia – mainly concentrated around Zenica – for more than two years.

We're desperate to get on our way, but in terms of intelligence value, this guy's giving us an Aladdin's cave of information.

He talks reverently about the two to three hundred Arab 'Afghans' who, along with the thousand or so non-Bosnian Muslims, have been helping the native mujahideen to fight the Serbs. 'They're amazing fighters,' he says. 'True soldiers of God.'

I don't share his admiration. The Afghans are believed to have been behind the murder of British aid worker Paul Goodall near Zenica last year. But Omar's on a roll now. He tells us about the Bosnian training camps set up by the Iranians, where mujahideen from Yemen, Algeria, Chechnya and the Middle East are trained in bomb-making, sabotage and guerrilla warfare.

I glance across at Shak, who sits impassively while Omar launches into another tirade, taking everything in.

'While our sisters were being raped in Bosnia and our brothers slaughtered, the enemies of Islam are living in a society where worshipping God has been replaced by worshipping money and sex.'

He scorns our drug- and alcohol-fuelled landscape, our encouragement of homosexuality, our lack of family values.

I'm trying to be objective, but the more he goes on, the more I feel myself getting wound up by his extreme revulsion towards the country that adopted him.

'There's only one thing that can save the West from destroying itself,' he says, 'a total conversion – by force – of all its people to Islam, and strict adherence to the codes of Sharia law. That's why we're here: to kill the *kafir* and the unbelievers; to kill them all. That is our *jihad*, and that is what will assure us a place in Heaven.'

Shak has been shifting in his seat, visibly disturbed by what he's hearing, and beats me to the draw. 'So, correct me if I'm wrong, but you're saying that all followers of Allah have been commanded to kill everyone who is not of our faith so they can have a place in Heaven?'

The expression on Omar's face completely changes. 'Yes,' he replies sheepishly.

Shak launches into him: 'Well, sir, I'm a Muslim, and a true believer, but I have a real problem trying to imagine the Pope commanding all Catholics to kill those of our faith or the Archbishop of Canterbury ordering all Protestants to do the same in order to guarantee them a place in Heaven! *Jihad* means 'struggle'. It's about one's inner struggle to be a better Muslim, not about politics and killing.'

He spends the next ten minutes trying to persuade our hosts that Islam is spiritual – it's about praying, reciting the Koran, giving to charity, and being kind to our fellow man. But the muj are having none of it. Realizing his message is falling on deaf ears, he stands up and demands that our hosts let us through their checkpoint – *now*!

When Omar asks why they should, Sergeant Khan responds with a brilliant quote from Edmund Burke: '"All that is necessary for the triumph of evil is for good men to do nothing." And if you don't let us through, more Muslims are going to die.'

10

Have a heart that never hardens, a temper that never tires, and a touch that never hurts.

Charles Dickens

25 August 1995

We continue on our journey for the next four or five hours, sitting in strained silence as we pass the mirror-surfaced Lake Prozor and on through the mountain roads to our RV. It's only when we pull into the lay-by at the head of the vast convoy that Sergeant Khan finally breaks his silence. 'Excuse my language, sir, but I'm fucking raging. Those cunts are to Islam what the Ku Klux Klan are to Christianity. They're fanatics – how can you possibly reason with people like that?'

He neither wants nor expects an answer, which is just as well. We've been in this fucked-up country nearly four months now and I still can't work out who's the oppressed and who's the oppressor. I don't know which side started it all, but I do know that Bosnia is a land of timeless conflict where every faction's been guilty of carrying out some of the most unimaginable acts of barbarity known to man. Croats, Muslims, Serbs. The finger of blame points at all of them.

As I jump out of the Land Rover, I'm met by the convoy commander, another RLC lieutenant, who tells me we're going to be here for at least another hour because the French Foreign Legion have reported Serbian snipers about a kilometre further up the road.

'We've got to get going the moment we're given the all-clear, though,' he says. 'The guns on Mount Igman are down to their last few pallets of ammunition.'

We spend the time planning the final leg of our route, poring over a map laid out on the bonnet of my Land Rover while the boys are busy rustling up some culinary delights on their hexamine stoves. Predictably, a group of kids gathers around them, begging for the remains of their ration packs, which the boys take great delight in sharing with them. Despite their emaciated frames and bloated bellies, the kids are positively beaming as they tear open the bags of boiled sweets and fruit biscuits. It's my favourite sound in the world, children's laughter.

I hear Dougie greeting one of them: 'Hi, Jesus, you want some chocolate?'

The youngster looks like all his Christmases have come at once.

'What's with the name?' Rob asks.

'He tried to sell me his mum a few weeks ago. "You want to fuck my mother, soldier? She number-one virgin!" I've been calling him Jesus ever since.'

Every time we stop in this lay-by, we're approached by flocks of starving kids. Children who literally have nothing. They walk barefoot and wear grubby, tattered clothes. Their entire existence is about survival – nothing more.

A little girl who couldn't have been more than six always used to bring Cleggy a flower whenever we stopped there. When he returned from R&R a few weeks back, he brought a big bag of sweets with him and has saved them all for her. But the little girl has died. She stepped on a landmine.

Rob's incessant piss-taking lifts the mood again. 'So I'm assuming you didn't get to shag the boy's mum, then, Dougie?'

'And what makes you so sure?'

'Because with hair like that you couldn't get a shag if you walked into Strangeways with twenty B&H and a father on the parole board.'

I leave the boys to enjoy their food and banter, and find myself a quiet spot under a tree. I got a bluey from my mum this morning and this is the first chance I've had to read it.

Dear Son,

Not a moment passes without you being in my every waking thought. I know I've never been to a war-zone but you're the second son I've sent to war and it definitely doesn't get any easier. I remember those feelings of futility when your brother was in the Falklands, and how I'd have done anything to keep him safe. It's exactly the same now that you're in Bosnia.

I'd trade places with you in an instant if I could. We spend all the formative years of your lives making sure you're neither too hot nor too cold, making sure you're protected from all the evils in this world. And then, when you become soldiers, we're expected to wave and smile as you leave for places that are always too hot or too cold, and where evil is the norm.

Some of the mums who come into the restaurant tell me that they couldn't begin to imagine what it's like, and that they'd be beside themselves with worry. I've become used to their stares when I tell them, 'I'm sorry, I have to take this . . . my son is calling from Bosnia.' I've become addicted to the news too. Even when I'm not watching it, the television's always on in the background. I find myself gasping for breath every time I hear those words: 'A UN soldier was wounded today . . .' It's truly awful.

Above: Graduating from Sandhurst, December 1994. Our colour sergeant told us that we were to drill what Genghis Khan was to human rights.

Below: The poignant photograph shown to me by Major Hudson at Sandhurst. An operator in a protective EOD suit makes the long walk towards a vehicle bomb in Northern Ireland.

"PREPARE TO MEET THY GOD"

Left: Bosnia, 1995. Brummie (*right*) discussing with Mac (*left*) how to discipline the *guilty fatherless* in his section after his boys were caught stealing from the supply area they were supposed to be protecting.

Right: Posing for the camera by Lake Prozor immediately before we discovered that the Muslim village of Rumboci had been ethnically cleansed.

Below: A short while later I stood, dry-mouthed, imagining the horrors experienced by the family who were evicted from this house in Rumboci.

Below: This little girl always gave Cleggy a flower when we stopped at the lay-by outside Sarajevo. When he returned from R&R he brought her a big bag of sweets, but he was too late: she had died after stepping on a landmine.

Above: The calm before the storm. Just after this photo was taken we came under intense sniper fire while trying to get much-needed ammunition to the UN mortar and artillery positions on Mount Igman. (*Left to right*) Rob, Woolly, me and Dougie.

Above: French Foreign Legion mortar crew firing their deadly payloads onto Serbian positions. For months we'd been at the heart of an impossible conflict and unable to do anything about it. That day, we felt like we'd finally contributed to something that had made a difference.

Right: Receiving our UN and NATO Balkans medals from HRH the Duke of Gloucester.

Above: On the ranges in civvies. During our pre-deployment 'build-up' training, Brummie had told us that 90 per cent of all shootings take place against victims entering or leaving their homes or places of work.

Left: Northern Ireland, 1996. An RUC police officer mans a cordon position following the Thiepval Barracks bombing. It was the first bombing I'd ever experienced.

Above: The ATO course. We took more than two hundred exams – on every aspect of ammunition and explosives. Here I am (*left*) having a practical assessment on a Lynx helicopter's weapons suite and (*right*) returning from a chemical munitions disposal task.

Below left to right: Preparing a demolition charge with plastic explosive and hand grenades, adding the finishing touches to a neutralized IED, and an Improvised Explosive Device Defeat practical assessment. It was the very last phase of the ATO course and everything hung on it.

Left: The Wheelbarrow robot is a 300kg tracked vehicle with an extendable robotic arm mounted on the chassis which can be fitted with a wide selection of disruptor weapons. It's saved thousands of lives.

Right and below: Ant Worrel arrives with operators from four teams to support me in a task to neutralize a hundred exploding chemical drums on the back of a lorry.

Below and left: The articulated truck was parked the previous night and hours later the first drum exploded. The explosion sent it hurtling through the roof of the truck and eighty feet into the air.

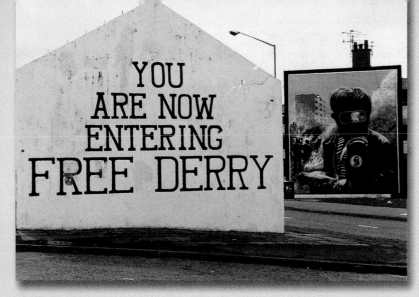

Above: Entering the hardline Republican estates of Londonderry, where an unskilled, unemployed Catholic man had two choices: sit around and do nothing, or join the IRA.

Below: Standing with the team in front of our Tactica EOD vehicles. Behind us, on the opposite bank of the river Foyle, the IRA snipers of Londonderry's Republican estates had a direct line of sight into our barracks.

Above: A suspected car bomb outside RUC Strand Road. A gunman had just driven it up to the front gate, opened fire with an AK47 and tried to escape on foot.

Below: Author carrying out a forensic clearance of the car before handing it over to the RUC scenes-of-crime officer.

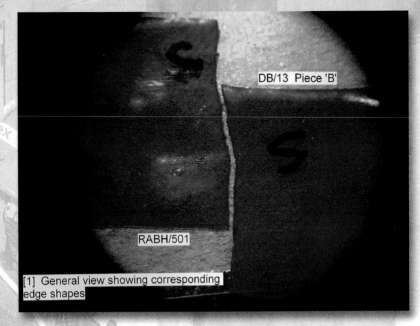

[1] General view showing corresponding edge shapes

Above: Handout issued by the Metropolitan Police showing the mechanical fit between an explosive detonator cord used by Richard Reid and found at 44 St James Street, Gloucester.

Below: Hostage rescue: Overseas Special Forces operators stack up against a wall ready to assault a terrorist stronghold.

I think about you day in and day out. And not just you, but all your men too. When I wake up each day, I find myself calculating the time in Bosnia and wondering what you're doing. And when Frank and I are sitting at dinner, I find myself thinking about what you had to eat today . . . and wonder if you've even eaten at all. Sometimes just thinking about it is enough to make me cry. I seem to do that a lot. I cry when you haven't called or written and I cry when you do. I find even the smallest of things make me teary-eyed these days . . . walking into your room . . . seeing your picture . . . even seeing other young soldiers home on leave. But in spite of all that, I also feel the most overwhelming sense of pride. I'm proud of you all for what you're doing over there and I'm proud that you manage to do so under the most difficult of circumstances.

Stay safe, darling boy. Our thoughts are with you.

Love

Mum x

Every now and again, being out here seems to throw up a special moment and receiving a letter from home definitely ranks right up there with the best of them. Reading a bluey always brings a smile to my face – but sometimes I can't help feeling an overwhelming sense of guilt too. I realize I've never really appreciated how difficult it must be for Mum: she's already lost one son, and came perilously close to losing another in the Falklands, so to cope with me being over here must be truly horrendous for her.

'Chris, it's time to roll.' The convoy commander doesn't need to tell me twice. I get the team together and give them a quick set of confirmatory orders. We're going to reconfigure. Dougie, Rob and I will ride in the lead vehicle and Shak and his guys will form the counter-assault team at the rear of the convoy. That way, if the shit hits the fan, they'll be in position for a counter-attack.

Before long our slow-moving convoy is snaking its way between the drab Soviet-style houses and apartment buildings that make up Sarajevo's suburbs. As we pass through the heavily fortified entrance to the airport, the foreign UN troops manning the sangar positions radiate disinterest. Most are lounging around doing fuck-all. Some are smoking; others are blatantly sleeping. And none of them seems to give a shit.

We head along a tree-lined boulevard, past hordes of concrete, flat-roofed buildings and badly shot-up planes, and continue onto the runway which – rather ominously – is known as 'Sniper Alley'. There are kilometres of run-down apartment buildings surrounding the airfield and all of them are a gift of a sniper position.

Seconds later, I feel the hairs rise on the back of my neck. I'm not sure why, but I have an overwhelming sense of impending danger. I look over to Dougie but he's completely oblivious. He sparks up a Lambert & Butler Silver and stares nonchalantly ahead.

As the cool Balkan air gusts gently through the Land Rover's window, I try to switch off and relax too, but something's not right. Maybe this is what they call combat intuition. Up until now, I've only ever heard about it . . .

Three or four shots crack open the air above our heads, kicking up dust as they ricochet off the airfield.

I'm unable to move. I'm numb with fear. I've never been shot at before. For the first time in my life I'm just inches away from becoming a statistic. Then my mind races as I try to regain the ability to focus and prioritize my actions.

The sky fills with gunfire – first a few loud pops and cracks, and then a roaring barrage; bullets are flying everywhere, screaming off the ground and the surrounding buildings.

I've never been so terrified. The tension in my stomach makes me feel trapped and sick with dread. I can't think straight; I've completely frozen.

The passing seconds have seemed like hours, but finally, now that the oxygen has started flowing back to my brain, I feel a surge of adrenalin. I grab the radio handset from Rob and yell into the mouthpiece: 'Zero, this is Papa Two Zero Alpha . . . CONTACT, over.'

There's no response.

'Fuck!'

Nobody can hear me. I've never felt so vulnerable in all my life.

'How do you want to play this one, Boss?' Dougie draws on his cigarette, still uncannily calm.

As far as surreal moments go, this one's beginning to take the piss. We've got to lead the rest of the convoy out of here. But it's suddenly dawned on me that, like most people, my only knowledge of armed conflict is from films, the news and from books.

'Put your fucking foot down, Dougie!'

The air is filled with dust and smoke as the deadly rounds continue to clip the tarmac around us. I find myself experiencing a whole range of emotions: anger, fear, rage, humiliation. But one thought is really playing on my mind: Why is someone who doesn't even know us so intent on killing us?

Dougie guns the accelerator and the Land Rover lurches forwards, engine shrieking. But as soon as we begin to build up momentum, Rob shouts through from the back, 'Boss, we've got to slow down – we've left the convoy behind.'

Jesus!

The rounds are still coming in thick and fast as the

gunmen unleash a savage storm of lead into the killing area.

The first rule in a contact is to return fire, to match aggression with aggression, and to kill people. We're supposed to kill people. The trouble is, we're completely blind. There's nobody to kill.

'Boss, can we start shooting yet?' Rob is desperate to see if his SA80 assault rifle really can fire upwards of six hundred rounds per minute.

'No, Rob! There's nothing to shoot at.' From the look on his face, I can tell he's frightened, excited and euphoric all at once. But, most of all, he's disappointed.

And so am I. My safety catch is off and I'm looking over my sights, scanning the area, but we're in a moving vehicle and the enemy gunmen are very well hidden and at least three hundred metres away. Even if we could see them, the chance of hitting them at this range is virtually zero.

Another burst of gunfire, and tracer crackles past our faces. I duck involuntarily into my body armour as a round punches into the road behind us.

'Anybody seen them yet?' I scream.

We can't debus and move into proper cover because there isn't any: we're completely exposed. We just need to keep driving.

My eyes flick back and forth over the area, trying to identify where the bastards are shooting from. All I want to do is get them in my sights and brass the fuckers up.

'Boss, we're good to go,' Dougie says. 'The convoy's caught up.'

'Then let's get the fuck out of here!'

Gradually, finally, the firing seems to subside as we make our way to the other side of the airport and begin winding our way up the road to Mount Igman.

I look at my hands. They're shaking uncontrollably. I'm still in a shit state.

Dougie sparks up another cigarette and hands it to me with a huge grin on his face. 'You'll get over it, Boss, everybody does. Later on you'll find yourself looking into other people's eyes and wondering if they had the same feelings as you did. You'll wonder if you were the only one who was scared. And once you realize you're human after all, you'll be able to accept that everyone was fucking terrified. Anyone who denies it is talking out of his arse.'

What he says makes perfect sense, but my first time under fire has been nothing like I'd expected. I was far more scared than I'd imagined I would be. I'm disappointed I didn't return fire, and absolutely amazed at how an episode that flashed by in little more than a minute seemed to last hours. I'm also amazed at how impossibly difficult it is to locate some bastard who's intent on killing you when you're in a moving vehicle. Thank fuck they couldn't hit a horse's arse with a banjo.

We climb the bleak mountain, carving our way through thick woodland and rocky outcrops, and eventually reach the summit – a barren plateau where huge strips of minefield line the windswept road. Moments later we reach the Mount Igman Hotel and the famous ski jump where Eddie the Eagle shot to fame in the 1984 Olympics. Row upon row of artillery pieces are dug into the muddy fields on its far side. We've finally reached the gun line.

'Get a fucking move on!' the battery sergeant major shouts. 'We need to get this ammo off the wagons NOW!'

Dozens of British, French and Dutch troops begin swarming over the convoy, tearing the pallets apart with pliers, bayonets and their bare hands. The guns have completely run out. There's no time to spare: each second that passes means another life claimed by Serbian snipers, artillery or mortar crews.

Everybody mucks in. Some of us are on top of the trucks, cutting through the banding wire, handing down the ammo boxes containing the artillery shells. Others are running the boxes across to the gun positions while their crews set the fuses and load the shells into their huge steel barrels.

I think of the hapless civilians, the old men and women, the mothers clinging to their children as they run the gauntlet through the middle of Sarajevo, zigzagging their way desperately through the exposed streets as the deadly salvoes rain down on them from the surrounding mountains.

Seconds later, the first massive explosions resonate across the mountain as the guns let loose a barrage of high-explosive hell onto the Serbian positions. Overhead, two Dutch F-16 fighters scream into view and fire off a lethal string of rockets – their deadly payload guided onto the Serbian tanks and gun emplacements by the British Special Forces dug into their hidden observation posts.

As my body shudders with each deafening boom, I think about the elderly Serbian couple I spoke to in Lipa who'd been robbed and beaten by the Muslims. I think about the Muslims in Rumboci who'd been raped, tortured and murdered by the Croats, and then I think about the seven thousand innocents massacred in Srebrenica and the scores of women and children in Sarajevo who've been slain by Serbian snipers and artillery.

Eisenhower said: 'I hate war as only a soldier who has lived it can, only as one who has seen its brutality, its futility, its stupidity.' For months now I've been in the heart of this impossible conflict and I've been unable to do anything about it. Finally, today, I feel as if I've actually contributed to something that's made a difference.

But it's still not enough.

11

History ... is a nightmare from which I am trying to awake.

James Joyce

15 March 1996

I'm standing opposite the house, shoulder to shoulder with the other villagers, helplessly watching the lifeless corpses hanging from the porch. The old lady said there were two adults and a child ... but I can see a fourth body swaying in the wind. I recognize the face. I feel sick to the pit of my stomach. Bile rises in my throat. My body goes into convulsions, faint at first, but quickly becoming so painful that it feels as if my chest is going to explode. It's my brother.

I have to do something; I have to cut Tim down. I take a step forward, desperate to help him, but I begin falling, spiralling down towards the lake.

I hit the water with incredible force, plunging into its murky depths. I can't breathe, I'm fighting to get to the surface, swimming in a sea of bodies, gasping for breath as I struggle to clear my way through layer upon layer of dead mothers and babies. I shudder as I come into contact with the wax-like cadavers, their pitiful faces obscured by the slimy weeds that have entwined us. I kick out repeatedly, desperate to free myself.

When I eventually break free and clamber past them, I find myself lying in a mass grave, surrounded by thousands of bullet-ridden corpses. There are mutilated bodies everywhere – and packs of dogs chewing the bones.

I let out a scream, and when I open my eyes, I'm sitting bolt upright in my bed, covered with sweat. My screams have jerked me back into consciousness. I grip my hands and bite my lip, trying to stop myself crying out again.

I feel confused, empty, exhausted. I look around me at the rows of books on my shelves; the photos of my family and friends adorning the walls; the furniture and souvenirs I've bought during my trips around the world. All my most treasured belongings are here. This is the place I'm supposed to call home. But it doesn't feel like my home any more. Nowhere does. I feel completely lost.

I look at my watch: midnight. My phone's flashing on my desk. It's a text message from Brummie, sent an hour ago.

'Boss, call me. Urgently.'

I punch in his number and after a couple of rings Brummie's cheerful voice comes booming down the line. 'Hello, Boss, how's tricks?'

I tell him I'm good and apologize for missing his call. 'I was sleeping.'

'Well, best you get suited and booted and drag your arse over here pronto. It's the Officers to Sergeants' Mess do and you're supposed to be here. The commanding officer's asking where you are.'

Bollocks. I'd completely forgotten. I've just been away on three months' leave and only returned this evening. I'd been warned about tonight's function before I left Bosnia, but it had slipped my mind.

'I'll be there in five, Brum.' I force a smile and try to mask my misery as best I can.

As I ring off, I realize I've forgotten to ask him about his Bosnia injuries. I'm so consumed with my own shit right now I'm finding it impossible to think about anybody or anything else.

I splash cold water on my face and try not to pay too much attention to the ghostly figure looking back at me. I pull out a suit from my wardrobe and grab a fresh shirt and a pair of shoes. I'm conscious of how much slower and more deliberate my actions have become. I feel like an old man. It's all I can do to get dressed. I feel completely fucked.

A few minutes later I make my way downstairs and head out of the Officers' Mess. The Sergeants' Mess is on the other side of the camp, past the guardroom and Regimental Headquarters. I enter its grand hall, adorned with oil paintings and battle trophies from centuries-old conflicts, and hear raucous laughter from the bar. The door swings open and Brummie appears, walking towards me with outstretched arms. He throws them around me like I'm a long-lost brother.

'You look like shit . . . but it's good to shee you, Bosh.'

He's blatantly as pissed as a parrot. I'm pleased to see him too. Right now he feels like my only friend in the world.

'How's your back, Brum?'

'Good ash new.' He goes into a drunken rant about the three months of extensive physiotherapy he underwent before being given a clean bill of health. 'Come on, letsh get a drink,' he says. 'You've got shome catching up to do.'

As we enter the room full of drunken officers, senior NCOs and warrant officers, I feel out of place. I experience a wave of anger and resentment as I look at all these people enjoying themselves. I know I'm being irrational but I can't help myself. How can they be so hedonistic when there's so much suffering in the world?

I need to curb my anger. I need to get a grip.

Brummie orders us both a large Bushmills and I neck mine in one.

'Easy, tiger . . .' He hands me his full glass and tells me to go and tip my hat to the CO. 'I'll order us another round.'

I head across the crowded room to Lieutenant Colonel Baker, a kindly grey-haired man who took over as commanding officer shortly before I deployed to Bosnia.

'Hello, Chris, how was your leave?' He extends his hand.

We exchange a bit of small-talk before I make my excuses and rejoin Brummie. He's holding a fresh round of drinks.

The regimental quartermaster sergeant (RQMS), one of the unit's most senior warrant officers, approaches as the two of us resume our conversation. Ignoring me, he whispers something in Brummie's ear.

'Not a fucking chance!' Brummie replies coldly.

I've got no idea what the RQMS has just said to him, but Brummie's clearly very pissed off.

'Sergeant Lees, I'm not asking you. I'm telling you.'

'Well, with respect, sir, you can go and get fucked.'

'What's up, Brum?' I ask, trying to ease the situation. Before he can reply the RQMS has grabbed me from behind and is trying to wrestle me to the floor.

'New officer!' he shouts. 'Get him naked!'

I'm suddenly surrounded by senior NCOs all trying to grab me. I've got no idea what's going on, but I'm fucking fuming. I start lashing out at them and Brummie wades into them too. One by one they peel off until it's only me and the RQMS, standing face to face.

'What the fuck do you think you're playing at?' I say.

The room goes completely silent. Everybody's looking at me. I can feel hundreds of pairs of eyes burning into the back of my head.

'It's part of your introduction into the regiment,' he says, with a curl of the lip. 'All new officers have to go through it. What makes you think you should be treated differently?'

I can't believe I'm hearing this. I've been in the regiment almost a year and I've spent most of that time on operations. I did four years as an NCO before that. There's no way I'm going to be treated like some fucking red-arse straight out of training.

I completely lose it. 'First, I've done my time, so you can shove your introduction right up your arse. And second, I don't give a fuck if I'm a guest in your mess. If you lay another finger on me I'll beat the living shit out of you.'

'That's enough!' Jake Garside's voice booms across the room. He comes storming over, grabs me and frog-marches me over to the door. 'What the fuck's got into you, Chris? The CO's just written you up for the Carmen Sword of Honour, and here you are – first day back – kicking off with a warrant officer. Completely out of order. Now go home and sort yourself out!'

My head hanging in shame, I leave the building and begin the lonely walk back to my room. Jake's right. I don't know what's got into me. All I know is that I've been suffering from increasingly severe mood swings. I wish I knew how to shake them off.

As I step into the Officers' Mess I hear a familiar voice behind me. 'Oi, Rocky, wait up!'

Brummie has followed me back.

'What happened to the happy-go-lucky boss I left behind in Bosnia, eh?'

'I'm sorry, Brum. I didn't mean to embarrass you.'

'You didn't embarrass me. The bloke's a fucking prick and I'd have paid good money to see you drop him. But, seriously, what's wrong?'

I motion him to follow me into the empty bar and grab a bottle of Bushmills from the shelf. I pour us a glass each and for a few moments we sit in absolute silence. Then it all comes flooding out. I tell him about the insomnia, the recurring nightmares and the mood swings. I tell him about my frustration, my lack of concentration and my total inability to readjust to normal life. 'I thought taking a couple of months out trekking in Africa and Norway would help me get my head straight. I thought the change of scenery would help, but it's made no difference at all.'

I'm conscious that I'm doing all the talking and Brummie's doing all the listening, but he knows I need to get it out of my system. I feel stupid saying it, but I tell him about how I've been on a kind of personal crusade since Tim's death; a crusade where I want to right the wrongs of the world; a crusade to crush the drug-dealer; a crusade to crush the terrorist.

'I just don't know which, and I don't know how. I thought becoming an ATO was the answer, but I'm questioning that now. Listen to me . . . I'm all over the fucking place, aren't I? I've even started toying with the idea of attempting SAS Selection. I just don't know what I want, Brum. I feel like I've completely lost my way.'

Brummie pours us another glass of Bushmills, sparks up a cigarette and takes a deep draw on it. 'It seems to me, Boss, you're a man searching for meaning. You're trying to make sense of your brother's death; you're determined to do the right thing by your parents, by me and by the world at large. You've got this burning desire to solve the problems of the world.'

He takes another draw.

'And that's all commendable stuff. The trouble is, you're also a man on the edge. Your life experiences have affected you, and you've become increasingly

112

frustrated by your inability to do the things you feel you need to do in order to give your life and Tim's death some meaning.

'I don't know whether yours is a war on drugs or a war on terror. I suspect it's probably a bit of both. But you know what? It doesn't matter. You're never going to solve all the world's problems in one go, but that doesn't mean you can't try to solve them one at a time. A lot of good men fail because they try too hard to be perfect. And you know what? It's all right to be good enough. You can be a good enough husband, father, soldier, and still be a success.'

I know we're both a bit pissed, but his words are really striking a chord.

'What I'm trying to say, Boss, is that you need to stop beating yourself up. The CO told me tonight that we're going to be deploying to Northern Ireland in a few weeks, and when we do, we're going to need you to be on top form. So do yourself a favour and start focusing on getting better and stop worrying about the things you can't change. I know you're suffering, but I promise you, I'll never let you suffer alone.'

He stands up, finishes his drink and leaves me to prepare myself for another dark night of the soul.

12

We only have to be lucky once; you have to be lucky always.

Patrick McGee, convicted IRA bomber

7 October 1996

My head's pounding. I'm nursing the mother of all hangovers and the lack of sleep and recurring nightmares are driving me crazy.

I gun the accelerator and overtake the Skoda I've been stuck behind for the past ten minutes. The drive – from our barracks in Antrim to the Army's HQ in Lisburn – normally takes less than half an hour, but today every driver in Ulster seems to be on a mission to make me late for my appointment. I know I should be more chilled out about stuff that really doesn't matter, but I'm struggling at the moment.

I just feel angry all the time. Angry at everything. Even the rain hammering against my windscreen is pissing me off. I'm sick of this road. I'm sick of this whole fucking place. I wish I was somewhere else. Anywhere but here.

For a moment, as I meander along this rolling country road on the outskirts of Belfast, I allow my mind to wander too. I wish I could think of something happy, something positive. But I just see the same images playing over and over again in my mind . . . the bodies in the lake at Rumboci; the mothers holding their babies with nooses tied around their necks; and my brother – his headless corpse lying underneath the bridge.

I've tried to follow Brummie's advice. I've tried to focus on getting better and worrying less about my future and the things I cannot change. But I'm still finding it impossibly difficult. Major Hudson told me to stay in the Army and fight terrorism. But I should have known better. He was a good man, and I've no doubt he meant every word, but I should have known it was never going to pan out that way. He sold me those pearls of wisdom nearly two years ago and in that time I haven't even so much as seen a terrorist.

A blue VW Passat comes screaming towards me as its driver attempts to overtake the car in front of him. Adrenalin courses through my veins as I slam on the brakes. He swerves back onto the left lane, missing my car by a fraction.

Tosser.

Now that I've been shocked back to reality, I begin blocking out the bad images and concentrating on something else. Something more important, like how the hell Brummie and I are going to sort out our troop.

Our last few months in Bosnia turned out to be pretty busy; at times there had hardly been time to eat, let alone sleep. And the lads loved it. They grew used to living with the danger and uncertainty and they thrived. But here in Ulster things are completely different. The Provisional IRA has been on ceasefire for more than two years and for months Northern Ireland has been holding its breath, wondering if the Provos will resume their long war.

And to top it all, my troop's been spammed with looking after camp security. Traditionally one of the most vital jobs in the Province, the ceasefire has made it one of the most mundane tasks imaginable. There's fuck-all happening and the cracks are beginning to show.

Two months ago, the security forces witnessed a single, solitary incident: a car containing a crude 250-pound bomb was found abandoned in Belfast, but the explosive was so poorly made it failed to go off. Some cowboy outfit calling itself the Continuity IRA claimed responsibility, but the word on the street is that they've neither the means nor the intelligence to pose any real threat and are basically a bunch of clueless clowns.

Other than that, there's been nothing. The boys are experiencing endless periods of boredom, and boredom leads to complacency, which in an operational environment invariably results in some poor fucker going home in a coffin.

Something needs to be done. Brummie and I spent most of yesterday smoking the world's supply of Lambert & Butler trying to come up with a solution, but unsurprisingly we achieved nothing more than a bad cough.

'This is bollocks, Boss,' he said to me, in his uniquely eloquent way. 'We're inventing tasks just for the sake of it. And no matter how much numb-nuts goes on about training, there's only so much PT, weapon cleaning and range work we can give the boys before one of them downs tools and goes AWOL. They've got a demanding day job, ceasefire or no ceasefire. They still need to remain one hundred per cent vigilant – and we can't keep loading extra tasks onto them just because that fucking space cadet thinks it's a good idea.'

Brummie rarely complains, but right now his outburst is completely justified. The commander of the Sapper Squadron to which we've been attached is a typical gung-ho Sandhurst cliché man who knows all the theory but has very little operational experience. He's also wired to the fucking moon.

What's worse is that he fancies himself as a bit of a

'Monty' type figure and regularly gets the blokes on parade so that he can talk at them. He loves the sound of his own voice and he's always feeding us bone lines. One of his favourites is: 'Your task in peace is to train for war . . .' Which would be fine if we were back home, but this is Northern Ireland. And, in spite of the ceasefire, the last time I checked it was still an operational deployment.

I totally agree that the blokes need to be kept busy. But, as Brummie said, adding to their workload in the form of training over and above their operational tasks is definitely not the answer.

As I drop down the hill I realize I'm going to have to put it all to the back of my mind – for now. I'm minutes away from the local Army Educational Centre, about to write the world's most pointless essay about *The Role of the United Nations in Future Peacekeeping Operations*. I've never understood why essays are deemed 'essential' to promotion but there's no compulsory continuation-training in either leadership or management techniques for young officers.

As I near the end of my journey, the horizontal rain gives way to a mild drizzle. I take a left into Duncan's Road, past rows of bungalows and red-brick terraced houses, and join the queue of anxious soldiers and support staff backed up nose-to-tail in unmarked cars, waiting to enter the camp. In spite of the ceasefire, and even on a journey as routine as this, we always do road moves dressed in civvies, driving unmarked cars. Brummie has hammered into all of us that we're never to let our guard down.

As I edge forward, I instinctively reach down and place my hand on the cocked Browning 9mm pistol that's tucked firmly under my thigh, ready to draw and shoot straight through the window at any attackers. During our pre-deployment 'build-up' training, Brummie had told us that 90 per cent of all shootings take place against victims entering or leaving their homes or places of work.

I know the chances of PIRA attacking anybody today are minimal, but I've no intention of confirming Brummie's statistics.

A pulse of brilliant white light silhouettes the watch-tower in front of me as a thunderous explosion and flaming whirlwind engulfs the car park ahead.

The car bomb – parked near the barracks' petrol point – fragments into thousands of tiny pieces of molten metal. Dozens of soldiers are blown off their feet, maimed and deafened, and rows of cars spontaneously burst into flames.

The roads are filling with screaming, blood-soaked people. Their agony is masked by the scores of car alarms set off by the bomb blast. The survivors wander around, dazed and confused. They're all in shock. They all need help.

The attack alarm sounds and one of the guards slams shut the huge iron gate.

I look in my rear-view mirror. People are getting into and out of their vehicles, gripped by panic and unsure what to do next. I'm stuck in the middle of a row of parked cars. Unable to move forwards or back.

There are injured bodies everywhere. Scorch marks on the paving are dotted with chunks of flesh. Soldiers and support staff are running out of the buildings, trying to comfort the survivors. Others are carrying the wounded to the medical centre.

While the wounded are being evacuated a small group of ammunition technical officers (ATOs) have begun smashing car windows with hammers. They're meticulously searching every vehicle, one by one, for secondary devices. But there are hundreds of parked cars. It must be like searching for a needle in a stack of needles.

A group of men are trying to give first aid to a badly burnt soldier at the petrol point. Others stand by them. They want to help, but are too overcome by emotion and shock to do anything but watch. A civilian is laid on a blanket nearby. His red and blistered body's been stripped naked by the blast.

There's another huge blast. All the oxygen is sucked out of the air as the second explosion rocks the barracks. Now the helpers are screaming and shouting and running for their lives too. The bombers have hit the medical centre with another 400-pound car bomb they've placed there to kill as many of the rescuers – and the rescued – as they can. There are charred and lacerated bodies everywhere.

I swallow hard. Bile sears the back of my throat as the nauseating stench of burnt flesh fills my nostrils.

On the other side of the wall a soldier is shouting for his friend. A few minutes ago they were standing next to each other – but since the second blast he's been unable to find him.

I wish there was something I could do to help him. But I can't. I'm stuck in a row of parked cars, locked out of the barracks.

Redundant.

Some time later, as the smoke and dust begin to settle, four soldiers come running out of a side gate and fan out into the road, each taking up a fire position. They're quickly joined by the rest of their section and, within seconds, their corporal has begun taking control of the situation, pushing back the hordes of onlookers and hacks and barking commands at the drivers of the parked cars, ordering them to return to their units.

Nobody's getting into or out of Thiepval Barracks today.

With a wave of his hand he motions me to do a three-point turn, then mouths the words: FUCK OFF.

* * *

I reflect on the carnage I've just witnessed as I drive back over Antrim's rolling countryside. I've never felt so useless in my life. I can still hear the screams of the victims, still see the charred civilian stripped naked by the bomb blast.

For months now I've been completely self-absorbed, getting pissed every night, so wrapped up in my own problems that I've been unable to see the bigger picture. I think of the ATOs – their coolness and calm under pressure as they searched hundreds of vehicles by hand for subsequent devices. They don't describe what they do as a job, they call it a vocation. And many of them describe the moment they decided to join the trade as a calling.

I'm in complete awe of them. Nobody ordered them to do what they did today. They just got on with it, fully aware that any one of the cars could have been packed full of explosives.

For two years theirs was the only job in the world that I wanted to do, but Brummie was right: I've allowed myself to lose focus.

Well, that's all about to change. I don't care if I'm sick. I'll get over it. This is my calling.

13

The true measure of a man is how he treats someone who can do him absolutely no good.

Samuel Johnson

8 October 1996

'How you feeling, Boss?'

'All right, Brum . . . I'm all right.'

He knows I'm not. He knows I don't want to admit I'm still suffering and I don't want those close to me to think I'm weak . . . or, worse, mad.

He can tell that the eight months we spent in Bosnia has affected me far more than I could ever have imagined. He knows I feel angry all the time, that I can't sleep, that I can't seem to hold down any sort of relationship for more than five minutes. He knows it's dominating every single aspect of my life. I've even thought about topping myself.

The trouble is, while I can precisely identify the

problem, I don't have the first fucking clue how I'm supposed to deal with it. There's a massive stigma associated with post-traumatic stress, and because it's such a taboo subject in the Army my only option seems to be to try to hide it. And yesterday's bombings only seem to have compounded the problem. I feel like shit.

'I've just read the incident report,' Brummie says. 'The bastards killed a REME warrant officer and injured a further thirty-one civilians and military. They placed the secondary in the path of victims fleeing from the first bomb. Those cold-blooded fuckers specifically tried to kill as many of the wounded as possible.'

'I know, Brum. They're scum.' I try to sound polite while making a beeline for the door. I just don't want to think about it any more. I feel as if every time I take a step forward, every time I manage to come to terms with the recondite shit I've experienced in my life, something else comes along and sends me hurtling back into the abyss. 'Listen, mate, I don't mean to cut you short, but I'll be back in half an hour. There's something I've got to do.'

One building in camp is out of bounds to all but a select few. I've frequently found excuses to walk past the ATOs' complex – occasionally catching a glimpse of their high-tech robots being deftly guided through car doors by operators with remote controls – but because I'd lost my way for a while and gone off the idea of becoming an ATO, I've never managed to find a reason to go and introduce myself. Until now.

As I approach the compound, I'm greeted by a young corporal ferrying boxes of explosives and equipment from his workshop to the back of his Tactica armoured EOD vehicle. I'd often heard the Tactica's blues and twos blaring out across the barracks as the ATO and his team screamed out of the camp gates to a waiting bomb. Even though there was an IRA ceasefire up until yesterday, these boys have been run ragged for months.

I introduce myself and ask if I can see the ATO.

'Certainly, sir, come on in.'

There are only six operational ATOs in Northern Ireland, only six men capable of taking on the most sophisticated bomb-makers in the world. They are the men who make the critical decisions during disposal operations. They live with their teams, separate from the remainder of the unit, and they go about their business quietly and efficiently.

Myths galore surround the courage and capabilities of these quietly unassuming soldiers. I deeply admire the way they operate. There's never any shouting, no bullshit, no parades, just a very tight team doing a very difficult job.

The corporal punches in a code and pushes open the thick security door, then leads me through a maze of corridors adorned with technical diagrams of IEDs and portrait photos of previous ATOs and their teams.

When we arrive at the crew room he tells me to take a seat while he goes and grabs the boss. Some of the lads from the team are in there but they're engrossed in conversation, so I don't interrupt. Instead I wander around the room looking at the photos and shelves of reconstructed IEDs used for training and identification. One of the boys, an animated Royal Signals corporal, is busy telling a story about his last leave. 'I was in Tesco and I see this busty blonde staring at me. I couldn't believe it – she was full-on staring. And then she started waving at me. So I thought, Fuck it. "Excuse me," I ask. "Do I know you?"

"I think you're the father of one of my children," she says.'

He's got our complete attention. He tells the team how he broke out in a cold sweat and racked his brain until he eventually remembered his one act of infidelity.

'"Fucking hell – are you the bird I shagged on me stag do, while your mate whipped me and your other mate stuck a brush up my arse?"

'"No," she says. "I'm your son's English teacher . . ."'

This is what I love most about the Army. Whatever shit life throws at us, however low our morale, there's always someone ready to crack a funny. In times of adversity it's the banter that sustains us. It puts everything else into perspective.

A tall warrant officer with a bushy moustache and a wide grin enters the room and extends his hand to me. 'Hello, sir, I'm WO2 George Wilkinson, ATO Antrim. How can I help?'

We go through to his office and sit down and shoot the shit over a coffee. I explain how I'd been desperate to become an ATO, but that after Bosnia I'd kind of lost momentum and briefly flirted with the idea of going for SAS Selection. 'I know this sounds crazy, Q, but I was at that bombing at Lisburn yesterday, and my whole outlook changed. It was almost as if I'd been given a message.' I feel my face redden, but he's surprisingly sympathetic.

Instead of making me feel foolish he tells me it doesn't sound crazy at all. 'It's the way it happens for most of us. And you should probably be aware, if you do need to get the whole Special Forces thing out of your system, we have ATOs serving with both the SAS and the Special Boat Service. It's all very sensitive so I can't tell you much about it, but I served with them myself before coming out here and it's the most fun time I've ever had. They even pay you for it!'

For the next half an hour, I fire question after question at him. He doesn't pull any punches. He tells me about life as an ATO: how you have to be totally committed – all the time, because not only does the ATO lead the team he's also the one responsible for walking down the road and defusing the bomb. No one else in the team takes the Longest Walk. 'That man cannot afford to take any chances. If he fumbles, or makes the wrong decision, there is no second chance. In this game it's either total failure or complete success.'

He goes on to explain that ATOs typically serve for six months in Northern Ireland and return home for a year or so before being called back. 'Only the most capable operators deploy to the Province. They're known as high-threat operators, and they're up against the most experienced bombmakers whose principal objective is to kill them.'

It's clear that a grudging respect has developed between these two sets of bitter enemies. Theirs isn't a war of attrition, but one of cunning and guile. PIRA has frequently faked devices or constructed concealed booby-traps specifically to lure an ATO to his death. In Northern Ireland the ATO is the star prize. If PIRA can kill a bomb-disposal man they can wreak havoc until he's replaced.

We head back into the crew room and he shows me some of the devices. He explains how the development of the IED has paralleled that of conventional weapons. 'Every technological advance improving the per-formance of conventional weapons has been utilized by bombmakers and incorporated into IEDs, either to directly improve their lethality, or to add sophistication to the triggering unit.'

The IED has developed from a comparatively crude weapon incorporating gunpowder and some form of pyrotechnic device to a high-tech remote-control system incorporating modern high explosives.

'Tactical advances developed alongside the technological advances – hence the proxy bomb, the come-on and the secondary device. Now the tactical use of the IED is limited only by the imagination of the bomber.' He tells me how bombs can be made to look like radios or other electronic equipment and how plastic and sheet explosive have enabled bombs to be constructed and placed in locations that were previously thought impossible. The Brighton bomb attack that nearly decapitated the British government in 1984 was constructed using sheet explosive hidden behind bath panels and initiated by a very accurate long-delay electronic timer.

'Other devices can be triggered using movement sensors and mercury tilt switches – one of PIRA's favourite methods of targeting ATOs.' He pulls out a file and flicks through the pictures, describing numerous incidents where operators have been personally targeted. 'They're what we call victim-operated IEDs – or booby-traps.'

He charts the evolution of the IED in the Province,

and how PIRA's mass production of radio-controlled devices led to the development of electronic counter-measures capable of jamming the IEDs.

Because of the success of ECM in Northern Ireland the terrorist groups turned to other means of detonation. The command wire, linking a bomb to a firer sited in an overwatch position, had been used from the very early days of the conflict, but was vulnerable to identifi-cation in advance of an attack. He shows me some aerial photography using infra-red false colour film, which clearly shows where vegetation has been disturbed by the process of digging in the wires. 'So, basically, our job is to get in there before these things go bang, and make them safe.'

I'm in awe of this guy. Men like WO2 Wilkinson aren't the gung-ho infantry types who go running around storming enemy machine-gun nests. Theirs is a far more refined form of combat – a game of extreme chess, in which every move, every action is meticu-lously planned and the consequences of those actions carefully weighed. I'm completely mesmerized.

WO2 Wilkinson is a very easy person to talk to. He's made me feel so completely at ease that I feel a bit of a fraud for not telling him about my post-traumatic stress disorder. I decide to come clean and, to my amazement, he tells me it's incredibly common in his neck of the woods. He touches me gently on the arm and tells me I should just deal with each day as it comes. 'You've got to stick it out. It will get easier, and you will get over it. But don't tell another living soul about it. If the shrinks find out, you won't make it past day one of the course.'

Before the thick metal door slams shut behind me I've made up my mind. No more indecision; no more fucking about.

Whatever it takes, I'm going to be an ATO.

14

Nothing in life is to be feared. It is only to be understood.

Marie Curie

14 December 1997

My hands are trembling and I've broken into a cold sweat. I've always wondered what it would feel like to stand next to a live bomb, and now I know: it's one of the most surreal and unnerving feelings in the world. I'm inches away from death – and desperately trying to work out what to do next.

I'm supposed to have separated the fuse from the neck of the artillery shell by placing an explosive cutting charge between the two components.

I thought I'd done it exactly as our instructor taught us. I shaped the cutting charge around the nose of the shell, slid the detonator into the explosive, then walked back to the firing point before initiating the small charge remotely.

After the explosion, I waited for the dust and smoke

to settle before making my way back to inspect my handiwork, but all I can see are the wires of a badly damaged fuse – fluttering dangerously in the wind – and a very unstable bomb that can detonate at any time.

This isn't good. I've completely stuffed the charge placement. At any moment I could be engulfed in a blinding flash of heat and flame as shards of razor-sharp bomb fragments tear through my flesh.

'Oh dear, Mr Hunter. You fucked that one up, didn't you? So what are you going to do now?' Knowing how dangerous this training assessment has become, WO2 Swaine, our demolitions instructor, should be taking over at this point, but we both know that if he does I'll fail the task for sure.

He's throwing me a lifeline. On the ATO course we take more than two hundred exams and face the threat of being returned-to-unit if we fail more than three. It's one of the few courses in the military where borderline cases are never given the benefit of the doubt. If you're deemed unsuitable in the classroom, the possible consequences of a mistake on the ground are highly likely to be terminal.

'So what's it going to be, sir?'

I've no experience of dealing with an unstable device like this, and very little in the way of knowledge. Every rational instinct tells me to leave it for the expert to deal with. But I can't help myself: in spite of my fears, I'm completely drawn towards it – which is just as well. After all, I don't have any choice: I'm damned if I do and damned if I don't. Even if I pass the course overall, failing any practical aspect of the EOD phase will almost certainly result in me spending the rest of my career as a 'Depot Donkey', storing and inspecting ammunition.

This course has been one of the most testing periods of my life. We spent the first six months covering the academic side of things at the Royal Military College of Science in Shrivenham. We were taught everything from explosive chemistry and advanced electronics to nuclear physics and terminal ballistics. I was way outside my comfort zone, rooted firmly in the class biff seat, so I had to work doubly hard, pinning all my hopes on the belief that what I lacked academically I would be able to make up in practical ability.

I don't know how, but I somehow managed to Forrest Gump my way through that first six months, and fifty exams, and make it to phase two: eight months of practical training here at the Army School of Ammunition in Warwickshire.

I'm still not sure if I'm cut out for this. Even getting on the course was a nightmare. I'd read the blurb about what the trick-cyclists were looking for, and figured I could probably bluff my way through their general questions, but when it came to the deeper stuff, I was in no doubt it was going to be a massive gamble. Thankfully, one of the guys on the course had managed to get his hands on the shrinks' selection criteria for ATOs:

> Candidates have to be of at least bright intelligence, satisfied with their careers, wholly identified with ammunition work, free from serious personal worries, in good physical and mental health, methodical and courageous, fairly adventuresome, thoughtful and decisive and free from group dependency. The ideal operator will also be socially at ease, have good impulse control and not suffer from nervousness or hypochondria, self-doubt, delinquent traits or perfectionism. Furthermore, an operator has to have an analytical mind. He has to be able to receive, digest and analyse information, then produce a response at the sweep of a finger.

I remember thinking, That's me fucked, then. 'Free from serious personal worries . . . in good physical and mental health'? I won't even get through the door. But somehow I managed to pull it off. And I'm still here.

Fuck it. I've come too far to fail now.

'It's too dangerous to move, Q,' I tell the instructor. 'So I'm going to blow it in situ.'

'Good man,' he says.

My heart tries to bludgeon its way out of my chest as I begin the render-safe procedure.

I select two packets of PE4 plastic explosive from my day-sack and remove the putty-like substance from its wax-paper wrapping. I mould the two six-inch sticks of explosive into two balls and place them on the ground, then take about a metre of detonating cord and cut it with a sharp knife. The cord looks not dissimilar to electric cable but is packed with powdered PETN high explosive. I place a sliver of tape over each of the sliced ends to stop the powder falling out, then tie a knot in one end and push it into one of the soft balls of PE4, folding the plastic explosive around the det cord as if I were kneading bread. Then I repeat the process with the second.

I take a deep breath and carefully place one of the charges next to – but not touching – the damaged fuse. Beads of sweat have formed on my forehead. Still trying to regulate my breathing, I slowly place the second charge against the body of the shell. When it's in position I tape the detonator to the length of det cord and head back to the safety of the firing point.

Moments later, the deafening blast resonates through my body as the shell explodes into a lethal whirlwind of white-hot shrapnel.

I've just neutralized a bomb for the first time.

15

The first step to knowledge is to know that we are ignorant.

Lord David Cecil

14 March 1998

I can't remember the last time I felt this happy. After fourteen sleep-deprived months we've finally made it to the end of the course, and I'm standing here with the most beautiful woman on earth.

'I'm so proud of you, honey.' She squeezes my hand and kisses me tenderly on the cheek.

Lucy and I met last year – a chance encounter in a hallway. A moment in our lives when we didn't have a care in the world. She was doing her degree at Shrivenham and was the most stunning woman I'd ever seen. She didn't wear makeup: she was what my mother called a natural beauty. I found her totally enchanting, not just because she was so pretty but because she was so warm and vital and didn't change her style for anybody. It took me about two minutes to realize she was the loveliest person I'd ever met.

We talked for hours that night. We talked about everything – our dreams, our desires and our disasters. She spoke with such passion; I hung on her every word. I was smitten, locked in the mesmerizing gaze of her piercing blue eyes.

'Thank you.'

She doesn't know it, but Lucy's brought a calm and balance back into my life that I never thought I'd experience again. She's saved me from myself.

My twelve course mates are sitting awkwardly in the lecture hall, chatting nervously with the members of their families who've arrived to witness our graduation. The rumour is that about half of us are going to be employed as counter-terrorist bomb-disposal operators at 11 Explosives Ordnance Disposal (EOD) Regiment. The other half are going to be working as ammunition staff officers. Considering what we've just put ourselves through, that's a real sickener.

During our eight months here at 'The School' we've sat more than a hundred and fifty exams and assessments and studied everything there is to know about ammunition and explosives, chemical, biological, radiological and nuclear weapons disposal, and the most prized module of all, the Joint Services IEDD course. Improvised Explosive Device Defeat. It was the very last phase of the course and everything hung on it.

'Ninety-nine per cent boredom and one per cent terror.' Those were the words we heard six weeks ago from Captain Steve O'Driscoll – the chief instructor of the counter-terrorist bomb-disposal training wing. His twenty-five-year career as an ATO is like something from a Bond movie. He's literally done it all: Northern Ireland, Special Forces, covert operations; the man's a legend within the trade.

Under his guidance we learnt how to identify and manufacture improvised devices; we were shown everything from traditional dynamite-type compositions to high-grade military plastic explosive. We were shown stacks of video footage of truck- and car-bomb attacks involving the use of ammonium-nitrate-based explosives, including the Oklahoma City bombing.

We also learnt about acetone peroxide, or 'TATP – The Mother of Satan', a favourite of urban terrorists because of the ease with which they can acquire the ingredients and defeat bomb-detection technologies. Thankfully, unlike most high explosives, TATP is dangerously unstable and an unusually high number of would-be terrorists have blown themselves to pieces while trying to manufacture it.

We received world-class instruction in IED defeat techniques. Our instructors were mega-experienced, and to a man they'd all rendered safe scores of live devices in high-threat theatres.

We were taught how to use robots to defeat a bomb remotely, and how to set up a complex hook-and-line system to move potentially booby-trapped items if necessary. We were also taught the black art of defeating devices by hand.

Practical lessons would normally follow the theory on the principles and philosophies of IEDD, the role of each team member and the conduct of an IEDD task. We spent many long days on the training ground, a mocked-up town with its own houses, pubs, petrol station, and a railway station, complete with train.

On arrival at a bomb scene we were tested on our ability to determine exactly what had happened, where it had happened and what had already been done about it – the crucial information needed to begin to get into the head of the bombmaker.

Scenarios, based on genuine incidents, ranged from dealing with simple incendiary devices like those constructed by animal-rights groups through to letter bombs and the more sophisticated devices used by PIRA on the British mainland. The instructors showed us devices from all over the world and, using their own experiences as case studies, offered fascinating insights in how to deal with every type of IED imaginable.

Within weeks, we'd learnt how to neutralize roadside

and buried bombs, car bombs, off-route mines, hostage bombs and even suicide bombs, sardonically known in the trade as 'not-so-smart bombs'.

We were tested over and over again; sometimes we'd sit exams or practical assessments four or five times in a day. Despite the unremitting information overload, every one of us loved it.

Last week was test week. Each of us was given four tasks, at least three of which we had to pass.

I passed.

IEDD was a discipline that seemed to come naturally to me. For the first time in my life, I'd found something I actually seemed to be good at.

The senior ammunition technician calls the room to attention, and we all rise to our feet.

I can feel the bile burning at the back of my throat. I glance around me. Everybody's putting on a brave face, but I know that deep down we all feel the same. All we want to know is if we're going to make it through the gates of 11 EOD Regiment.

Colonel Harry Flannigan, the commandant of the school, takes his place at the lectern. 'Ladies and gentlemen, it gives me great pleasure to be able to stand here today and award you the coveted ATO flash.'

The colonel served as an infantry officer during the Bloody Sunday riots and spent years working as a high-threat IEDD operator in Northern Ireland. He's one of the most respected in the trade.

'To this day,' he says, 'the standards demanded of our operators are something we are not prepared to compromise on. All of you should feel justifiably proud of your achievements.'

Lucy squeezes my hand. She knows I feel sick with nerves.

The colonel awards a couple of prizes. I'm chuffed to bits that Will – one of my closest mates on the course – has received the prize for best operator. He goes on to give us some words of wisdom delivered with his trademark Irish charm – congratulating us all on how well we've done and telling us how vital the work we're about to undertake will be in the fight against domestic terrorism.

Much later we're each called into his office.

'Sit down,' he says.

Fuck it. His face says it all. My heart sinks.

'Chris, you're going to Shorncliffe Troop.' He gives me a mischievous smile.

It takes a moment for his words to sink in.

Shorncliffe Troop is one of the best jobs in the regiment. I'll be responsible for all EOD operations in Kent and East Sussex, including the Channel Tunnel and Gatwick airport.

I can't believe it. I'm in.

'Congratulations.' He extends his hand. 'Out there on the streets you'll be given a huge amount of responsibility. Never let it go to your head. EOD takes a lifetime to master. And the more proficient you become, the more you realize you don't know. But don't let that put you off.'

16

Don't waste time learning the tricks of the trade. Instead, learn the trade.

H. Jackson Brown, Jr

10 April 1998

'Sir, grab your kit. An eight-line's just come in.'

This is it: the moment I've dreamt of ever since leaving Sandhurst. I grab my toolkit and hurry outside, silently running through my last-minute checks as I stride into the secure compound. Corporal Steve Parker, my number two, is already trundling the Wheelbarrow robot onto the bomb wagon as I pack our kit into the cab.

Adrenalin pumping, I unfold the printout of the eight-line EOD report and begin checking the co-ordinates on the map as I scribble down the name and mobile-phone number of the police incident commander.

'Boss, can you hit the blues and twos?'

As the EOD compound's steel blast-door clanks shut, we roll out of the gates into the heart of the Garden of England, dog-legging our way out of the tiny village of Shorncliffe.

As we scream along the streets lined with rows of parked cars – barely wide enough to get the bomb wagon through – Corporal Parker deftly manoeuvres the vehicle in and out of the traffic and onto the M20.

We pass the Channel Tunnel terminal with our two-tone sirens wailing and head west. Dozens of cars pull over to let us pass. As I read through the contents of the report I can feel my stomach performing somersaults.

'So what does it say on the dream sheet then, sir?' Parker asks.

'Line One: DATE-TIME GROUP: 080900ZAPR98.
Line Two: Unit and Grid Location of Device: Kent Constabulary, Sittingbourne Vehicle Park. Grid SU 456 355
Line Three: Contact Method: Sergeant Mike Wilkes, Mobile number: 07967 . . .
Line Four: Type of IED/Ordnance: Exploding gas cylinder
Line Five: Target/Resources Threatened: Vehicle park workers/ civilians/emergency services
Line Six: Impact on Mission: Requirement to

neutralize threat and return the situation to normal
as soon as possible

Line Seven: Protective measures/Action: All
buildings and personnel within a three hundred
metre radius currently being evacuated by Police
call-signs on-site

Line Eight: Recommended priority: Immediate.'

'Well, this should be interesting, then,' he says.

As we continue along the M20 Corporal Parker
explains the importance of confirming the contents of
the eight-line report with the man on the ground as
quickly as possible. 'Virtually every device I've ever
deployed to has been completely different from the
initial description.'

The police – who themselves are usually informed by
a member of the public – confirm the presence of an
explosive device before reporting it to their incident
control room. From there it goes to the Joint Services
Explosive Ordnance Disposal Operations Centre based
at HQ 11 EOD Regiment RLC in Didcot, who in turn
send the eight-line tasking message to one of the twelve
EOD troops based around the country.

According to Corporal Parker, who's been serving
with the troop for almost two years, the process often
results in a case of Chinese whispers and by the time the
eight-line gets into the hands of the operator a small

firework has often metamorphosed into a large car bomb.

'The main advantage of calling the man on the ground while you're en route,' he says, 'is to confirm what actions have been taken so far.'

It makes sense. Our area of responsibility covers Kent, East Sussex and parts of Surrey and for that reason we could easily be in the middle of one incident while being tasked to another two hours away. If I can establish the size and type of the device over the phone I can make a number of possibly life-saving recommendations there and then – like how far to cordon and evacuate.

I'm going to like Corporal Parker. He's got a lot of experience and I admire his ability to share his knowledge without a hint of condescension.

I grab the vehicle phone and punch in the number for the police commander. Sure enough, as we begin chatting through the detail of the incident, it turns out the eight-line is wrong.

'An articulated truck carrying a hundred chemical drums parked up late last night and one of the drums exploded,' he tells me. 'The explosion sent it hurtling through the roof of the truck and eighty feet into the air. It landed on a parked car, destroying it completely. Since then, at least a dozen others have exploded.'

The fire service won't go near the truck and

everybody is waiting with bated breath for the next explosion.

'FUUUUUCK!' As we drive off the motorway a car pulls out of a side road and stops right in front of us. We're a split-second away from colliding with him and at this speed, with four tonnes of EOD equipment in the back of our bomb wagon, we'll almost certainly write him off – and us with him.

Corporal Parker is known affectionately as 'Flash' because of his pronounced drawl and apparently slow reaction times – but he executes a perfect defensive driving manoeuvre, jolting us left into the slow lane, then right just before we collide with another vehicle.

But in his effort to avoid the two cars, he loses control of the bomb wagon and the back starts skidding left then right. As I brace myself for the inevitable crash, Parker calmly dips the clutch and carries out a brilliant counter-steer manoeuvre, bringing us straight back in our original direction of travel.

It's a hell of a conjuring trick.

Ten minutes later we drive through the gates of the vehicle park and pull up at the incident control point (ICP).

'Mike Wilkes?' I ask the police sergeant who meets us.

The look of relief is wiped off his face as a deafening explosion resonates through the park. Another oil drum shoots up into the air and everybody dives for cover as it comes hurtling back down onto the tarmac.

Mike takes me over to the owner of the truck, who's as white as a sheet. He nervously explains that the drums were supposed to have been emptied and cleaned out with a supposedly innocuous chemical. 'The drums were supposed to have been left to vent off any remaining gas before being loaded onto my truck,' he says. 'But somebody's fucked up.'

I turn to brief Corporal Parker, but he's several steps ahead of the game. He's reversed the Wheelbarrow off the wagon and fitted it with two loaded EOD disrupters.

'Ready when you are, Boss,' he says cheerfully.

'OK, Corporal P. You know what to do. Get the Barrow down there and start giving those drums the good news.'

He's in his element. He sends the robot trundling down across the park. The three-foot-high miniature tank's cameras are transmitting fuzzy pictures back to our grainy monitor screens in the incident control point.

He approaches the truck from the rear, then takes a wide berth around the left-hand side of the vehicle and comes in for a perpendicular attack. He pauses about a metre short, takes a deep breath and slowly lowers the robot's weapons mount so that the disrupters are almost touching the ground. With the deftness of a school-kid on a games console he nudges the paddles on his remote-control unit, edging the weapons very slightly upwards. He's aiming to shoot up, into the bottom of the drums, hoping to enable the gases to vent out.

He inches the Wheelbarrow towards the first drum. All eyes are on him and he's sweating like ten men.

The pig-stick disrupter is in place, its water-filled steel tube aimed at the heart of the drum. With any luck the supersonic jet will punch straight through it.

'Boss, I'm on. Are you happy for me to take the shot?'

I give him the nod. He yells a warning, pans the camera away from the oil drum and selects the firing circuit.

Even though we're a hundred metres away we can hear the crack of the controlled explosion and the thud as the pig-stick's high-velocity water jet smashes into the side of the drum. Corporal P pans the camera back. All we can see is a small dent.

Bollocks.

'OK,' I say. 'Time for Plan B. Let's try the Hotrod.'

He selects the next firing circuit and prepares to fire the larger disrupter into the drum. But just as he's about to take the shot, there's another almighty explosion and the target disappears from view as it hurtles skywards through the roof of the truck.

Without waiting to be told, he manoeuvres the Wheelbarrow quickly onto another drum and takes the shot. This time, instead of an explosion, there's a whoosh of gas.

'Nice work, Corporal P. Now let's get the Barrow back and reload it.'

'We might have a slight problem, Boss,' he says sheepishly. 'We've got another Hotrod, but only enough ammunition for ten more shots . . .'

Fuck. I hadn't thought of that. There are at least seventy drums on the back of that truck.

I call Ant Worrel for a bit of advice. In the few weeks we've been working together my new troop staff sergeant has come across as a great team player. When I asked him to teach me some tricks of the trade he told me I should concentrate on the trade rather than the tricks – so he's no push-over, but he's been very patient with me.

'No worries, Boss, leave it with me,' he says. 'You crack on with the ammo you've got left and I'll round up the cavalry. We'll be with you as soon as we can.'

We send the Barrow back and forth for the next thirty minutes or so, shooting the drums. A local TV crew rocks up just as we run out of ammo and another drum launches itself into the sky. My heart sinks. We're going to be all over the six o'clock news, looking like prize pricks, doing absolutely nothing.

Then the 7th Cavalry arrives. Three EOD wagons scream into the park, sirens wailing, led by Ant Worrel.

He's brought the world's supply of Hotrods and ammunition and tasked three of the squadron's reserve teams to bring their robots too. Our PR disaster is about to become a reality TV epic. Within minutes, we've got four Wheelbarrows weaving in and out of the target area like a Broadway chorus line in full view of the rapidly expanding audience of press, public and largely redundant emergency services.

I'm so impressed with Staff Sergeant Worrel. As the more experienced operator, he'd be well within his rights to take over the running of the task, but he knows it's my first job and he's not that sort of bloke. He leaves me to crack on while he and the other operators sweat away at the back of the ICP, opening boxes of disrupter ammunition and reloading weapons, as the number twos clock up more kills.

Once we get down to the last thirty or so barrels, Corporal P informs me they can't shoot any more. The Barrows can't get to them: the vented drums now obstruct the remainder. I'm going to have to neutralize them manually.

As Corporal Parker inserts the last Kevlar plate into my protective bomb suit, I snap shut my visor and ready myself for the walk. Outside sounds become muted and I am aware only of the sound of my own breathing and the drumming of my heart.

I'm carrying ninety pounds of equipment and the

bomb suit's cumbersome armour weighs about another eighty-five. I can feel the sweat soaking my back and dripping into my eyes as my visor begins to mist up. The long walk to the truck seems to be taking for ever.

I try not to hold my breath as I take each step, but it isn't easy.

Fifty metres to go. I'm halfway there.

My mouth is dry and I'm struggling to see. My visor has completely steamed up now. I wipe away the condensation with a cloth.

Twenty metres.

For a brief moment I allow myself to think about Lucy. She's driving over to stay with me tonight and I'm imagining how the conversation's going to go when she asks me about my day.

This is beyond surreal.

Ten metres.

If one of the barrels launches now I'll be blown off my feet.

Five metres.

I compose myself, take a deep breath, and climb up onto the back of the truck.

It's decision time . . .

I've got two disrupters with me, but it's going to take me at least an hour to work my way through the barrels two at a time. And the longer I leave them, the greater the chance of them exploding in my face.

Fuck it. I'll open them by hand.

I grab the vented barrels closest to me and start throwing them over the side. I need to clear some space. As I get to the first of the gas-filled monsters, I realize this is a rite of passage in more ways than one. Lucy's been a really positive influence in my life, but the demons inside me still haven't surrendered.

I try to focus on the task in hand. I extend my trembling hand and begin unscrewing the cap of the first drum.

A jet of gas blasts out with a high-pitched whine.

Seconds later, it's safe.

I make my way to the next drum, my burst of optimism clouded by the knowledge that if it explodes while I'm unscrewing it, it'll take off my hand and a fair chunk of my arm as well.

I take a deep breath and try to block out the negative vibes.

By the time I reach the final barrel, I'm absolutely terrified. Yet the rush I'm experiencing is awesome. It's like a drug, and I'm already an addict. I'm living on the edge. I'm in a truly elemental place, a world in which everything is black and white, a world of straightforward choices.

As I stumble back into the ICP, I glance at my watch and realize I've been down at the target for thirty minutes. I'm physically and mentally fried, but I feel good. I feel good because today I belonged to a team of people who were doing something good.

I'm starting to believe that Major Hudson was right all along. Maybe by doing this I can make a difference.

17

28 April 1998

During the Second World War the Garden of England became 'Bomb Alley'. Kent was the primary route to target for both Nazi and British aircraft. Those who weren't able to make it as far as land often had to drop their payloads into the Channel, so fifty years later the dredgers that scour the coast for aggregate routinely scoop up unexploded ordnance.

Our troop receives an endless stream of taskings to neutralize them. It's so full-on that Lucy and I have only seen each other once in the last three weeks and she's not impressed. I've just returned from a UXO task in Dartford and tried to call her, but she's not answering the phone.

At least the task went well. I questioned the witnesses, located and identified the munitions – a pair of foot-long Second World War anti-aircraft shells – and asked the police to put in a cordon and temporarily stop the shipping in the Thames Estuary. Then I made a manual approach, fashioned an improvised sandbag blast-wall around the devices and gently placed a series of plastic explosive charges close to – but not touching – them.

I asked Air Traffic Control to temporarily divert any aircraft overflying the Thames, got everybody under hard cover and fired off the charge. It went like clock-work. I feel I'm really starting to get the hang of conventional munitions. Thanks to Ant and the other operators, my knowledge and confidence have grown immeasurably. But there's still something missing. I haven't been tasked to an IED.

I'm now hoping that's about to change: a few minutes ago I received a secure call from our squadron duty officer. We're on immediate stand-by for a combined op with the Metropolitan Police. They're calling it Operation Heath. For the past three years the suspect – a white middle-aged man named Edgar Pearce – has planted close to forty devices in and around London. Between December 1994 and December 1995 he targeted Barclays Bank with packages bearing a 'Mardi Gra' calling card. The guy's an absolute headcase. In January 'ninety-six he sent twelve devices to random addresses across the south-east; within six months he'd sent letters demanding ten thousand pounds a day to Sainsbury's head office and begun planting devices near supermarkets across the capital.

Unlike most criminals, Pearce was extremely patient. He became an expert at disguise; he even razored out the tiny serial numbers on the Sainsbury's carrier bags he used. Now he's instructed police to issue ATM cards on the cover of *Computer Shopper* magazine. He's insisted they should look like magazine promotion items but be programmed to work in Nationwide cash machines. The police have followed his instructions and issued Pearce with a four-digit PIN number. They've been waiting for him to use it ever since.

'This morning Pearce bought a copy of the magazine and drove to a Nationwide branch,' the duty officer told me. 'He was heavily disguised and hid his face behind a clipboard, but they knew they had their man when he withdrew seven hundred pounds.'

Scotland Yard had the National Crime Squad install some specialized software that would notify them within three seconds of his PIN being entered. And the balloon's just gone up.

'They've deployed the greatest number of mobile surveillance units in their history. Almost every Nationwide cash machine in the country is under surveillance and a thousand London police officers are searching for him as we speak. I've placed every single EOD team in the south-east on standby.'

I walk into the EOD compound to brief Corporal Dave Campbell, the duty number two. He also tries to play it cool, but he's not kidding anyone. I can tell he's as excited as I am.

For the rest of the day we check and test every piece of kit on the bomb wagon. We make sure every single battery for every single piece of electronic equipment is fully charged and good to go. When we can check no more we grab a selection of mock-ups of previous Mardi Gra devices from our bomb store. Inert versions of IEDs are regularly issued to EOD teams for training purposes, just in case the bomber strikes again.

We work out what makes it tick and then – having had eyes on – we configure the Wheelbarrow with the optimum weapons and manipulation equipment and practise dealing with that specific device.

Then we wait. And wait. And wait.

While the other members of the troop go about their business, Corporal Campbell and I are rooted firmly to the television in the crew room, watching for any news of Mardi Gra activity.

But there is none.

Another hour or so passes and I begin to drift off. My nervous excitement is sapping all my energy.

My wake-up call comes in from Bruce, the squadron duty officer.

'Stand down, Chris. They got him.' As Pearce tried to escape he was apprehended by one of the surveillance teams and arrested. Immediately prior to being caught, he'd placed a shotgun IED inside a bin bag with the barrel pointing at a bus stop in Eltham High Street. It was sheer luck that no one was standing in the line of fire when it exploded at midday. A child in a wheelchair had been pushed past the device just moments before it was activated by a kitchen timer.

I'm over the moon that they've caught the crazy bastard, but gutted that we didn't get to deal with a live IED today. The frustration is really getting to me. I know that if I'm going to be any good at this job, I've got to learn some patience, but I can't help feeling disappointed. I thought I'd be pitting my wits against the world's leading bombmakers by now, fighting a raging battle against the mad, the bad and the sad.

18

He who sedulously attends, pointedly asks, calmly speaks, coolly answers and ceases when he has no more to say is in possession of some of the best requisites of man.

Johann Casper Lavater

15 August 1998

Ant Worrel was swimming the Channel earlier today in aid of a school for blind children. He's been training for months. But just as he was about to reach the halfway point, a boat pulled up alongside him and he was arrested by the Royal Military Police Special Investigation Branch. The heartless bastards didn't even let him finish.

As his troop commander, I've been called in to act as his 'accused adviser', to ensure he has the full range of support from the military system during his charge interview. I'd represent him even if I wasn't duty-bound to do so. He's a brilliant guy, and I know that whatever he's done, there'll be a good reason for it. I'm finally coming to terms with the fact that things aren't always black and white, and I'd like to think I can see beyond the minutiae of these shiny-arsed pen-pushing disciplinarians.

As I listen to the investigator reading out the charge, I can't help feeling an overwhelming sense of sympathy for Ant. In our trade EOD doesn't just stand for Explosive Ordnance Disposal, it's also a sardonic acronym for Everyone's Divorced. I discover his wife has just left him and completely stripped their bank account. His car tax has just expired and in his desperation he borrowed a disc from one of the bomb wagons, hoping that nobody would notice until he gets paid at the end of the month. Unfortunately, one of the MoD Police patrols spotted it while they were carrying out a security patrol on camp and neither the Army nor the SIB investigator has any sympathy whatsoever. In fact the SIB man seems to particularly relish the opportunity to accuse this brave, proud man of being a common criminal.

There have been so many occasions when I've looked up to Ant, even envied him for being such an amazingly grounded, decent and successful guy. Yet the poor man has been in absolute turmoil and now risks losing everything in his professional and personal life.

Ant's also one of the hardest men I've ever met and I

can tell from his body language that he's about to flash. Sure enough, as the investigator starts laying into him again, he completely loses it and ends up calling him a cunt.

I put my head into my hands, thinking the investigator's going to throw the book at him. Amazingly he replies, 'I never heard that.'

But instead of quitting while he's ahead, Ant takes it to the next level.

'Deaf cunt.'

This really isn't going well.

For the last few months we've actually managed to reach a state of relative calm within the troop. There has been a steady flow of conventional munitions disposal tasks and even a few criminal IED tasks, but we've had five operators for several months now, and until today only one of them was unfit for duty, so we've all been able to get at least a week per month off the pager – allowing us to spend some much-needed time with our loved ones.

It seems that's about to change. Ant will almost certainly be suspended from EOD duties until his court martial – and Buddy Holiday won't be able to operate for at least another month. Last week he was tasked to deal with a shell at an aggregate yard where he did everything by the book – except for the sandbag filling. He asked the police and his new number two to fill the sandbags for him and they used gravel instead of pure sand. When he carried out the controlled explosion Sergeant Holiday inadvertently created the world's biggest claymore mine and wrote off four parked cars. It's only by the grace of God – and because his cordoning drills had been so thorough – that nobody was killed.

As Ant and the policeman continue to cross swords, my pager starts beeping. I glance at the screen: IED SEARCH ASSIST TASK. CALL JSEODOC IMMEDIATELY.

'I'm so sorry, Staff. I've got a job on. I'll be back as soon as I can.'

Back at the Detachment I find Corporal Parker loading the bomb suit and a whole load of ops kit into our Land Rover Discovery – the troop's unmarked EOD vehicle.

I punch in the door code and head into our ops room before dialling the number for the Joint Services EOD Operations Centre. The ops officer tells me we've been tasked by Kent Police to assist them with an arrest op in a travellers' encampment just outside Maidstone. We're to meet up for a mission briefing at the Traffic Police compound just off the M20.

I take down the details of the task and within five minutes of receiving the pager message we're screaming out of the gates.

Just as Corporal Parker taught me, I call ahead to

speak with the incident commander, but he tells me that this particular task is so sensitive he can't discuss anything over an unsecure line.

It's a fair one.

Thirty minutes later, we take the Maidstone exit off the motorway. A firearms cop – all dressed in black, tooled up and ready to go – takes us into the compound briefing room. His colleagues sit in rows along with a smattering of Royal Engineers Search personnel.

Pictures of the target area and the suspects we are about to go and arrest are displayed on boards at the front of the room. The groundplan of what looks like a travellers' camp is being pinned up alongside a series of aerial photos.

At the other end, police snipers are busy preparing their kit. I ask their commander if he can shed any light. He and his team have clearly already been briefed and are about to move onto the target. He tells us that we're going in to arrest two hard-core criminals who also happen to be bare-knuckle boxing champions. They've got drugs and weapons hides on their site, as well as a dead body buried underneath a chicken coop, which – according to their informants – is protected by mines and IEDs. He and his team are going to deploy as far away as they need to be for the purposes of concealment but close enough to provide covering fire and forward observation.

'That's as much as I know.'

The senior police investigating officer confirms what the sniper has told us. He points out the compound on the map; it's only a mile away from our current position. The firearms teams will go in first to make the arrest. The Royal Engineers, accompanied by unarmed police search teams, will locate the buried hides using their specialist ground-penetrating radar equipment. Then I'll go in and clear any devices protecting the hides.

He spends the final few minutes of his briefing explaining our actions-on – and in case we hadn't got the message: 'These men are extremely dangerous. They're hardened, organized criminals and they're almost certainly going to put up a fight.'

Minutes later, we're on our way.

The firearms teams hurtle off down the dusty wood-lined track towards the target with the rest of us following, a tactical bound behind them. Flashbangs explode around the compound. We pull up just short of it and can barely make out the firearms teams through the trees. They've stacked up outside the travellers' caravans, backs against the walls, covering doors and windows with their Heckler & Koch assault rifles. I pity anyone who tries to take them on.

More flashbangs are thrown.

Go!

'Get down, get down!'

The women scream as they're dragged to the floor and cuffed. The police aren't taking any chances – this is no time to be warm and cuddly.

They clear each caravan and then move on to the outbuildings.

Within two minutes of the initial 'Go, go, go!' the sound of flashbangs ceases. Not a single shot has been fired. These boys are good.

'Area secure!' one of the cops shouts. The teams exit the caravans leading the two handcuffed suspects to a waiting police van.

So much for putting up a fight. These hardened criminals both had huge piss stains around the groin.

For the next three hours Corporal Parker and I sit waiting as the Royal Engineers scour every inch of the camp. They're absolutely meticulous in their search patterns and if there's something hidden in this woodland clearing, I have no doubt they'll find it.

Sappers and police search teams scour every cavity of every building with mirrors and probes. Others pace up and down the clearing and surrounding woodland with their hand-held ground-penetrating radar equipment.

'ATO – we've found a cache.'

We're in business.

I brief Corporal P on the kit I'm going to require and

prepare to face the task ahead. My redoubtable number two gathers the working equipment I'm going to need: a mini pig-stick disrupter, my tripwire feeler, operator search equipment and a bagful of other hand-held tools including a hook-and-line set.

He helps me on with my bomb suit. It's designed to provide protection on the approach to a device, but not when you're up close and personal. If it explodes when I'm on top of it, the shockwave will tear the limbs from my torso and use what's left as a basketball.

Fifty metres isn't far, but on this approach I'm carrying about sixty pounds of equipment in addition to my bomb suit, so operator degradation is something I have to take into account.

Sweat pours off me as I shuffle through the leafy woodland towards the suspect cache. Every step is an effort of will. I try to regulate my breathing, to get my pulse down. I inhale deeply through my nose and exhale slowly through my mouth but after just ten metres my visor is already steaming up.

I stop to wipe it with my rubber glove and then move on.

The walk seems to take for ever. I try not to hold my breath, but it's not easy. I don't feel scared, but however much I try to convince myself that I'm not in danger, I know I can't take anything for granted.

I go over the threat assessment repeatedly in my

mind. There are three options. There's the timed IED, which could go off at any moment. There's the command-initiated device, usually detonated by wire or radio control; I hope I can discount that as the baddest of the guys are firmly in police custody. Finally there's the VO, the booby-trap. The searchers have walked all around the cache, so there's unlikely to be anything buried in the ground, but there's still every chance of a VO inside it.

Five metres short, I set down my equipment, lie on my stomach and prepare to search for tripwires and buried pressure IEDs. Even the smallest device can be powerful enough to blow a man's leg into his stomach and blind him with the shrapnel of his own bone fragments.

I'm crawling on my belt-buckle, scanning the ground for any hint of disturbed earth, the tip of a plastic box, a piece of fishing line. I remember the lifesaving phrase from training – *look for absence of the normal and presence of the abnormal*. In this job, Murphy's Law rules. Always expect the unexpected.

I slide my tripwire-feeler gingerly forwards. I keep the foot-long telescopic rod close to the earth, but not touching it. I focus on its tip. Everything else becomes a blur. I raise it an inch, then two, until eventually I am standing. I am totally oblivious to outside sounds now. I move the feeler left . . . slowly . . . then right . . .

No tripwires. I lay the rod down and begin searching the ground beneath this virtual 3D box. I use a small metal detector to locate pressure-plate devices. It's painfully slow, laborious work.

Sweat is pouring off me . . . running into my eyes . . . stinging them. My pulse is racing. I begin to search with my fingertips, leaf by leaf, inch by inch, before crawling forward a foot and then repeating the whole process.

I'm finally at the cache.

As I search all the way around it with my hand-held metal detector, a little red light suddenly flashes and its tiny buzzer vibrates in my hand. Bingo.

I slowly, carefully, lift a leaf, and then another, and my eyes are immediately drawn to the pressure mat, wedged just underneath the lid of the hide's trapdoor.

For a moment, I visualize the blinding flash as the explosive device contained inside the cache detonates – taking me with it in a violent whirlwind of heat, flame and lethal fragmentation.

I have to break the circuit.

I can't cut into it by hand because I can't see everything I need to see. I'd normally cut the wire to the power supply – job jobbed. But a pressure mat is almost certainly on a relay circuit, and if I cut that by hand I'll be killed instantly.

I'm going to place a flying scalpel and cut the pressure mat out of the circuit. Which means I can fire it from the safety of the ICP. I choose my precise target and edge my weapon up to the wire leading to the black plastic pad.

My stomach lurches. I tell myself to keep going.

The flying scalpel is in place.

I wipe the sweat from my visor and make my way, light-headed, back to the ICP.

I remove my helmet and Corporal Parker hands me a bottle of water. As I glug down the cool liquid, he orders everybody to get under hard cover.

When I'm satisfied, I give him the nod.

He takes control of the Shrike firing device. '*STAND BY . . . FIRING!*' His thumbs come down simultaneously on the circuit and fire buttons. There is a whip-crack as the mini pig-stick unleashes its blades.

The ground-shaking boom of an IED would tell us we've failed. But there's nothing. I wait for a few moments, trying to throw as much water down my neck as I can. I've got to get back to the device. I need to make sure we're good to go. The EOD weapon might have blown over in the wind and completely missed, or it might only have partially fired. The flying scalpel might have done nothing more than nudge the device. I take another weapon with me, just in case, and make a second approach.

I find a perfect cut in the wire.

I pull out my reel of insulating tape and wrap a strip

around each bare end. The mat is now harmless – which means at least one firing switch has been removed from the circuit. But it isn't yet over. There might be another anti-handling device to prevent the contents of the hide being moved. There might even be a secondary booby-trap, triggered by the disruption of the first . . . Doubtful, but possible. I clear my mind and press on.

I pull out the line from my kitbag and fasten it to the edge of the cache's trapdoor and up through a pulley I've attached to a nearby tree. Then I head back to Corporal Parker and get him to grip the line and pull it with all his strength. Seconds later, the lid is dangling from the tree and everything is still silent.

I let the device soak.

Another fifteen minutes pass. Still no explosion.

I make my way back down to the cache and find two rifles and about ten kilos of brown powder – almost certainly heroin. Next to it is a long copper pipe, crimped at the ends, with wires coming out of one end. One of the wires is leading to a battery and the other to the severed pressure mat. The pipe bomb is filled with confined low explosive and an improvised initiator.

I feel myself shiver. If I'd activated that pressure mat, I'd have been blown to pieces.

Back in the EOD compound I leave Corporal Parker to

unload the kit while I call my OC and type up my incident report. I'm exhausted, but thrilled to have finally neutralized my first live IED.

I head back to the Mess where Lucy's been waiting all day. We spend the rest of the afternoon catching up over a bottle of wine, then make the mistake of switching on the early-evening news.

At ten past three this afternoon a car bomb containing around five hundred pounds of explosive detonated in Omagh, County Tyrone. The place was crowded with shoppers and spectators awaiting a carnival about to pass through the town centre. Forty minutes earlier three telephone warnings had confirmed that a bomb had been planted outside the courthouse at the top of the high street so the police were busy evacuating the crowds to a safe area at the junction of Dublin Road and Market Street – several hundred metres away – precisely where the device was actually parked.

The blast was devastating. Twenty-nine people have been killed and 330 more – including dozens of children – are injured.

We can't tear our eyes from the blood-soaked images that fill the screen. The surrounding buildings are completely wrecked and people are still trapped inside them. Dead and injured line the streets while panic-stricken onlookers search for their families and friends.

My mind races back to the Thiepval Barracks, then through a cavalcade of horrors I've witnessed over the past few years. I'm once again transfixed by the bodies in the lake at Rumboci, the mothers holding their babies with nooses tied around their necks, the mass graves in Srebrenica and all the other senseless killings . . .

I know I must go back to Northern Ireland. I want to stop something like this happening again. I want to do my bit.

I'm going to volunteer to become a high-threat operator.

19

Go confidently in the direction of your dreams. Live the
life you have imagined.

Henry David Thoreau

1 March 1999

I've got no idea how I managed to pull it off, but last
night I popped the question to Lucy and she said yes.
This is the happiest day of my life.

It's also the most terrifying.

In the past year our troop has neutralized thousands
of items of explosive ordnance, I've dealt with live IEDs,
we've been in raids on criminal bomb-making factories
and I've even spent a week at Sandringham on royal
protection duties. I've evacuated entire city centres,
rerouted aircraft at Gatwick airport and stopped
shipping at countless docks across the south-east. I'm
really beginning to love this job.

Now I'm at the end of the high-threat operators
course. Essential for any of us who wish to stay on active

service, it has one of the highest failure rates of any course in the Army.

Major Brian Jeffries is the new senior instructor here at the Felix Centre. He's a highly decorated operator and his introductory address still rings in my ears. 'The average pass rate for this course, gentlemen, is about twenty-five per cent. And for those of you here for the first time it's only ten per cent. But don't let that put you off. If you make the grade, you'll be joining the most exclusive club in the world.'

If successful, we'll be taking our places in the legendary 321 EOD Squadron, whose ATOs have responded to more than 47,000 tasks, neutralized almost 5,500 IEDs and recovered over 200 tonnes of explosives since the Troubles began. It's the most decorated unit in the British Army. During its twenty-five-year existence, the ATOs serving in 321 Squadron have received nearly three hundred gallantry awards, including two George Crosses, twenty-nine George Medals and sixty-seven Queen's Gallantry Medals.

Our course began five weeks ago with instruction on searching for victim-operated IEDs. Booby-traps were used to devastating effect against the Allies by former SS troops in the early years of the occupation of Germany. The Viet Cong and NVA used IEDs extensively in South Vietnam, often making use of unexploded ordnance recovered from American bombing raids.

They accounted for around a third of US casualties.

We've closely studied how terrorist groups around the world have used them to assassinate heads of state, VIPs and large groups of civilians. Perhaps most chillingly of all, we have been left in no doubt that the Provisional IRA are the most sophisticated proponents of the dark art – and are currently using the full spectrum of technology specifically to target ATOs.

I know that if I'm going to stand any chance of surviving in this landscape, I must get into the minds of the bombmakers. I'm learning everything I can about what motivates terrorists on both sides of the sectarian divide. I must have a detailed understanding of their strategic and operational objectives to know how and why they conduct their targeting.

I need to understand the history and philosophy of the Republican movement. I've hoovered up *Provos: The IRA and Sinn Fein* by Peter Taylor and *Rebel Hearts* by Kevin Toolis.

I've spent every waking minute of every day studying the intricacies of high-threat bomb disposal. In Northern Ireland, even a hoax device is part of an elaborate 'come-on' for the ATO, linked to a booby-trap or covered by a sniper.

We've been taught how to use complex hook-and-line arrangements to gain access to vehicles, caches and buildings. We've spent hours clambering through vans and cars, wading up rivers and shimmying through culverts attaching ropes and pulleys to improvised mortars and other suspected bomb components, to the point where it's now second nature never to remove anything by hand, even if we don't suspect a booby-trap. Our instructors have taught us that if we move items ourselves, the enemy will almost certainly attach a victim-operated IED to them in future. There appear to be only two options in this environment: complete success or total failure.

By the start of week two, we'd progressed to advanced search techniques. 'They only have to be lucky once; you have to be lucky always,' has become the course mantra. Our instructors went into painstaking detail about the case histories of operators who'd fallen in the line of duty. Like thirty-five-year-old WO2 Michael O'Neil, killed when an IRA bomb exploded in a car he was examining near Newry on 31 May 1981. The booby-trap – hidden inside one of the cavities – detonated as he made his eighth manual approach. It was supposed to be his final action on target before handing over to the scenes-of-crime officer.

WO2 John Howard was killed in Belfast in July 1988 when he stepped on a pressure plate on the Falls Road. He'd been carrying out a follow-up search of the area after an IED had killed two people the previous day.

Twenty ATOs have been killed and twenty-four

seriously wounded during a campaign that's seen almost 16,000 IEDs explode in Northern Ireland since the Troubles began.

As we've fine-tuned our skills, each of us has been putting them to the test; every day our four-man syndicates have watched a colleague being put through his paces during a complex IED task, which could last in excess of ten hours. Now, after five and a half weeks, we face the final assessment.

A warning has been phoned in to Radio Ulster and RTÉ news stations from a pay-phone. The caller has refused to give any details other than the location of the device . . .

The culvert is another ten metres away and I'm already knackered. I lift my visor and wipe away the condensation.

Walk, pause, observe; walk, pause, observe.

Breathe.

The self-induced pressure is far more stressful than anything I've experienced in the presence of a live device. We're not being tested purely on my ability to render safe: we're being assessed on every action and thought from the moment we arrive at the scene right up until we pack away our kit and declare, 'Task complete.' This includes the command and control of the incident, our ability to evaluate the problem, to re-evaluate when things go wrong (as the instructors throw a notional problem into the mix at the last minute) and to prosecute the numerous legal and post-incident procedures relating to the gathering of forensic evidence.

I would usually fire up the Wheelbarrow in a situation like this, but my instructor has informed me that it's notionally broken down and a replacement won't be available before the end of the week.

I shuffle forward again.

My combats are drenched in sweat. It's not just carrying close to 200 pounds of equipment that causes fatigue: it's the intense concentration and the knowledge that even though this is an exercise it's based on actual IRA tactics in real incidents, so someone somewhere has almost certainly placed a hidden device that's designed to kill me.

I've got to stay focused. My entire future depends on how I perform right now.

Walk, pause, observe; walk, pause, observe.

A few metres short of the culvert, I drop onto my belt-buckle and take out my binoculars. Like a tracker hunting prey, I scan the ground for any detail that may give an indication of what lies ahead. *Absence of the normal, presence of the abnormal . . .*

I search for disturbed earth, downtrodden vegetation, discoloration of the ground – any suggestion that something may have been dug in here recently.

I'm lying in the middle of an open field, surrounded by tree-covered hills, so it's fairly obvious the trigger-man will be able to see me, but the culvert is pretty much obscured by bushes and vegetation, so he'll definitely have had to mark the location of the bomb – and any secondary devices – with something identifiable. It could be a small pile of stones, a discarded Coke can, even a lone tree.

But I can't see anything.

Fuck.

I take out my tripwire-feeler and carry out an operator search. I raise it an inch, then two, until eventually I am standing. I move it left . . . slowly . . . then right . . . I'm not expecting any tripwires in this sort of terrain, but I still have to go through the motions. If I fail to do so on a real task, there will almost certainly be one in place next time round.

Next, I scan the ground beneath me with my hand-held metal detector. Every few seconds it sounds an alarm, and when it does, I search the area with my fingertips, lifting leaves and small clumps of loose grass, until I can see what's caused it to activate. The edge of the stream is littered with buried beer cans, bits of old tin and rusted circuit boards. A scrapyard hidden beneath the English countryside. Every item has to be meticulously checked before I remove it from the ground and place it to one side. I wipe my misted visor and repeat the whole process before inching forward. Twenty seconds later it's misted up again.

I check my watch: 4:50 p.m. I've been on task for almost three hours – an hour of which I've spent carrying out this manual approach. It only feels like ten minutes. It's what we call operator time. Another world where outside sounds become muted and operators are aware only of the sound of their own breathing and the drumming of their hearts.

I creep forward a little further and begin to search down the slope towards the stream-bed. Once I'm in the water, I'll be able to see all the way inside the culvert and then I'll have a far better idea of what the primary device looks like.

My chest tightens.

I can see drag-marks and footprints on the side of the bank leading down towards the culvert. Next to them, a neat square cut is visible in the earth. I'm immediately drawn to it . . . *Presence of the abnormal* . . . It's almost certainly a secondary.

I check for tripwires. There are none. When I wave my metal detector left and right about an inch above the ground, it belts out an electronic shriek.

I don't give it a second thought. It *has* to be a secondary.

I reach behind me and ease my disrupter towards the bomb. I extend the tripod's steel legs one at a time, then manoeuvre the weapon right up to the bottom edge of the cut. The disrupter will shatter the firing pack before the explosive can detonate. I'm going to take a shot facing up the bank so I'll be able to recover all the components rather than risk them being fired into the stream below me.

The disrupter's in place and I'm making my way back up the road to the ICP. I'm desperate for a cigarette, but I'm under assessment and don't want to look unprofessional.

I take off my helmet and run my hands through my sodden hair before telling the instructor – who's playing the part of the incident commander – that I'm about to make a controlled explosion and will need everybody under hard cover.

Moments later, my number two is pressing the tit on the Shrike. The Hotrod roars in the crisp spring air. I can feel the disrupter deliver its supersonic blast into the bomb's circuitry through my boots. The high-pressure water jet will have torn the device apart – separating the components before the initiation mechanism had time to function.

I grab a hook-and-line set and another loaded disrupter and make another manual approach, carefully retracing my steps. I can see the shattered TPU and explosives spread across the edge of the bank.

First things first – I need to find the detonator. I may

have disrupted the device, but there are components all over the place. If a battery comes into contact with the detonator's leads, I'll be blown to bits.

I systematically comb the area. Nothing. I eventually find it inside the still smouldering hole, hanging off the remains of the TPU, surrounded by plastic explosive. The TPU has been blown to pieces and I can see the few remaining components inside it. Good. I can do this by hand.

I know I won't be cutting into a collapsing circuit but force of habit still makes me think twice. I rummage in the toolkit for a pair of snips. The twin-flex wire attached to the detonator must be cut precisely. If the bare copper strands touch each other and complete the circuit, it could be game over. I'll sever one first, then move an inch further down the line and deal with the second. That way, there's no possibility of the two arching together.

My heart is racing. I take a breath, hold it for a few seconds, exhale and make the first cut. Nothing. Good.

I move the snips an inch to the right and repeat the process. Still nothing. Even better. I cut the detonator out of the explosive and pull it free.

'OK, sir, stop there!'

Jesus. My instructor's just frightened the fucking life out of me. He was standing right over my shoulder the whole time. He tells me to remove my helmet and passes me a lit cigarette.

'How do you think you've done, then, sir?'

I can't believe it. I've only completed half the task and my instructor's just called the assessment to a halt. But I'm certain I've not fucked up.

'Er . . . All right, I think . . .'

'You think? Or you know?' His expression is completely deadpan.

'Er . . . I know.'

'Would you have done anything differently?'

I hate these mind games.

'Well, no . . . Actually, I wouldn't.'

He asks me what actions I'd carry out next and I tell him I'd have searched all the way into the culvert and taken a shot against the second TPU then used a hook and line to remove the explosive charge from the culvert and onto the bank. 'Once I'd made everything safe, I'd hand the area over to the scenes-of-crime officer.'

He stares at me for a full minute . . . then breaks into a huge grin. 'Well, in that case, sir, you'd better go and pack your bags. Looks like you're going to Northern Ireland.'

20

Listen and be led.

L. M. Heroux

1 April 1999

'One minute!'

The RAF loadmaster barely has time to get the words out before the pilot carries out a terrifying banking manoeuvre and descends low over the trees and rooftops into Ebrington Barracks.

Within seconds we're on the ground and the blast of the Puma's rotor engines scorches our faces as we spill out onto the rain-covered parade square.

The pilot begins his ascent as the last man leaves the chopper. I shield my eyes and close my mouth to ensure I don't get a lungful of grit as the Puma roars over us and beats its way up over the city. Moments later it has disappeared from view.

I'm met at the heli landing site (HLS) by Gavin, the outgoing ATO. We've known each other for several years – both of us were on the same potential officers' course before we went to Sandhurst – and we've now got two days to complete our handover-takeover.

He's only a couple of years older than me but has far more experience as an operator, having served as a number two in the trade before being selected for officer training. He's quiet but has a fearsome sense of humour. I like him immensely.

'Welcome to Londonderry, mate . . . and welcome to the monsoon season.'

'You mean the one that lasts about twelve months of the year?' Some things never change. Northern Ireland is the wettest place I've ever been in my life.

We exchange a bit of small-talk as we dash across the parade square to the Officers' Mess – a white-fronted Victorian edifice.

'How did Staff Worrel get on at his court martial?' he asks. In this trade nobody has any secrets.

'He had a bit of a result. The judge saw sense and let him off with a severe reprimand.'

Gavin takes me inside and leads me along the maze of corridors to my room. 'I'll kip in the Det tonight, so you can move straight in.'

I ask him about the number on the door. The rooms along the magnolia-painted hallway are numbered 11, 12, 12A, 14.

'Fucked if I know,' he replies. 'But it's always been the

ATO's room. Maybe someone just changed it one day 'cos he woke up and saw a magpie.'

'Fair one.' I think of the Mary Stewart quote: *There are few men more superstitious than soldiers. They are, after all, the men who live closest to death.*

After a whirlwind tour of the Mess we make the hundred-metre dash past the 1950s-style accommodation blocks and prefab offices that line the road to the Det. As we punch in the simplex door code and go through the steel blast door, raucous laughter spills out of the two crew rooms. The boys are watching a Peter Kay video in one; in the other, a card game is in full flow.

I feel instantly at home.

Gavin gives me a quick orientation of the Det before taking me into the TV room to meet some of the blokes I'm going to be working with. Corporal Al Cunningham jumps up and offers me his hand. He's going to be my number two, responsible for helping me with the day-to-day running of the Det and deploying my EOD equipment when we're out on task. Gavin really rates the tall, kind-natured Jock and is keen to see him promoted to sergeant. As soon as he is, he'll be eligible to become a number-one IEDD operator.

Joe Harrison, another big rugby-player type, is the team bleep: the Royal Signals expert whose job it is to operate the top-secret electronic counter-measures equipment that will protect us all from the IRA's sophisticated radio-controlled IEDs.

After apologizing for interrupting their card game, Gavin then introduces me to Banksy, a Royal Engineer search specialist who's going to double as my infantry escort. Originally from Bristol, he looks every bit the gentleman farmer, but behind his rosy cheeks and country-bumpkin accent, I'm told, is a shrewd and capable soldier.

Sergeant Pete Mundy, the Royal Engineers search adviser, Corporal Mickey Burnham, my covert driver, and Corporal Dave West, the team's Wheelbarrow technician, are out on a recce.

Introductions over, we get straight into the handover brief. We step into the operations room, its walls adorned with laminated maps of the city and surrounding countryside. Gavin pulls out a thick lever-arch file full of IEDD reports and takes me through every single incident over the past seven months. 'I don't mean to teach you to suck eggs, Chris, but I need to brief you on every action I've carried out on every task, as well as the location of every incident control point.'

It's standard practice during a handover to be briefed on exactly what our predecessors have done in case they've inadvertently set any patterns – like using the same ICP twice. It's a lesson we've learnt the hard way.

In August 1979 six members of the Parachute Regiment were killed at Warrenpoint – close to the border with the Republic – when a 500-kilogram bomb hidden under a lorry-load of hay was detonated as their convoy drove past. Twenty minutes later a second device exploded on a cordon position close to the gate lodge on the opposite side of the road, killing a further twelve. The IRA had been analysing how we responded to bombing incidents and correctly assessed that the soldiers would set up an ICP in the nearby gatehouse.

We run through the classified documents and equipment in the safes, all of which need to be signed over, and finally head into the briefing room where Gavin talks me through the most recent Loyalist and IRA devices used in the city and shows me montages of the local terrorists.

Gavin disappears to get a brew on and leaves me with Corporal Milsome from the brigade's weapons intelligence section. WIS's sole job is to work out who's planting IEDs, what they're capable of and how to defeat them. They're some of the best int operators in the business. A couple of the newer lads on the team come and join us as Milsome flashes up a detailed map of the country and gets straight into the meat of it.

'In July 1997 the Provisional IRA announced a cease-fire but many of the rank and file were unhappy with the Army Council's decision and broke away to form splinter groups. One of those groups – the Continuity IRA – carried out a number of bomb attacks during 'ninety-seven and 'ninety-eight, but it appears to have calmed down a little since then. What the headsheds are really worried about right now is the existence of the Real IRA – an extremist splinter group we believe to have been behind the car bombing in Omagh last year.

'Our major concern is that while PIRA are currently honouring the ceasefire, and we know who pretty much all their players are, nobody has the first fucking idea which of them have broken away to RIRA.'

'So how much do you know about the Real IRA?' I ask him.

'We're told it's led by Michael McKevitt, who we believe is the former quartermaster-general of PIRA.'

McKevitt, he says, has regularly and publicly stated his opposition to Sinn Fein's involvement in the Good Friday Agreement but, more worryingly, had allegedly been responsible for all PIRA arms caches and the supply of weapons and explosives to every PIRA cell in Northern Ireland. The caches are said to contain around six tonnes of Libyan-supplied Semtex, six SAM missiles, six general-purpose machine-guns, about 600 AK-47 assault rifles, 200 pistols and an unspecified number of M-16 rifles and 12-gauge shotguns.

Corporal Milsome brings up a series of slides depicting the location and contents of known arms dumps. He and his team have also identified underground bunkers in County Kerry and the Irish Republic, and a number of smaller ones south of the border. Small quantities of weapons are believed to be held in up to fifty buildings along the border as well as safe-houses in Belfast and Londonderry.

'McKevitt resigned from the Provisionals in October 1997 and agreed not to make use of their arms caches, but recent reports suggest he's reneged on that agreement. The 500-pound bomb planted by the Real IRA in Banbridge in January was fitted with two detonators, one of which was from a batch purchased by the Provos in the United States in 1989 and the other was a "PIRA Mk.3 improvised detonator". It appears that McKevitt has recruited several of their most experienced bomb-makers. Recent incidents in Moira, Portadown and Newtown-Hamilton are reportedly all the work of the Real IRA, so I think you're going to have your work cut out during your time here in Londonderry.'

After a quick brew and a cigarette, Gavin and I resume the handover, but I'm distracted almost immediately by a tall, shadowy-looking bloke who's just walked into the Det.

Gavin raises a hand. 'Chris, I want to introduce you to a good friend of mine: Connor Dooley.'

Connor is a Special Branch officer from the RUC's HQ across the river at Strand Road, and he's going to take me out for a familiarization drive around the Republican estates. Corporal Cunningham hands me a Browning 9mm pistol and three twelve-round magazines, and minutes later Connor and I are pulling out of the camp's huge steel gates in an unmarked police car.

As we drive south through the Protestant area of the city, we pass dozens of buildings adorned with murals of armed men in combat fatigues and Loyalist 'No Surrender' slogans. A few hundred metres later, we head west, cross the river Foyle over Craigavon Bridge and enter the IRA's Catholic heartland.

'This is the place I was born and one day hope to return to,' Connor says. He tells me he was born into a large Catholic family on the Republican Brandywell Estate, where he spent the majority of his youth involved in petty crime and fighting with Protestant kids. But unlike the majority of kids on the estate, he became increasingly sickened by the atrocities he witnessed. Instead of joining the IRA he became a policeman.

'A letter addressed to me arrived at my mother's home one day. Inside was a Roman Catholic mass card, usually sent by relatives and friends when a person they know has died. On it,' he says, 'was my name.'

As I listen to his story, I find myself feeling incredibly sorry for him. He neither wants nor asks for my sympathy, but I can't help feeling deep sadness for a man reviled by his own people for turning against them and mistrusted by his colleagues for being a Catholic.

As we pull into the Creggan, a run-down, post-war council estate, Connor sees me shifting nervously in my seat. 'Try to relax, Chris. We tell all our new guys that the secret to working undercover is to remind yourself that you've as much right to be in a place as the next man. If you feel out of place, you'll look out of place.'

I'm sure he's right, but it's easier said than done.

As if reading my mind, he goes on to explain why only the two of us are in the car. 'The only time you'd expect to see more than two men in a car is during rush-hour, when they're sharing one on the way to or from work. Outside of that, they're either going to be criminals, terrorists or cops.'

We pass the rows of pebble-dashed terraced houses that line the edge of the cemetery and continue past the drab shopping centre and factories in Bligh's Lane Industrial Estate.

'Nice view, isn't it?' he says drily.

But were it not for the burnt-out cars and rusting iron beds that seem to line every back-street, he wouldn't be far from the truth. From the Creggan Heights we can see all the way down to Craigavon Bridge and right across the river to the Waterside.

We continue down the hill, past rows of

disintegrating concrete fences and minefields of broken bottles and scrap metal. Connor begins pointing out the homes of known 'players' and of IRA members he knew as a kid: Paddy Deery and Eddie McSheffrey, killed when the bombs they were about to emplace detonated prematurely; Mairéad Farrell and Sean Savage, shot dead by the SAS in Gibraltar; Hessie Phelan, shot dead by a policeman in the USA in 1996.

'Good enough for the bastards,' he says grimly.

Half a mile or so later, we're driving down the middle of Westland Street in the middle of the Bogside. I'm immediately struck by how many hostile and miserable-looking men there are standing around on the street corners.

As he continues pointing out the players, Connor says that 80 to 90 per cent of men in the Catholic estates are unemployed. Most of them have no qualifications so can only labour or do menial work. 'The Prods still have all the good jobs here in Northern Ireland. An unskilled, unemployed Catholic man has two choices: sit around and do nothing, or join the IRA.'

He then tells me why I've been singled out for this tour of Londonderry's most hard-line estates.

'You're going to be out on the ground regularly, and you're going to be vulnerable. These men are hardcore fanatics and they wouldn't think twice about topping you. Out here you're a high-value target. So you need to know who they are. If you're on the ground and you see even one of them standing on the edge of your cordon, consider it a combat indicator – because those fuckers are all out to make a name for themselves and, believe me, they'd love nothing more than to score some points by sending you home in a wooden box.'

21

We can never obtain peace in the world if we neglect the inner world and don't make peace with ourselves. World peace must develop out of inner peace.

The Dalai Lama

10 April 1999

As I stand in the shadows of the heavily fortified watchtowers, the rain beats down from a low grey sky. The rolling clouds feel as if they're resting on my shoulders.

'Whatever you are, be a good one,' my father used to say. But, inspiring as he was, as I've grown older I've realized that sometimes it's just not possible. We've been on immediate notice to move twenty-four hours a day ever since I arrived, but we've not been tasked to a single IED incident. I hope we can remain focused, because we all know that at the drop of a hat our world could switch from full-off to full-on.

I never thought sitting around doing fuck-all could be so stressful. We try to fill our time constructively –

preparing our equipment or training for possible tasks – but we're all waiting for that call from the ops room. We're never able to relax; we've always got to be poised, ready to respond.

I suspect today will be no different. It hasn't been so far. I woke up, went for a run, a shit, a shower and a shave, and now we're about to embark on another training stint as we wait for the call that never comes.

'So what's on the cards this morning, Boss?' Al Cunningham asks cheerfully, as he steps out of the Det to join me for a cigarette.

'Car bombs, Corporal. I thought we'd have a crack at car bombs first. The doc's agreed to run some patrol medic training for us later this afternoon.'

Al's eyes light up. Every soldier is trained in basic first-aid techniques, but the patrol medic course is a specialist qualification, and the boys, many of whom left school early, love getting qualifications. For many of them, it's one of their principal reasons for joining up.

'He's going to run a series of half-day modules for us.'

'Nice one, Boss. But how the fuck did you get him to agree to that? A place on one of those courses is rarer than rocking-horse shit.'

I smile. 'He's a mate of mine.'

Mark is a captain in the Royal Army Medical Corps. He arrived at Ebrington Barracks a month or so before I did. He also happens to be a big fan of our team.

I met him about a week ago when I sat in on a briefing he was giving to a load of new arrivals. 'And unless you want a nasty dose of Cupid's measles,' he concluded, 'I suggest you stay away from the local girlies.'

We hit it off instantly.

Despite bearing a mischievous resemblance to Dennis the Menace, he's one of those guys who's naturally brilliant at everything he does. He's fiercely intelligent and very funny. He rattles off jokes like a stand-up comedian and plays the guitar like a rock-star. Basically, he's everything any normal man would hate, but it's impossible to do so because he's such a genuinely decent bloke.

Al sets off to find us a suitable training area in a corner of the parade square and Banksy drives one of the old training cars over and rigs it up with the first device of the day.

As I stare out over the river Foyle, I'm conscious that every time we do our stuff on this square, someone from the IRA is watching from the safety of an upstairs window somewhere in the Creggan Heights.

But fuck it. It will have to do.

I start by giving the boys a bit of background. 'Because of their inherent manoeuvrability and their capacity to stealthily deliver large quantities of explosives to a target, the vehicle-borne IED has become one of the most prolific precision weapons in the terrorist's arsenal. Between 1992 and 1998, car bombs killed over a thousand people and wounded nearly twelve thousand.'

'But I thought the IRA didn't target people,' Joe says. 'My understanding was that they prefer commercial targets.'

He's a sharp operator.

'You're not wrong. They don't target civilians per se, but when it comes to attacking the Army and the RUC, they'll happily kill as many people as possible – just like they did when they attacked Thiepval three years ago.'

My mind flashes back to the horrific images of that vicious attack.

'And they're not shy of economic targets. The IRA inflicted billions of pounds' worth of damage on the City of London in just three attacks between 1992 and 1996. All it takes is a second-hand vehicle, some crudely assembled electronic components and a few hundred pounds' worth of commercially available chemicals.'

We rattle through a series of different scenarios. After a couple of hours we have a fag break and a brew and I rig the car up with an under-vehicle booby-trap.

'OK,' I say, 'we've just been tasked to a vehicle that's owned by a member of the security forces.' I tell them that the owner has discovered an IED beneath it. This is a task primarily designed to test Joe's electronic counter-measures skills and Al's flair with the Wheelbarrow.

Al is sitting in front of the monitors in the back of our armoured Tactica EOD truck. He's reconfigured the weapons on the robot and moved it to the front of the ICP, ready to deploy to the target. He's holding the remote-control unit, patiently waiting for the go-ahead.

Joe shouts out of the back of the ECM wagon, 'Boss, I've done a complete sweep of the vehicle. There's no signal. It's clean.'

Good. Radio-controlled bombs are a favoured form of attack for the IRA and Joe's correctly identified that none are present.

'OK, Al, the target is about a hundred and fifty metres down the road. The owner's told us that the device is under the driver's door. Get the Barrow down there and give it the good news.'

He's in his element. He sends the robot trundling along the road and, as we sit glued to the grainy monitor screens, the car comes into focus. He inches the Wheelbarrow towards the device and lines it up ready to take the shot. He knows this is only an exercise, but he's still sweating like ten men, caught up in his own private world.

The pig-stick disrupter is now in place. Any second now, its jet is going to punch a hole through the plastic Tupperware box and rip out the heart of the bomb.

'Boss, I'm on. Are you happy?'

I give him the nod.

He takes the shot and pans the camera back to the area where the under-vehicle car bomb once sat. Hundreds of tiny bomb components lie scattered on the tarmac.

'Good job, Al.' Within three minutes of being given the go-ahead, he's driven the Wheelbarrow out of the ICP, acquired the target and neutralized it. This boy's the business.

As he begins scanning the area for secondary devices, I hear a shout from the back of the ICP. It's Mark, the doc. 'Hello, Bombs,' he says. 'I just heard a loud bang and thought you might need some medical assistance.'

'We're all good, thanks, Doc. Just doing a bit of training. But you can put on the suit and go and make the bomb safe, if you like . . .'

'Fuck that,' he says. 'I'd rather flick the balls of an angry tiger.'

Having packed up the kit and shovelled down our lunch, we're with Mark and his team of medics. So far they've taught us how to set up and insert an IV line into each other's arms, and have now moved on to gunshot wounds.

Each of us takes it in turns to listen to chest auscultations through a stethoscope as Mark explains that under normal circumstances – if we've not been shot through the chest with a high-velocity bullet – our breathing should sound clear. 'But if there's an absence of lung sounds on one side, along with a raised jugular vein in the neck and a gaping gunshot wound in the chest, then you're almost certainly going to be dealing with a tension pneumothorax.'

You could hear a pin drop. The boys are soaking up every word.

Using each other as patients, and with Mark's medics keeping us straight, we practise applying Asherman's chest seals to patch up the entry and exit wounds. We then move on to a dummy and take it in turns locating the space below the second rib on the outer side of the collarbone and inserting two 14-gauge cannulas all the way into the chest cavity.

'Easy, isn't it?' Mark says cheerfully.

Sure enough, when we listen to the dummy's breathing again, the lung has re-inflated and sounds as clean as a whistle.

The boys think it's amazing. And so do I.

The opportunity to learn all this new stuff is one of the things I admire about the Army. But I still can't help feeling that I've spent most of my career training instead of *doing*. I know I need to let it go. I try to imagine that I'm somewhere other than here. I tell Mark I need to nip out and make a quick phone call, but wander over to the edge of the parade square. I sit looking out over the river Foyle and think about home. I think of Lucy and the picnics we've had together on the heather-clad ridges of the Black Mountains. I miss her so much.

I decide to call her, but when she answers, she sounds harried and impatient. Foolishly, I put it down to the pressures of her degree course and go straight into permanent-send mode, telling her about our medical training and all the other cool things we've been up to since I arrived.

She doesn't want to hear any of it.

She stops me in my tracks. Her voice is ice-cold. It's been ten days since I last called. Do I realize we're supposed to be getting married in a few months?

I go on the defensive, and sound like a terminal arse-hole. The conversation goes from bad to worse and both of us become totally unreasonable. Even when one of us does try to placate the other, all we seem to do is make things worse.

I try to see it from her perspective. I know it's hard for her. I'm going to be here for five months while she arranges the wedding and finds us somewhere to live, then I'll come home for a week, dash up the aisle and come back here to see out the rest of my tour. It's not exactly the stuff of fairytales.

I know I need to get to grips with the complexity of her high-wire act. She's busy studying for her finals and

I'm getting miserable because I can't save the world. The combination of missing your loved ones and getting on with your own life must be virtually impossible for those we leave behind.

If only I could communicate it.

I wish I could get to grips with my own insecurities too. Absence doesn't make the heart grow fonder: absence makes us grow more distant. Right now all I can think about is coming back to an empty house and finding a note from her saying she's sorry but she's decided to call it a day.

I tell her I miss her terribly. But it's too late. The line's already dead.

22

In today's world, no one is innocent, no one is neutral. A man is either with the oppressed or he is with the oppressor.

George Habash, leader of the Popular Front
for the Liberation of Palestine

11 April 1999

I'm lying in bed, staring at the bare walls of my tiny room and wishing I was at home. It's 3 a.m. and I've not slept a wink. *How have I let things get so out of control? Why is my life such a fuck-up?* I wish I knew how to get it back on track.

I close my eyes and imagine Lucy's beaming smile. It seems so distant, so remote. I hate being away from her. I miss talking to her. I miss laughing with her. I would give anything to hold her in my arms right now.

The phone rings and my heart skips a beat.

'Lucy, is that you?'

'Er . . . no, Boss . . . it's Al. You need to get yourself over here. We've got a job on.'

By the time I arrive at the Det the boys are already suited and booted and raring to go.

'Jump in, Boss.' Al hands me my pistol and SA80. 'I'll brief you en route.' As we pull out of the gates, the roar of the Tacticas' engines is overridden only by the wailing sirens of the RUC Land Rover that's been sent to escort us to the incident.

'This is a bit of a strange one, Boss,' Al says, struggling to keep up with the police vehicle in front. 'Shortly after two a.m. a taxi was apparently hijacked from Columcille Court in the Bogside by two masked men claiming to be from the Continuity IRA. The driver was held at gunpoint while one of them placed a large bomb in the boot. The other took the driver's taxi licence and told him his family would be killed unless he drove the car to RUC Strand Road. They said he had fifteen minutes before the device was due to detonate.'

'OK . . . so we're dealing with a proxy bomb, right?' Car bombs are sometimes driven to the target by someone who may have been coerced into the role, or is completely unaware that the vehicle contains an IED. It's a tactic we've seen in Northern Ireland, Colombia and Turkey. The driver's foot is often taped to the accelerator, or his hands are chained to the steering-wheel. In one case, he was welded into the cab.

'No, Boss. That's what doesn't add up. The bloke drove his car back into the Bogside and left the bomb on a pavement – right in the middle of a Catholic residential area. Then he drove the empty car to RUC Strand Road to report it to the police.'

I feel a tingling between the shoulder-blades. He's right. It definitely doesn't add up.

We continue our journey in silence, heading first through the north-eastern part of the city, then crossing the Foyle Bridge and heading south through the Republican Shantallow Estate. As we pass the rows of tired-looking council houses, I'm immediately struck by the emptiness and the darkness. Nobody is about and every single one of the street lights has been smashed.

We continue through Pennyburn and eventually drop down onto the Strand Road. As we pass the rows of offices, shops and bars overlooking the quayside I run through my mental checklist of arrival drills: the need for caution and vigilance when approaching the area; the risk of gunmen lying in wait to ambush our vehicles; where the device is, what time it was laid, how long the area's been secured, what else was seen and heard. I also think about our greatest enemy of all – concealed secondary devices. They might be on the cordon position, on the route to the device, or in its immediate vicinity.

Seconds later, we're pulling into the ICP.

'Fuck me,' I say. 'What's wrong with this picture, Al?'

Unlike the rest of the sleeping city, the Bogside is absolutely heaving. A large crowd has formed at the edge of the cordon and entire families have congregated in their first-floor bedroom windows to watch the show. The closest of the terraced houses can't be further than thirty metres away from the device.

'Jesus, Boss, it looks like every man, woman and child in the Bogside has stayed up to see you do your thing tonight. Have they been flogging tickets?'

Maybe it's a coincidence, or perhaps I'm just being paranoid. Either way, I've got a nasty feeling something sinister is waiting for me.

I jump out of the wagon and I'm met by the cordon commander, a young-looking RUC sergeant called Billy Moore. Al and Joe park their Tacticas to form a protective V and drop the blast skirts to prevent explosive debris shooting underneath the vehicle. The RUC's armoured Land Rover pulls in across the back of us to close the triangle.

Banksy and a platoon of infantrymen from the Royal Regiment of Fusiliers are carrying out checks for hidden devices.

Good. They're doing everything by the book, sending out the message to any would-be aggressors: *Don't fuck with us, because if you do, you're going to get hurt.*

I introduce myself to the RUC sergeant, exchange

a few pleasantries, and we get straight into the task.

He runs through the chain of events prior to our arrival, confirming that the taxi had been hijacked and its driver held at gunpoint before he drove up to Abbey Street – where he removed the bomb from the car before continuing to RUC Strand Road.

'So where exactly is the bomb right now?' I ask.

'If you take a right at the end of this street, it's about thirty metres further down, opposite the only derelict building in the entire estate.'

'And the driver?'

'He's right behind you.'

Unbelievable. Witnesses are supposed to be segregated and kept out of earshot.

I turn and introduce myself. The boyo offers me his hand and tells me his name is Francis McGuire. He appears to be a little nervous, but I give him the benefit of the doubt and put it down to the ordeal he's just endured. Other than that he seems like any other normal bloke – early forties, dark, unkempt hair, average height and build.

But as I begin questioning him on his version of events, I notice he's getting more and more agitated and there are some inconsistencies in his story. He tells me he couldn't bring himself to drive the car bomb to RUC Strand Road, because there are dozens of bars opposite the police station and he couldn't live with himself if he was responsible for so many innocent deaths.

'OK . . .' I check my notebook. 'I may have written this down incorrectly, but didn't you say that you were hijacked at two in the morning?'

'That's right.' His eyes dart up and to the right.

'So why were you so reluctant to deliver the bomb to Strand Road, knowing the bars are all closed at that time of night, and yet perfectly happy to bring the bomb back to your own estate – full of innocent Catholic families?'

'Er . . . I don't know,' he says, his eyes darting so far up and to the right I thought they were going to bounce out of his head. 'I was worried for my family. I guess I just wasn't thinking straight.'

There are several ways to tell if someone is lying, and eye movement is one of the most reliable indicators of all. If you ask somebody to recall an event and they look up and to the left, it means they're searching for an image they've seen before. But if they look up and to the right, it means they're lying their arses off.

I leave him with the policeman and go round to the back of the Tactica from which Al is controlling the robot that's already trundling down the road. 'Al, have any of these coppers bothered to check out the driver on the Police National Computer?' I ask.

He stops what he's doing, flashes me a look of utter contempt and says, 'Boss, my balls are pink 'n' hairy, not made of crystal. How the fuck would I know that?'

He's right. It's a bone question, and the last thing he needs when he's trying to do his job is me asking stupid questions.

As the robot turns the corner, we can see from the monitors that the street ahead is eerily silent. Deserted, empty.

A few seconds later, our eyes are drawn to a large black bin-liner standing up against a lamp-post.

'Good work, Al,' I say. 'If you can line up the Barrow for a shot, I'll go and tell the RUC to get everybody under hard cover. I just want to ask our driver a couple more questions first. But don't worry, we're not in any hurry. I'll bet a month's wages there's fuck-all in that bag.'

'If I was a gambling man,' he replies, 'I'd bet two!'

I take the sergeant to one side. 'Billy,' I say, trying to sound as upbeat as possible, 'please don't take this the wrong way, but has anybody P-checked Francis McGuire?'

His face reddens. His sheepish expression tells me he hasn't. Fucking hell, this is day-one, week-one stuff. The Provos have been on ceasefire for five minutes and Billy seems to have forgotten every lesson the RUC's learnt in thirty years of conflict. Everybody gets P-checked. Jesus, if ignorance is bliss, this boy must be completely euphoric.

A minute or two later, Billy reappears. He looks absolutely mortified.

'Er . . . it's not good, I'm afraid. It seems our kidnapped taxi driver isn't quite what he claims to be. He was sentenced to eighteen years in prison for murdering a Brit soldier. He's a former member of the Irish National Liberation Army and is now suspected to have ties with the Continuity IRA.'

I have to restrain myself from tearing shreds out of this boy for not doing his job properly the first time around.

'We also checked his taxi licence and it's registered to his old address. A completely different family lives there now. His family were never in any danger at all.'

'OK, thanks for that, Billy.' I try to remain calm. 'Could you bring him back over to me, please? I've got a few more questions I need to ask him.'

While he's sorting out McGuire, I get the team together at the back of the ICP and give them a quick heads-up. They seem even more annoyed than I am that the RUC needed a kick up the arse. Only Al remains completely unruffled. 'Fuck it, Boss, what's done is done,' he says. 'Just remember that muddy water becomes clear if you leave it to stand – so take your time and don't go wading in with both feet.'

'Thanks, Al. I've got it covered.' Sometimes I think working with Al is like doing a task with Confucius.

I step back out onto the moonlit street and head straight up to McGuire. I stand opposite him, my face just inches away from his. 'The one thing you can give and still keep is your word . . .' I tell him, staring coldly into his eyes. 'And I give you my word that unless you tell me exactly what's waiting for me around that corner, you're going straight to Castlereagh for some one-on-one with the Special Branch boys.'

Castlereagh police station is the huge stone fortress that strikes fear into the heart of every IRA man. I'm told that nobody, no matter how tough they are, is impervious to the interrogation techniques practised there by Special Branch.

McGuire's eyes narrow, and for the first time I notice the anger and cruelty they contain. He's clearly a man who doesn't like to be defied, and definitely not by a British soldier. 'Fuck you,' he says.

'It's your call, McGuire, but it seems to me your plan is rapidly starting to go to ratshit, and if I decide to ask my pals at Special Branch to begin spreading the word that you're working for them, who do you think your internal-investigations people are going to believe?'

'Fuck you,' he says again, just in case I haven't got the message.

'So be it.' I do my best to mask my own fear. 'It's your choice.'

It's not the outcome I'd hoped for, but his silence

speaks volumes. There's definitely something waiting for me out there.

Decision time.

Do I sack it now, or should I take time to mull it over? Is the device on a timer?

According to McGuire's story, it was supposed to detonate after fifteen minutes, but how can I believe anything the lying bastard's told me? Ideally I should let it soak until tomorrow.

Fuck it. I'll only be putting off the inevitable. Let's get it over with.

I get on the radio and request a high-risk search team from the Royal Engineers to carry out a search of the derelict buildings and check for cables leading into the target area. The last thing I want to do is make a manual approach to the device, then be blown to bits by a hidden command wire.

I'm told by Brigade HQ that no search teams are available.

I'll just have to do what I can.

'OK, Al, I know this may sound a bit stupid, but I want you to take the shot on that bag. Then I'm going to request a heli-teli to see if there's anybody inside that derelict. I'll make the manual approach once we've flushed them out. What do you think?'

'If it's stupid but works, Boss, it isn't stupid.'

We stand side by side, glued to the grainy monitor.

The black bag fills the screen as the robot's extending arm closes in for the kill.

'OK, Boss, I'm on. Are you happy for me to take the shot?' The disrupter is in position, its water-filled steel tube aimed at the heart of the black bag.

I go through a quick mental checklist. Everybody is under hard cover; the residents are as well protected as they can be. We're less than a hundred metres away from the device, but relatively safe. It's not going to get any better than this.

'Go for it,' I tell him.

He bellows out his one-minute warning, then selects the circuit and uncovers the firing switch on the control box. 'STAND BY . . . FIRING NOW . . .'

I hold my breath.

There's a pause . . . then a deep roar as the disrupter pummels the night air.

And then silence.

Al pans the camera back towards the bag and confirms it's been completely disrupted before scanning the surrounding area with the Barrow for secondary devices and command wires. He finds nothing but rubble and bits of plastic where the bag once stood.

'So that was our bomb. A bag of bricks and sand. Nice work, Al.'

Well begun is half done, I think to myself.

Now it's time to use the ace up my sleeve. I call in a

heli to over-fly the area. The Provos hate helis – particularly at night, and especially when they're equipped with infra-red cameras. If there's a sniper waiting for me, the heli is going to flush him out. And by now he probably knows it.

Minutes later, the bird swoops down low and hovers a few hundred feet above the rooftops. The distinctive beat of its rotor blades echoes around the houses like cannon fire. So far so good.

I turn back to the police sergeant.

'Billy, this is almost certainly a come-on, and I'm fairly certain I'm their target. I'd like you to deploy some of your police call signs, supported by infantry if possible, to the back of the derelict and ideally position a few guys on the rooftops. I want all lines of sight into the device covered. And I want to reduce the cordon to fifty metres. I suggest we shift the ICP closer towards the end of this street. Does that sound workable?'

'I can definitely send some guys to cover the derelict. But covering all lines of sight into the device? There are just too many potential firing points. I'll do what I can . . .'

A few more locals have rocked up on the cordon position. I wonder what they know that I don't.

I tell Joe to switch on the ECM kit and fry the city. I want him to pump out everything he's got while Al prepares my kit and Banksy begins dressing me in the bomb suit.

The cumbersome armour looks like an astronaut's outfit and is made up of layers of Kevlar and ceramic. I put on the over-trousers first, then the jacket, then the plates and helmet. On the plus side, it's designed to offer limited protection from small-arms fire, and right now that's exactly what I need.

Al hands me my bag of EOD tools and places a disrupter under my arm. Then he snaps my visor shut and taps me twice on the shoulder. 'Good to go, Boss.'

As I begin the long walk, I remember Major Hudson's words. *You'll need moral courage, compassion, judgement and determination . . . and, most importantly, you'll need to be able to remain calm . . . to think clearly and act decisively.*

I wish I could, but right now I feel as nervous as a Para on a spelling test.

I'm carrying the world's biggest array of EOD weapons, tools and electronic counter-measures, and all I can hear is the heaving of my lungs and the sound of the blood rushing in my ears. I'm back in the zone.

I take a few steps forward, then stop to scan the scene for any hidden threats. *Absence of the normal, presence of the abnormal.*

I continue on. Walk, pause, observe; walk, pause, observe.

As I take each laboured step along the darkened street, passing the rows of terraced houses, I feel an incredible sense of vulnerability. I'm completely exposed. A soldier's life often depends on nothing more than intuition, the indefinable feeling that tells you when the shit's about to hit the fan, and right now that's exactly where it seems to be heading.

There are dozens of people looking at me from every window and the area is perfect for a sniper's shot. For all I know my team and I could have been in the middle of a gunman's cross hair from the moment we arrived.

I'm halfway there.

I stop again and try to regulate my breathing as I take in the scene once more. I'm just about to turn the corner when the whole street lights up in front of me. For a moment I'm blinded by the heli's powerful spotlight. It's like night has turned into day.

People begin shouting all around me.

'ARMY . . . halt or I shoot.'

I freeze.

The voices are coming from behind the derelict.

'Boss!' Al shouts. 'Get your arse back here. NOW!'

I turn, still rooted to the spot. It's like a bad dream.

'*Run!*'

My heart is thudding like a jackhammer. This is insane. I snap out of my zombie-like trance and begin pounding my way, low and fast, towards Al and the team.

Twenty metres.

Adrenalin and fear are pulsing through my body in equal measure. I'm running faster than I've ever run before. I'm running for my life, trying desperately to block out the paralysing images of a high-velocity bullet entering my body, as it creates a vortex behind it like the wake after a boat, tearing through my flesh.

Ten metres.

Banksy runs out towards me and drops onto one knee, taking up a fire position in the street and covering me as I scream past him. Seconds later, we're both doubled over, panting for breath, in the back of the ICP.

Outside, infantry and police patrols are running down the street, shrieking and yelling as they enter the maze of alleys and side-streets that criss-cross the Bogside. The helicopter continues circling above the estate, sweeping its beam over the jagged rooftops.

'What the fuck happened, Al?' I ask.

'It's just come over the net . . . the heli-teli picked up a possible gunman inside that derelict and sent in an infantry team to flush him out.'

'Did they get him?'

'Sorry, Boss . . . No, they didn't. It seems he legged it through some houses in the Bogside and they've lost him.'

My heart sinks. They'll never find him now. The streets have suddenly filled with people – presumably as part of a pre-arranged plan to allow the gunman to blend in among them. Even if he was still hiding in one of the occupied houses, it's not as if the RUC are going to start kicking down doors to find him. They're terrified of starting a riot.

He's long gone.

Back at the Det, as I sit typing up my incident report, I see a familiar face in the doorway. It's Connor, the Special Branch detective.

'I thought you might be in need of this.' He waves a bottle of Bushmills in front of me.

'Madness not to,' I reply.

The Irish whiskey tastes good, but I can't kick the arse out of it; one glass, two at most.

'I'm sorry you were put in that position tonight,' Connor says. I can tell he feels personally responsible for the lack of warning about the attempted shooting.

'Really, it's no big deal.' I hope I sound more relaxed than I feel. 'Shit happens.'

He apologizes again before explaining that he'd received some int a couple of days ago that members of CIRA were planning a spectacular, but that was all he knew. 'It wasn't until you and your guys were out on the ground tonight that our source confirmed it was going to be a shoot, and you were the target.

'By the time I was in a position to tell you, you'd already figured it out for yourself.'

It's nice to know we've got people like Connor looking out for us, and even though his intelligence wasn't timely on this occasion, I can't get het up about it. OK, so it was a bit of a baptism of fire tonight, and I was scared half to death, but fuck it, we managed to disrupt a CIRA plot, nobody was killed or injured and I got to experience the headiest, most extreme adrenalin rush I've ever had in my life.

23

To conquer fear is the beginning of wisdom.

Bertrand Russell

24 June 1999

'What time is it, Bombs?' Mark asks.

I glance down at my watch and realize I don't even know what day it is. Our routine seems to have become so grinding and repetitive it feels as if the nights are melting into days and the weeks are drifting into months. 'Nine fifteen,' I reply.

We've been forward-based here in the canteen of RUC Strand Road since four thirty this morning waiting for Sergeant Goode – the Royal Engineers search adviser (RESA) – to give us the all-clear. He's spent the night running a major operation with the new infantry battalion's ops company to clear a route for the two hundred or so Loyalist Orangemen about to exercise their centuries-old right to march through the city.

'Just another hour to push, then,' he says. 'Thank fuck for that. This is about as exciting as listening to your hair grow!'

Ninety-nine per cent boredom and one per cent terror. The monotony is killing me too. Thankfully, Mark's medics and my team are keeping each other amused with a near-constant stream of banter. I've got a new number two, Nick Foote, who replaced Al a couple of weeks ago, but even though he's a relative newcomer to the group, he's happily trading insults with the best of them. Until a couple of minutes ago, they were all trying to upstage one another with outrageous stories of their shagging conquests on leave, but now they're grappling with the fundamental differences between men and women.

'If two women meet in the street, one will say to the other, "Hey, you've had your hair done. It really suits you. Did you have the rinse? I really like it!" Whereas if two men bump into each other, one will say to the other, "You've had a number two, haven't you? You look like a right cunt!"'

Seconds later, after a bout of raucous laughter and several nods of agreement, the conversation somehow shifts to vegetarians.

'It's just wrong,' one of the medics says. 'I mean, if we aren't supposed to eat animals, then why are they made out of meat?' More nods of approval. 'Don't get me wrong, I love animals. I just love to eat them more. Fun to pet, better to chew . . .'

These boys are priceless.

Before long, we've shifted to the perceived demise of the British family unit. When one of the lads makes the controversial suggestion that a widespread return to Christianity is the answer, another pipes up, 'It's so obvious, isn't it? A celestial Jewish zombie, who happens to be his own father, says he can make you live for ever if you just keep eating his flesh and drinking his blood and agree for him to be your eternal master, so he'll remove the evils of the world, which are only there in the first place because a woman made from a rib was persuaded by a talking snake to steal an apple from a magical tree. I can't understand for the life of me why so few people go to church!'

Right on cue the commanding officer of the new infantry battalion appears. I've only met him a couple of times, but I get the impression that Lieutenant Colonel Richard Kemp is very much old school. Approachable yet strong-minded, he is the archetypal Sandhurst officer and gentleman; a highly experienced combat soldier who's adored by the men of the 1st Battalion, The Royal Anglian Regiment. He's driven them hard during their preparation for this two-year tour, training them thoroughly in all aspects of counter-insurgency but also ensuring every officer and man knows that first and foremost they're here to protect the civilian community.

'Right, which one of you scruffy gits is the ATO?' he asks, knowing the answer full well. The boys start pissing themselves with laughter; they know what's coming next.

'That'll be me, sir . . .'

'Aaah, Captain Hunter . . .' He looks me up and down and shakes his head. 'Have you tried turning the iron on when you press those combats?'

The colonel has obviously spent some quality time alongside Colour Sergeant Maclaren. There's only one thing for it: I give him my best Clint Eastwood impression. 'Combats are for dyin' in, not ironin', Colonel.'

'Fucking good answer, ATO. But I haven't come in here to sort out your laundry. The RESA has just located an IED and I need you to make it safe.'

The canteen bursts into life.

While we're shrugging on our kit, the colonel says that the two hundred Orangemen currently gathering at the Guildhall are due to begin their parade at ten thirty, and if they're delayed by even a minute, they'll definitely kick off.

He pulls out a neatly folded map and spreads it on the table. 'The suspect device is situated here, behind a telephone box on Shipquay Street, up the hill between the Guildhall and the Diamond. I'm told it's a Clansman radio battery with a fishing line trailing off into a pile of sand beneath it. It's almost certainly a VO. The problem is, there are five hundred or so Republican protesters at the Diamond, and although they've assured the police they're feeling all warm and fuzzy, if the Orangemen kick off, we're going to see the mother of all riots. I need you to render that bomb safe, and fast.'

I imagine the petrol bombs lighting up the Londonderry night as his soldiers try in vain to keep the age-old enemies from killing one another. I look at my watch: nine thirty.

Exactly seven minutes later I'm walking towards the suspect device. I'm carrying the king-size party-pack of EOD weapons, tools and electronic counter-measures, and once again I can hear the heaving of my lungs and the blood rushing in my ears.

I'm back in the zone.

Columns of Orangemen in dark suits, white gloves and bowler hats are pressed up against the cordon behind me. Their band members are beating out all their favourite hits: 'The Sash' and 'The Green, Grassy Slopes of the Boyne' blare out from their pipes and drums, every note a deliberate provocation, fuelling the hatred of the Catholic Republicans poised two hundred metres up this hill.

Banksy and one of the Royal Anglian privates come with me for the first fifty metres to provide a bit of extra firepower should things suddenly go tits-up. Joe is pumping out enough radio waves to sterilize every man in Londonderry. I'm completely reliant on my team. So much of being a bomb-disposal operator is about placing your life in other people's hands and I've struck gold with these boys.

A Gazelle circles overhead, its navigator peering through the thermal-imaging sight of the heli-teli, ready to warn me of any sudden threats. Lieutenant Colonel Kemp has thought of everything. I just hope the crowd doesn't get too excited. I'll be royally fucked if they decide to surge now.

My heart muscle feels tauter than an Orangeman's snare drum.

At the halfway point, my two escorts give me a nod and peel off to their fire positions.

I try to regulate my breathing. To get my pulse down. I inhale deeply through my nose and exhale slowly through my mouth.

Now I'm standing next to the bomb. The green military radio battery and the fine filament trailing off into the mound of builders' sand beneath it. Every nerve-end snaps to attention and a bead of sweat runs down my back. Thank Christ Sergeant Goode's boys are switched on. Any one of them could have picked this thing up, thinking he was doing a favour for one of his mates.

I switch off my radio and edge forwards. My gaze is transfixed by the green battery, no larger than a pack of cards. There's no one else in the world: just me and the bomb. My hands are shaking; my breathing is deep and fast. I'm really starting to feel the fear now. But it feels good; I feel alive.

I drag my tripod to the edge of the phone box and extend its legs, one at a time, then edge my disrupter into place. I'm going to take a downward shot into the sand directly beneath the battery. I want to take time over the weapon placement. I want to line it up perfectly. But I remember Brummie's words the night I unravelled in Bicester: *A lot of good men fail because they try too hard to be perfect. But, actually, it's all right to be good enough.*

A second or so later the disrupter's in place and I'm making my way back down to the ICP. Nick hands me a ciggie and the bottle of Diet Coke he liberated from the police canteen before we left. I take off my helmet and run my hands through my sodden hair.

'Go for it,' I say.

He bellows a warning. The roar of the Hotrod rolls down the hill as the disrupter delivers its low-pressure blast into the bomb's circuitry. I know it's done the trick without even seeing it.

Sure enough, I walk back into the ICP after my

second manual approach with a bagful of components.

'Not bad, Boss,' Nick says. 'Twenty-four minutes.'

The march was completed with barely a ripple. The boys have spent the rest of the day chilling out at the Det, writing letters home and furiously trying to beat their previous top scores on the PlayStation. Everyone's laughing and joking, and the place is absolutely buzzing.

I haven't felt this happy in ages. I'm still fired up from this morning's task and I've just had a brilliant chat with Lucy. She's on great form today and has just told me some amazing news: a letter arrived in the post this morning saying I'm being posted to 22 SAS next April, which means we're going to spend the first two years of our married life in Hay, the place we've always dreamt of settling. Maybe we'll get that fairytale ending after all.

The boys and I slot in the DVD of *Saving Private Ryan*. At the end of the movie, as the camera pans across row upon row of Normandy war graves, the elderly Ryan kneels in front of the grave of his former platoon commander, turns to his wife and says: 'Tell me I've led a good life. Tell me I'm a good man.'

There's not a dry eye in the house. It must be particularly dusty in the Det tonight.

Just as I'm having a moment – wiping the tears from my eyes and taking stock of my own life – Mark the doc strides in and does a double-take. He's obviously not used to seeing a roomful of fully grown men blubbing.

'Er, Bombs,' he says awkwardly, 'are you coming over to the Mess for a quick snifter?'

I tell him I'd love to but it's just not worth taking the risk when we're on immediate notice to move.

'Go on, treat yourself. The int cell says the city's going to be completely dead tonight.'

It seems like a bit of a bold statement, but he explains that the Provos have been on the piss all day, and the last of them has just staggered home. The int boys have been monitoring them all day through the city's CCTV cameras.

I definitely don't need to be asked twice.

'Prepare yourself,' Mark says. 'It's *Showaddysquaddie* . . .'

Even before we reach the Mess, we can hear the rhythmic beat of 'Three Steps To Heaven' blaring out of the open windows. A few of the Royal Anglian officers have flown their girlfriends over for the week and they're partying big-time.

As we step inside the bar, we're greeted by a horde of drunken maniacs, fucked out of their heads to a man and desperately trying to impress the girls with their two-step dance routines.

It's totally surreal. The only person not dancing is the families' officer. He's sitting in a corner with the padre, trying to teach him the alcoholic's version of the Lord's Prayer:

> Our lager which art in barrels, hallowed be thy drink. Thy will be drunk, at home as in the tavern. Give us this day our foamy head, and forgive us our spillages, as we forgive those who spill against us. And lead us not into incarceration, but deliver us from hangovers. For thine is the beer, the bitter and the lager, for ever and ever, barmen . . .

A few of the dance gurus eventually break away from the floor to meditate profoundly on different types of courage. This is drunken philosophizing at its sparkling best. As Mark hands me a large vodka Red Bull, one of the captains says, 'We've all heard about people having guts or balls. But is there really a difference?'

After a couple of minutes' earnest reflection, the Anglian officers spend the next ten or so talking complete gibberish. Then one of them says, 'Ask the ATO, he should know . . . He walks up to things that go bang for a living . . .'

Sensing my awkwardness, Mark steps in: 'Guts,' he says, 'is arriving home late after a night out with the guys, getting smacked over the head with a broom by your missus, then asking, "Are you still cleaning up, or are you about to fly somewhere?"'

'Balls, on the other hand, is coming home late after a night out with the guys, stinking of perfume, with lipstick on your collar, then slapping your missus square on the arse and yelling, "You're next, Fatty!"'

The man's a genius.

We spend the next four hours knocking back vodka Red Bulls, dancing like men possessed and talking extreme bollocks. The next time I look at my watch it's four thirty – and I'm as pissed as a parrot. The birds are firing up the dawn chorus and the first rays of sunshine are fighting their way through the curtains. 'Jesus, Mark, we've been awake for twenty-four hours and drinking solidly for the past four. It's fucking daylight outside!'

'I know,' he says reverently. He reaches over and pats me on the back. 'Live every day as if it were your last. Eventually you'll be right.'

I decide that enough's enough. As I stagger back to my room and begin stripping off, my ops phone starts ringing.

For a brief moment I think I'm imagining it.

No such luck. I pick up the receiver and hear Nick's voice.

'Boss, there's a car bomb outside RUC Strand Road. A gunman's just driven it up to the front gate, opened fire with an AK47 and legged it.'

Fuck me. I'm in all sorts of trouble. I can barely

speak. 'Please . . . tell me this is a wind-up, Corporal Foote . . .'

He tells me it isn't.

I can't believe it. The only thing ATOs fear more than the possibility of dying is looking unprofessional, and right now I'm about as amateur as they come. I'm so pissed I can hardly stand.

When I arrive at the Det, the boys are raring to go.

'Here you go, Boss.' Nick hands me my weapons and a mug of steaming coffee. 'I thought you could probably use a brew.'

As we race towards RUC HQ I think of the car parked outside it and imagine the pulse of stark white light silhouetting the watchtowers, the thunderous explosion tearing everyone and everything to shreds. In expert hands, even the smallest of cars can be apocalyptic.

We turn into Strand Road and pull up at the police checkpoint before being ushered through the cordon tape to our own incident control point.

There in front of us is a red Vauxhall Astra with its engine running. It's no more than ninety metres away. I'm sobering up fast.

While Nick and Joe park their Tacticas in the standard protective V, I attempt to debus to get a brief from the cordon commander. Unfortunately, either because the vehicles are moving, or more likely because I'm still half-cut, I tumble out of the cab and land on my arse. I feel like a complete loser. I make a promise to myself that I'll never get pissed on duty again.

Trying not to breathe on him, I ask the police incident commander to prepare to get everybody in the danger area under hard cover. Then, just as we're about to spark up the Wheelbarrow, he asks me if I want to speak to the gunman.

'What . . . ? You've *caught* him?'

'We certainly have,' he replies. 'And if he's an IRA hit man, I'm the shagging Pope. The old feck's as blind as a welder's dog and couldn't hit the side of a barn with a handful of gravel. He emptied an entire mag at the station and didn't hit a thing.'

I tell Nick to hang slack on the Barrow.

I can tell the gunman is no terrorist as soon as he arrives in the ICP. He doesn't have killer eyes: he has the same dead eyes as my brother Tim. The eyes of a man who sees no future.

When I ask him if there's a bomb in the car he says there isn't. And when I ask him to tell me in detail what happened, he lets out a gut-wrenching howl and falls to the ground. Tears stream down his face as he rocks backwards and forwards, mumbling to himself.

'Look,' I say, 'we both know you're no terrorist, but you're in a lot of trouble. You need to tell me in your own words exactly what happened.'

He turns and looks deep into my soul. Then he tells me his story.

His nineteen-year-old son was sent to prison eighteen months ago for joyriding. When he was released earlier today, he wanted to surprise his dad by turning up unannounced, but didn't have the money for the bus fare home, so stole another car and drove it to Derry. Only he didn't make it that far. He collided with another vehicle four miles outside the city and was killed instantly.

'I'm so sorry,' I tell him. I mean it sincerely, but I know it's completely inadequate: there's nothing I can say to ease his despair.

The dead boy was his only child. In his turmoil he decided to remove an AK47 from an IRA hide and use it in a suicidal attack on the RUC HQ. He'd obviously watched *Butch Cassidy and the Sundance Kid* a couple of times too often: he'd thought he'd leave this world in a blaze of glory. Instead he got a stoppage and was immediately nicked.

'I just wanted to die,' he says simply.

I know that time often heals what reason cannot, but as I stare into his lifeless eyes, I fail to see how he'll ever get over this. The weight of his sorrow is just too much for him to bear.

And the irony is that now he's stolen a weapon from the IRA, he's pretty much a dead man anyway.

*   *   *

As I climb into bed for the first time in almost thirty-six hours, I find myself thinking about *Saving Private Ryan* again. I replay in my head the scene in which Captain Miller talks about wanting to get home to his wife. 'I guess I've changed some,' he says. 'Sometimes I wonder if I've changed so much my wife is even going to recognize me whenever it is I get back to her, and how I'll ever be able to tell her about days like today.'

As I drift off to sleep, I dream of being home with Lucy, and wonder how I'll ever find the words to tell her about my surreal day.

24

For it is written that a son of Arabia would awaken a fearsome Eagle. The wrath of the Eagle would be felt throughout the lands of Allah; while some of the people trembled in despair still more rejoiced: for the wrath of the Eagle cleansed the lands of Allah and there was peace.

Verse 9.11 of the Holy Koran

11 September 2001

I touch the tip of the soldering iron against the wire filament and a pungent puff of white smoke drifts up from the circuit board sitting inches from my face. The tiny globule of molten metal sets hard, instantly fixing the components firmly into position. The bomb is now primed and ready to go. It's a classic mobile-phone device, an international terrorist's favourite.

I've just returned from the school in Kineton, where I've spent several weeks attending the coveted manual-IED defeat course. To start with we were taught how to be terrorists. We learned advanced electronics and IED construction and how to mix and manufacture home-made explosives. Once we'd become suitably adept at bomb-building, our instructors then took us through the process of neutralizing them by hand. We covered every type of bomb imaginable and it was a real eye-opener.

It's been a humbling experience too. Like most operators in our trade, once I'd passed the high-threat STT course and completed a tour of Northern Ireland I thought I was the mutt's nuts. But the beauty of the manual-skills course is that it shows you just how much you don't know. When I graduated from the ATO course the commandant warned me about this. I now know exactly what he meant. And my thirst for know-ledge has become unquenchable.

I glance up at the clock on my wall. It's ten thirty and I need to get my skates on. We've got an aircraft-hostage-rescue exercise this afternoon and I've still got to make the forty-five-minute drive to the training area and prepare my kit.

As I weave my way through the warren of country lanes I decide to give Lucy a call. She's pregnant with our first child and due to go into labour any day.

She's as cheerful and radiant as ever, and switches immediately into permanent-send about who she's met up with over coffee this morning and who's doing what to whom. Since we moved to Herefordshire she's been happier than at any time in our relationship. Originally, our plan had been to rent a place in Hay-on-Wye, but because it's twenty miles from camp and I'm on immediate notice to move, we've settled for a married quarter in Hereford. Thankfully, she loves it; she's settled in really quickly and made some great friends.

I love it too. And right now I'm especially happy because we're closer to the hospital than we would be in Hay.

'And how's our little bump?'

'Still kicking me constantly,' she says, 'but all good.'

Just then the signal dips and we get cut off. I try calling her back but sack it after a couple of failed attempts. I don't really want to play phone tennis while I'm at the wheel.

Twenty minutes later I pull onto the training area. I grab my kitbags and slide into the temporary operating base, a large concrete building about a mile away from the target aircraft. The place is absolutely frenetic. All around me blokes are donning their black coveralls and assault vests. Some are preparing explosive entry charges while the team commanders are tapping away at their laptops, preparing their orders for the assault.

I'm told today's training serial is going to be based on a real incident that took place a few years ago in France. On Christmas Eve 1994, four *jihad*ists from the Armed

Islamic Group seized an Air France flight from Algeria, taking 173 hostages. They placed twenty sticks of TNT around the plane and threatened to detonate them if they weren't allowed to take off.

The incident was finally resolved by French GIGN police commandos during a dramatic hostage rescue in Marseille. It emerged later that the terrorists had planned to crash the aircraft into the Eiffel Tower.

I find myself a kit-prep area and begin donning my equipment. On ops we wear a shed-load of protective clothing and equipment.

I walk over to the briefing area – giving a pretty reasonable impression of Peter Weller in *Robocop* – and prepare to receive our orders.

'Fuck me! How long have you been here?' says a familiar voice beside me.

It's Tam Maclaren – my legendary Sandhurst colour sergeant. We spend the next few minutes catching up on what we've both been up to over the past seven years and he tells me that after his stint at the Academy he had a crack at SAS Selection and has been here living the dream ever since.

I can't believe how different he is now that he's out of the training environment. I used to think he was a bit of a megalomaniac, but as I listen to him now I see that was all a façade. He's every inch the quietly unassuming professional soldier that epitomizes our Special Forces.

*   *   *

As the squadron commander stands up and begins our formal orders for a deliberate assault, my pager begins beeping furiously. **PHONE SSM CRW IMMEDIATELY.**

I take out my mobile and punch in the number for Matt Foster, the CRW Wing's sergeant major, but my screen just keeps coming up with *Call Failed*.

Trying not to draw attention to myself I slip outside and spend the next ten minutes pissing about trying to get a signal.

Eventually I get through.

'Chris, you need to get your arse back to camp,' he says. 'Your wife's been trying to get hold of you. She's just gone into labour.'

I can't believe it. I only spoke with her half an hour ago and she was absolutely fine. A million thoughts race through my mind. I'm panicking here. I'm at least forty-five minutes' drive away. What if I don't make it back before the baby's born? She'd never forgive me.

Matt's got it covered.

'There's an Agusta on its way to you. The pilot's going to fly you back to camp and I'll be waiting by the heli landing site to drive you home.'

I thank him profusely and run back inside to strip off my kit. The squadron commander scowls at me for disturbing his orders and carries on regardless. Sensing something's up, Tam sidles over to me and asks if I'm OK.

'No, mate. My wife's just about to give birth to our first and I've got to pack all this away and get back to Hereford.'

'Right,' he says. 'Leave all that shit to me and get yourself home. I'll drop your stuff off when we're done here.'

The man's a star.

An unmarked helicopter swoops low over the building and drops down onto a patch of wasteground about twenty metres away. The distinctive beat of its rotor blades echoes around the training area.

I drop to one knee and turn my head away to avoid the clouds of dust and grit being churned up by the downdraught. When I look back the loadmaster's giving me the thumbs-up. I run over to the heli and climb inside. Seconds later we're powering over the rolling countryside.

As we drop down into Stirling Lines, the loadmaster slides open the side door and gives me the thumbs-up again. But Matt's nowhere to be seen. There's no sign of anyone. I make the hundred-metre dash to CRW Wing. His office is empty. I race down the corridor, checking each of the normally busy offices. They're all empty too. The whole place is dead.

When I reach the crew room, I find the answer.

Every single member of the Wing is in there, rooted to the spot and shocked into silence by the scenes playing out on the TV screen in front of them. Smoke billows from the Twin Towers of the World Trade Center into a blindingly blue Manhattan sky. Desperate office workers hurtle hundreds of feet to their deaths. Live camera feeds follow the mayhem in the streets with an intimacy that borders on voyeuristic. And grainy images of first one aircraft then another striking at the heart of each iconic building punctuate the coverage of a story that we are already in no doubt will permanently fracture the landscape of our certainty.

As the inferno rages, the news teams switch from Manhattan to Washington DC, where a third plane has crashed into the Pentagon, then back again as the South Tower – inconceivably – collapses before our eyes.

It's truly apocalyptic. I never thought I'd see anything like this in my lifetime. I'm completely overwhelmed.

'Really sorry, mate, I got tied up.' The sergeant major grabs me by the arm. 'Come on, we need to get you out of here . . .'

Miraculously, Lucy and I make it to the hospital in time and later that afternoon, as the world is reeling from the devastating events of this September morning, she gives birth to the most beautiful little girl I've ever seen.

As we lie on the hospital bed, cradling the baby, Lucy

turns to me and says, 'I feel guilty for being so happy.'

I kiss her forehead and stroke our daughter's perfect, unblemished cheek. There's nothing I can say. The destruction of the World Trade Center has changed our lives for ever.

25

Take time to deliberate, but when the time for action has arrived, stop thinking and go in.

Napoleon Bonaparte

8 August 2002

I hate to admit it, but my years of service have made me a creature of habit. Lucy gets up for Sophie during the night and I do when she wakes each morning. I change her nappy, give her breakfast, throw a strong coffee down my neck, spark up Ceefax and then watch the news.

I'd never really been interested in current affairs as a young soldier but now I can't live without it. I have to be ready to deploy anywhere in the world with little or no notice, so keeping abreast of crises in the making is the only way I can keep one or two steps ahead of the curve. The breaking story right now is Colombia.

'As President Ulribe – an Oxford graduate and personal friend of Tony Blair – was being sworn in as the new President, a massive mortar offensive was launched against the presidential palace, killing twenty-one people. An estimated two to three hundred shells were fired at the complex from several points around the city. Experts say the attack was remarkably similar to the one carried out against Number 10 Downing Street in February 1991, and that this is the first time mortars of this type have been seen in Colombia. Until now such technology has been exclusive to the Provisional IRA, strongly suspected of having a role in the incident . . .'

I think for a moment about old dogs and new tricks.

Once Lucy is up I throw on my phys kit, run for an hour, then shower and go to work. I'm in a good place right now. I love being able to spend time with the family, and I love my work.

I walk the two hundred metres to my office and stroll into the crew room. I'm greeted by Phil, one of my old staff sergeants from Shorncliffe. Originally from Cheshire, he's fiercely loyal, very funny and one of the best operators I've worked with. He's just been through a messy divorce but is grinning like an idiot. Looks like he got lucky last night.

'Bit of a spring in your step this morning, then, mate?'

'I was awesome.' He kisses his biceps. 'And she was a honey. The sex was so good even the neighbours had a cigarette afterwards.'

'She was a minger, Boss,' Duffy chips in. '*Baywatch*

body, *Crimewatch* face.' Duffy is hunched over the table making some modifications to his assault kit. He's another fearsome operator. The two of them have been sharing a flat for the past six months.

'And what the fuck would you know, Forrest?' Phil jeers. 'When was the last time you had a shag?'

Duffy doesn't turn a hair. 'Put it this way, Boss, if she worked in a cake shop, it would be making the gorilla biscuits. And in answer to your question, Staff Sergeant, I'm a man of science, less easily tempted than you by the transient pleasures of the flesh . . .'

'Fucking homo, more like,' Phil says, under his breath.

The office begins to fill for the weekly briefing. In virtually every unit a drama of some sort tends to surface at this point in the proceedings; someone's always in the shit for getting pissed and gobbing off to the police or jumping the queue at the chippy. But Alpha Troop is different. Even the young bleeps – the junior NCOs from the Royal Signals who provide our electronic counter-measures capability – are utterly dependable. They're all barking mad and have a deeply twisted sense of humour, but they're highly motivated and thoroughly professional, and I'm immensely chuffed to be their troop commander.

The squadron clerk appears when I'm in mid-flow, makes a grovelling apology and asks me to go and see the OC.

David is a fiercely proud Welshman with a larger-than-life personality and the ability to drink like ten men. He's also completely devoted to the soldiers under his command. We've not seen each other for well over a month, but there's clearly no time to catch up.

'I've had a call from the ops officer. Lothian and Borders Police need you to get your arses up to Edinburgh for some Op KRATOS-related stuff. Your point of contact is Inspector Alec Rennie, the head of the L and B firearms unit. Oh, and don't blue-light up there. The CO doesn't want you drawing any attention to yourselves.'

His tone is so matter-of-fact he might be asking me to fetch him a packet of cigarettes. But Op KRATOS is about as far from normal as you can physically get. It's the Home Office response to a suicide bomber on UK turf.

'I don't suppose you have any more info than that?'

'Sorry, bud. That's all I know.'

He must think I was born yesterday.

I brief the lads and they scoop up the team kit. We keep our grab-bags in the troop garages: holdalls containing both civvies and military clothing so we're good to go, irrespective of the type of operation. I tell the boys not to bust a gut, though. This is obviously an exercise, so Andy, the troop warrant officer, and I will go ahead in the command car and get things organized while they sort their shit out.

I phone Lucy and tell her I'm going to be away for a few days. Since starting at Hereford I've tried to keep the farewells short, but this time there's a distinctly uncomfortable silence at the other end of the phone. She's still coming to terms with being a young mum, and she's definitely not impressed.

On the seven-hour drive to Edinburgh, Andy and I talk through the scenarios we could encounter when we get there. I've studied suicide terrorism obsessively since 9/11 – pretty much all my time at Hereford. In the previous twenty-five years, three hundred suicide attacks were recorded worldwide. Since the Twin Towers the level and frequency of suicide bombing has increased at an alarming rate. There have been more than fifty incidents in the last year alone – and they're spreading westwards. An Al Qaeda operative called Richard Reid boarded an American Airlines jet three months after 9/11 and attempted to detonate a shoe bomb halfway across the Atlantic. It was only by sheer luck that he failed to do so.

The UK counter-terrorist community has always believed it will never happen here, but I know it's only a matter of time. Alpha Troop and the Metropolitan Police are covertly developing the skills required to meet the challenge. We've travelled nationwide with police firearms teams, rehearsing every possible scenario and formulating new ways to defeat a terrorist intent on taking the lives of multiple innocent victims. We've studied the tactics, techniques and procedures of all the countries around the world who've suffered decades of suicide attacks and developed a series of procedures based on their hard-won lessons. It's been a massive undertaking.

Andy and I arrive at Edinburgh Police Headquarters and drive into the familiar compound off Fettes Avenue. I ring the doorbell at the back of the building and we're welcomed by a giant of a man – Alec, the firearms inspector. He offers us a coffee and takes us through to the secure briefing room.

'Time is short, gentlemen, so I'm afraid I'm going to have to crack straight on with the exercise brief. We've received high-grade int that a cell from Ansar al-Islam is going to detonate a suicide device outside the McDonald's restaurant in Princes Street at 1600 hours tomorrow. They believe that attacking Edinburgh will send a fierce message to the European countries supporting what they see as a US-led war against Islam. They believe it will offer them retribution for what they perceive to be the atrocities carried out by British troops against Afghan civilians.'

It's a chilling scenario.

'Ansar al-Islam – Supporters of Islam – is a radical group that also supports Saddam Hussein's regime. It stems from Northern Iraq and has strong ties with both the Taliban and Al Qaeda. It has about seven hundred members and its current portfolio includes numerous suicide bombings, the razing of beauty salons, burning schools for girls and murdering women in the streets for refusing to wear the *burka*. In addition, it is responsible for the kidnapping and beheading of a number of civilians working for aid agencies.

'According to some reports, the group has received six hundred thousand dollars from Al Qaeda to conduct operations in Europe, as well as a delivery of weapons and vehicles. There are also reports that Ansar al-Islam received thirty-five thousand dollars from the Mukhabarat, the Iraqi intelligence service, in addition to a considerable quantity of arms, to attack Western Coalition targets. Gentlemen, this is a seriously dangerous organization . . .'

He nods, inviting our questions.

We don't even pause for breath. What are the capabilities and *modus operandi* of the group? What devices have they used previously? How many of them are in the cell? Who, if anybody, is known to the security services and what training in IED construction has the group received? Andy and I quiz him about every single aspect of the impending attack.

He then goes over the plan in detail so that we can integrate our part of the task into the overall concept.

Once we've agreed every detail, we sack it for the night and grab a couple of well-deserved beers.

We arrive at West End Police Station bright and early the next morning and the place is already buzzing. About two hundred people are crammed into the briefing room. A mate of mine from one of our sister EOD squadrons, Staff Sergeant Gary O'Donnell, waves at me from the corner.

Gaz has been heavily involved in devising the procedures for a conventional EOD response to a suicide bomber and we've been trying to drive it forwards together for several months. The trouble is, quite a few of the old and bold remain sceptical; they think we're just wasting time and valuable resources on something that's never going to happen.

I ask him how it's going.

'Living the dream, Boss. Living the dream,' he replies. But I know he's not.

We've been attempting to transfer him to Alpha Troop but, not surprisingly, his OC has been fighting tooth and nail to keep him. Gaz spent three tours working in ammunition depots before coming to 11 EOD Regiment as a sergeant, but his technical ability was blindingly obvious and he was quickly promoted. He's now amassed stacks of operational experience in Sierra Leone and Northern Ireland.

The incident commander, a Lothian and Borders superintendent, begins his meticulous exercise brief. The intelligence services have managed to infiltrate a suicide bomber cell and an attack will take place today in Edinburgh City Centre.

'The bomber, Mustafa al-Khazraji, is going to be driven from Leith docks along the A900 and into the north-east of the city. As he enters the city centre, the driver will turn west into York Place and take a left turn into North St Andrew Street after about four hundred metres. He'll continue along that road until he reaches St Andrew Square. Once he's made a complete 360 of the square and is satisfied that no security forces are present, he'll stop the vehicle outside Harvey Nichols. The bomber will dismount and continue on foot into South St Andrew Street, heading towards the Scott Monument until he reaches the corner of Monsoon and the Old Waverley Hotel. There he'll turn right, cross over the road to Jenners and continue west along Princes Street. He'll walk through the crowds for a mile or so until he reaches his target.

'Once the bomber arrives at McDonald's, he'll turn to face the plate-glass window and detonate his device, shredding everybody inside with shards of glass and thousands of ball-bearings projected at supersonic speeds by the high-explosive blast wave.'

The atmosphere in the room is electric.

'From the moment he leaves the vehicle until the moment he detonates the device he'll be watched by other members of his cell, dickers armed with remote firing switches and tasked to look for the unusual presence of security forces. If any of them think that the bomber has been compromised at any stage of the operation, they're under strict orders to detonate the device remotely – killing as many civilians as possible.'

The superintendent outlines the police interdiction plan.

The operation itself goes like clockwork – barring a couple of hiccups – right up until the moment the 'suicide bomber' turns to face the firearms cops and says 'Fucking hell, fellas, I'm impressed. I didn't see a fucking thing.'

Then the police commander's voice crackles over the net. 'ENDEX, ENDEX. All personnel return to West End Police Station for a debrief.'

We complete the exercise in one of the busiest city centres in the world. And none of its inhabitants have had a clue what we were up to.

I only hope we never have to do it for real.

26

Being on the tightrope is living; everything else is waiting.

Karl Wallenda

17 December 2002
Jobs like this have become a regular occurrence since 9/11. We get the call, speed to some inner-city police HQ for the briefing, work out our part in the plan and then wait – sometimes for days on end. It could be anywhere in the world. Two months ago, fifty heavily armed Chechen terrorists took eight hundred hostages in a Moscow theatre and I was on stand-by to deploy there.

Today we're in the tourist-packed streets of Blackpool, waiting for a bomber to emerge from the pub. McCallion is getting pissed in there with his cronies, bragging about how he's going to blow his target into a million pieces.

We've been told he's going to collect a device from

the outskirts of town. He's going to place it under a car belonging to Johnny 'Mad Dog' Adair's cousin and watch his victim get blown to bits the moment he turns the ignition.

But that's not going to happen. We aren't going to let it. Not on British soil. And definitely not today.

The security forces had a bit of luck last time: the bomb was discovered before it detonated. They're not taking any chances now. McCallion is a very nasty piece of work and we're here to make sure he's enjoying his last glass or two of freedom.

Months of painstaking surveillance are coming to an end; in a matter of hours this operation is going to be over. We've booked into a local hotel, been given the ops brief and we're waiting for the nod. We know the terrorist is being watched by the surveillance teams. We'd normally stay out of the way until needed, but this time it's different. The police want us close to the target area, just in case. So we've changed into our shopping rig, split up and begun 'blending in', wandering around the shops while we wait for the call.

It's been thirteen years since I was in Blackpool and not much seems to have changed. I still think the place is a dump. There are different shops here now, but they're full of the same crap. No wonder the people in them look so miserable. It's bitterly cold and grey and depressing.

Andy gives me a bell on my mobile. I can see him at the opposite end of the pedestrian walkway.

'Any news?'

'Nope, nothing.'

It's starting to get dark and I can see my breath billowing in front of me. I've walked every possible combination of routes through and around the town centre. My gut instinct is telling me it's time for us to get off the ground. We've already been here too long; unless we can get our skates on we're going to be compromised big-time. As far as I'm concerned, the sooner we lift this scrote the better. It's edge-of-the-seat stuff when these guys are under surveillance in the movies; in truth, it's painfully boring and frustrating.

Most modern terrorists are well trained and highly motivated. Like organized-crime cartels, they're acutely aware of police procedures and often trained in counter-surveillance techniques. They often deploy dickers to forewarn them of the presence of security forces. We don't know whether McCallion has or not; another reason Andy and I are keen to get off the ground. The last thing we want to do is compromise the op. Far better to move to a stand-off position. We have a van full of specialized EOD equipment and a turbo-charged estate car, both unmarked civilianized vehicles fitted with blue lights and sirens so that we can crack on when we get the go-ahead. It just doesn't make tactical sense to be here.

I call the super who's running the operation – an SO13 officer called Jim Stanton – and explain my concerns. He totally agrees. Within minutes the boys and I rendezvous in a car park and head back to the hotel.

McCallion may be some big-time terrorist but he has no real interest in politics and he certainly isn't fighting for a cause. Not any more. Money is his sole motivation. He's using his position within the Loyalist movement to trouser as much as he can on the drug-smuggling circuit. And that's why he's here: to remove the competition and to do a bit of business.

He's been drinking for ten hours. He's pissed out of his head. All of a sudden, and without saying a word, he staggers out of the bar. We get the call seconds later. We're in business. McCallion is going to be followed to the exchange point; we'll split ourselves up among the firearms teams, move to a pre-arranged RV two streets away and then stand by for the 'Go, go, go'. The police 'shooters' will give McCallion and his accomplice the shock of their lives and whichever one of us is closest when the firearms teams are ordered to move in will neutralize the device.

The bombmaker is still unknown to the security forces at this point, so nicking him as well is going to be a real bonus – but if our guys find the bomb first, and the bomber is not in the immediate vicinity, I'll move in and neutralize it covertly.

Until about ten years ago, covert neutralization was a closely guarded capability. Then the press published a story about the attempted assassination of the leader of Sinn Fein in Northern Ireland. In March 1984, specially trained soldiers were involved in an operation to thwart a Loyalist attempt to murder Gerry Adams, the newly elected MP for West Belfast. Military Intelligence officers had received information from an informer in the UDA that an Ulster Freedom Fighters hit-team would gun him down as he left the magistrates court in Belfast, where he was due to appear on a charge of obstruction.

The information was passed to the Royal Ulster Constabulary's Tasking and Coordination Group by one of the intelligence units in theatre. An informer had given his handlers details of the weapons to be used in the attack and the location of the cache in which they were concealed. Operators from the intelligence services found pistols and ammunition in an outhouse at Ballysillan, a Loyalist area on the outskirts of Belfast. On 15 March Adams left the court as it adjourned for lunch and drove down Howard Street accompanied by three companions, Sean Keenan, Kevin Rooney and Joe Keenan. A brown Rover overtook Adams's car and two gunmen opened fire at close range. Some rounds struck the passenger door and Adams was hit in the neck, shoulder and arm. Sean Keenan, in the rear seat, was also wounded. But the driver kept control of the vehicle and drove immediately to the Royal Victoria Hospital, where Adams and Keenan were treated for their wounds. Several Military Intelligence operatives kept tabs on the shooting and shortly afterwards the two UFF gunmen were arrested with their driver.

Covert neutralization remains a potent weapon in the fight against the bombmakers. I've recently completed my training. We were taught the basics of tradecraft – the art of being a spook – how to deceive, role-play and exploit. More importantly, we learnt how to survey and covertly gain entry into a target, then clandestinely neutralize the devices inside it without leaving any trace of our presence.

My phone buzzes. It's Andy.

'We're on.'

Good. Time to focus.

I've cleared my mind of all the trivia that swirls around in it when we sit around waiting for something to happen – what household bills have to be paid, where I'm going to take my family on holiday this year, what we're going to be doing at the weekend . . .

In a matter of minutes I could be face to face with a bomb. But I've come to realize that euphoria now lies at the heart of my intense cocktail of emotions, not fear.

We board the vehicles and put on our covert radios. We're completely silent, each of us in his own world. We're a surprisingly diverse bunch, but our feelings at moments like this are identical. When he knows he's about to be confronted by a device, every bomb tech in the world experiences a kind of calm before the storm. But every one of our senses is working overtime as we pull away.

We're silent, watching, listening, taking in every detail. You can hear a pin drop in the vehicle. Without thinking, any one of us could tell you the number of people in the street, what clothes they're wearing, how old they are. All the things one would normally miss while driving along an inner-city road suddenly become blindingly apparent. We're taking in every detail, computing every item of incoming information. The only thing we're not thinking about is what might happen if we get it wrong.

There's no margin for error in our profession. We can all handle the prospect of a sudden, violent death; somehow it seems easier to accept than the prospect of a life sentence in a wheelchair. That's still my greatest fear. But it's one I can never dwell on. Most of us keep it hidden away. We certainly never speak about it openly to one another. It's a kind of unwritten rule.

We're racing along the main road into Blackpool. Seventies-style concrete blocks and rows of council houses crowd in on us from all sides. Dogs roam wild. Kids holler at each other from their pushbikes and kick balls against the walls. Mothers scream blue murder at them. The place is a shit hole. I phone Phil, the firearms inspector, and let him know we'll be with him and his team in two minutes.

'Haven't you heard?' he says. 'McCallion's fucked off – he's driven out of town and is heading for the M6 as we speak.'

What the fuck's going on? Is he employing some sort of counter-surveillance manoeuvre?

Instinct tells me otherwise. He's gone for good. Maybe something's spooked him. Or maybe somebody has tipped him off.

And why didn't anybody tell us? We were dragged off Christmas leave for this op at a moment's notice. One minute we were relaxing at home with our families, the next our pagers were going mental and we were out of the camp gates. To say my wife is unimpressed is an understatement. *EOD* . . . I think. *Everyone's divorced* . . .

We slip back to the local Special Branch offices for a debrief. McCallion's decision to get up and fuck off threw the SB into a flat spin. There was no point in arresting him because they had nothing evidential that would secure a conviction. The police couldn't even arrest him for drink-driving – though they certainly wanted to. Surprisingly few people actually get stopped on the motorway for drink-driving, so if they had done, he'd have probably guessed they were on to him for something else. The operation would have been instantly compromised.

So for now McCallion is on his way back to his house in Birmingham – still under surveillance – and none of us has any idea if or when he's going to strike again.

27

Although prepared for martyrdom, I preferred that it be postponed.

Sir Winston Churchill

16 January 2003

The lads are calling it Operation Certain Death. We're going to parachute under enemy fire into Iraq's heavily fortified Ramallah oilfields to find and neutralize hundreds of demolition charges wired into the pumps by Saddam's M18 bombmakers. During the last Gulf War, the retreating Iraqi army set dozens of wells on fire in an attempt to disguise their troop movements and slow up Coalition forces.

It worked so well for them that this time they've decided to up the ante. If the intelligence reports are correct, Saddam's boys have rigged up more than four hundred devices.

We've only had a parachute EOD capability since 1972. In the spring of that year an American phoned

Cunard Headquarters and informed them that six bombs had been placed aboard the QE2. They would detonate while the ship was at sea unless a $350,000 ransom was paid by the following day.

At the time, the liner was mid-Atlantic, on its way from New York to Southampton with 1438 passengers and 850 crew. In a blatant abuse of the Special Relationship, the FBI persuaded the British government that they would run with the criminal investigation while we should send in a team to deal with the explosives.

According to legend, the ATO didn't have any military parachuting experience, so had to be taught the basics during the 1400-mile flight across the ocean. Worse still, he was only told the nature of the task when they were airborne. Having already evacuated the entire contents of his stomach, he refused to jump and had to be forcibly thrust out of the plane. Amazingly, the mission ended successfully, but it had highlighted a glaring capability gap in our armoury, and the concept of airborne EOD was born. For the past ten years, that role has fallen to the men of Alpha Troop.

After weeks of training we've honed every drill we're going to be carrying out on the day, from boarding the aircraft and exiting under fire to landing and carrying out our actions on target. Our final rehearsal is a night parachute drop. I can't think of anything I'd rather be doing on my twenty-fourth birthday.

We wait nervously in the hangar, strapped into our state-of-the-art low-level chutes. One of the corporals in the stick next to me tries to lighten the mood. 'I think I'd rather leave this world as I entered it,' he says to his mates. 'Bald, fat, and with a mild boob fixation.'

I want to laugh, but my stomach's doing cartwheels at the thought of a 500-foot drop out of a C130 Hercules. From the looks on their faces, I know the lads are feeling pretty much the same.

We hear the drone of the Hercules taxiing across the runway. Our parachute-jump instructor orders us to stand up and follow him. He leads us in a straight line towards the C130. Its engines are turning and the stench of aviation fuel catches in my nose and throat.

Two of the bleeps behind me begin to grapple with the mysteries of the universe as we head towards the aircraft. 'Why are piles called haemorrhoids?' one asks the other. 'Shouldn't they be called asteroids?'

The rear ramp opens and we're guided inside in two rows. As we approach the front of the aircraft we're told to sit in our stick order and put our seatbelts on.

There's a huge amount of concurrent activity. The RAF loadmaster and his crew are busy with their pre-flight checks and the PJIs are scrutinizing the parachute cables. The engine noise drills into my frontal lobes. As the tail ramp whines shut, I think about the invasion. I'm in no doubt whatsoever that Saddam and his Ba'ath

Party cohorts are evil bastards who need to be ousted, but I can't help thinking that things have been rushed at the strategic level. The duty rumour is that Tony Blair and his three-ring circus have known about it for months, but refused to allow the generals to begin their preparations for fear of compromise.

Churchill said: 'Let us learn our lessons. Never, never, never believe any war will be smooth and easy, or that anyone who embarks on that strange voyage can measure the tides and hurricanes he will encounter. The statesman who yields to war fever must realize that once the signal is given, he is no longer the master of policy but the slave of unforeseeable and un-controllable events. Antiquated War Offices, weak, incompetent or arrogant commanders, untrustworthy allies, hostile neutrals, malignant fortune, ugly surprise, awful miscalculations – all take their seat at the Council Board on the morrow of a declaration of war.'

I can't help feeling the politicians have failed to heed the lessons of history once again.

The engine gradually changes pitch and the Hercules rolls onto the runway. The drone becomes a roar and we're forced sideways in our seats as the bird gathers momentum. Moments later I feel the nose starting to rise and within seconds we're airborne. There's a sound somewhere between a whine and a hiss on both sides of the fuselage, followed by a menacing thud. It's the Herc's wheels folding in. The first time I heard it I almost shat myself.

My stomach feels like it's doing the best of three falls with my kidney as the aircraft gains speed and climbs steeply into the sky. Soon afterwards the pilot levels off and the Hercules is heading towards the drop zone. The PJIs are working frantically at the back of the ramp to prepare for our first exit.

For a moment I think of Lucy. I'm desperate to get into Iraq and experience real combat for the first time, but I know she's going to go crazy when she finds out I've been spammed for this imminent suicide mission. How on earth am I going to tell her?

I try to concentrate on the here and now. My senses sharpen: I can hear every creak of the airframe and smell the tension. I focus on what's happening at the back of the Herc. The PJI gathers a couple of armfuls of strops – short pieces of rigging line with a small metal ring at each end, one of which is attached to a long metal cable that runs the length of the aircraft. The other is what we'll clamp to the static line on the back of our parachutes, triggering our canopies to open automatically when we jump. The PJI looks each of us in the eye, shouts a strop number and moves on. We give him the thumbs-up to acknowledge that we know it's ours.

Once everyone's accounted for, he gestures upwards

with his hands. I can just make out the words, 'Port stick, stand up, prepare for action.' We can't hear him too well above the noise of the engines, but this is where the drills that we have been taught over previous weeks start to kick in.

We unfasten our seatbelts and the PJI works his way through the aircraft again, releasing our static lines from the back of our parachutes and placing them firmly in our hands.

I'm standing now, trying to maintain my balance as the Hercules rocks in the turbulence.

I imagine being peppered with high-velocity fragments from the Iraqi anti-aircraft guns. I hope to God the fast jets and attack helicopters can neutralize them all before we get stuck into the mission proper.

The PJI tells us to hook up and check equipment.

I attach my static line to the cable above our heads. We make sure that our parachutes are OK, that our lines are clipped correctly to the strops and that our helmets fit snugly. We then check the chute of the man in front.

The PJI goes through his final safety routines. 'Port stick, tell off for equipment check.' The countdown gets louder as it passes down the cabin, until the man standing behind me gives me a hard tap on the shoulder and shouts his number, then 'OK.'

As the officer, I'm going to be the first man out of the door. 'One OK,' I yell. 'Port stick OK.'

The weight of the main and reserve parachutes combined with my sixty-pound Bergen, not to mention the heat, smell and cramped conditions, are making me piss sweat.

But it doesn't last long.

There's a blast of cold air as the doors at the rear of each side of the Hercules are opened. The PJI sticks his head out and scans the drop zone while his colleague listens to the pilot and waits for confirmation of the drop zone (DZ) approach and wind speeds. The PJI blows heavily on his hand and holds up four fingers: wind speed four knots.

I can't wait to get out. I'm increasingly desperate to escape the confines of the aircraft and get some fresh air in my lungs.

There's another muffled shout – 'Port stick, action stations' – and everyone starts to push towards the door. The PJI holds me in position, as we speed over rural Oxfordshire. My heart starts to pound as I watch both the PJI and the red and green lights positioned by the door. His sidekick in the middle of the aircraft holds up one finger and mouths, 'One minute, one minute.'

The red light glows, then the green.

This is it.

My aim is to jump as far out of the door as I possibly

can, but I've got a sixty-pound pack strapped to my legs and only make it a few feet before the slipstream cannons me sideways.

I try to keep my eyes open during those first seconds but I'm totally disoriented. Initially I can see only sky, then ground, then I get a quick glimpse of the Hercules and can just about make out another para hurling himself out from where I'd been standing only seconds ago.

I'm yelling, 'ONE THOUSAND, TWO THOU-SAND, THREE THOUSAND . . .' at the top of my voice. Then I feel a slight tug and the world begins to slow as my parachute opens. I look up, shout, 'CHECK CANOPY,' and sweep my eyes across the business end of my parachute.

No problems there.

We've been taught how to avoid other parachutists by manipulating our harness lift webs to manoeuvre into our own air space. Once there we can assess our drift. But it's easier said than done when every inch of dark-ness seems to be occupied already.

I lower my Bergen and try to work out which direction the wind is carrying me.

I position my feet and knees for a 'rear right landing'. I've always been crap at judging how far away the ground is and at night I'm worse than ever.

Suddenly the ground comes rushing up to meet me,

and not in a good way. Every ounce of air is driven out of my lungs. As I pick myself up, fighting for breath, I can't say I'm looking forward to doing this for real, under fire, facing a highly trained, well-equipped enemy.

28

Life is a flame that is always burning itself out, but it catches fire again every time a baby is born.

George Bernard Shaw

26 November 2003

'Chris . . . we need to go . . . we need to go *now* . . .'

'Right . . .' I'm trying to sound calm. 'I'll get your things.' I wish I was as together as she is, but I feel like a gibbering wreck.

As we pull out of the gates of our house in Vauxhall Barracks, Lucy's mood suddenly lifts. She's had an awful pregnancy and looks relieved to be in labour.

We've lived in this camp opposite Didcot power station for just over a year, and although she puts on a brave face I know she hates it. I can't blame her. Living behind the wire and having to wake up to a view of drab cooling towers every morning, a million miles away from the dramatic beauty and freedom of

Herefordshire, is eating away at her. And there's absolutely nothing I can do to change it.

We were all gutted that the Iraq deployment didn't go ahead, but now I'm grateful. The powers that be decided to bin the mass airborne assault in favour of a ground offensive. Saddam's forces were defeated in three weeks and the oil infrastructure was seized largely intact, with only forty-four of the four hundred oil wells destroyed or set ablaze by Iraqi explosives.

We pull onto the A34 and head north along the dual carriageway towards Oxford. Lucy's looking decidedly uncomfortable now and I'm conscious that anything I say is likely to backfire, so I take the cowardly option and switch on Radio 4.

'Last week while President Bush was in London meeting Tony Blair, suicide bombers detonated two truck bombs at the HSBC bank and the British Consulate in Istanbul, killing thirty people and wounding four hundred others. The bombers deliberately attempted to inflict the maximum number of casualties by waiting for the traffic lights in front of the HSBC headquarters to turn red before striking. While most of the victims were Turkish Muslims, several Britons were killed, including the senior British official, Consul General Roger Short . . .'

Without saying a word, Lucy leans forward and retunes to Radio 1. I'm not surprised: she gave birth to

Sophie on the day of the World Trade Center attacks. The war on terror seems to be providing the soundtrack for what should be the happiest moments of our lives. I much prefer Black Eyed Peas.

We pull into the car park of the John Radcliffe Hospital and weave our way through the busy reception area to the maternity ward. We're greeted by a friendly nurse who ushers us through to the delivery room. An hour or so into her labour, Lucy is squeezing my hand and screaming in agony as the nurse and I try to offer her the usual futile words of encouragement.

'Well done, honey . . . you're almost there . . . one more push . . .'

But no sooner have the contractions started than the moment passes and they tail off again.

I nip into the corridor to get her a bottle of water from the vending machine, and use the opportunity to check my mobile for any missed messages. The moment the phone powers up, it starts ringing.

'Chris, it's Phil. I'm just calling to let you know I'm back from the McCallion job.'

A few days after we'd got back from the Blackpool task, the police intercepted McCallion's mobile phone and discovered he'd called off the bombing because the target was out of town. They kept him under surveillance by a skeleton crew. Two weeks ago it became obvious that the whole thing was sparking up again, so the police asked us to send up an Alpha Troop operator to assist them. Phil was the natural choice.

'Mate, I'm sorry to have to cut you short—' Before I get the chance to tell him Lucy's in labour, he's on permanent-send. He goes into painstaking detail about every aspect of the task, until eventually he cuts to the chase: 'We got the fucker! We put in an assault on his house last night. He was so frightened he physically shat himself.'

McCallion was arrested for the illegal possession of a firearm in the end. The bomb was never found, but he's behind bars – at least for now.

'Nice work, Phil. Listen, I've got to go, I'm at the John Radcliffe. Lucy's in labour.'

'Fucking hell! Why didn't you say so?'

By the time I walk back into the delivery suite, Lucy is in the final stages of labour. 'Where the fuck have you been?' she says.

Before I've finished getting the words out, she's given birth to our second beautiful daughter.

As I pull into the driveway, I'm greeted by my mother and a very excited Sophie, who's desperate to see the photos of her new baby sister. We're joined by Sophie's godfather Chris and his wife Catherine. He's an army chef and we've been best mates since we were young NCOs. He rustles up an amazing celebratory dinner, but just as I'm pouring the first glass of champagne, my ops phone rings.

It's David, my OC.

'Chris . . . I need you and your boys to get over to Gloucester ASAP. An op's going in to take down a suicide bomber cell.'

Yeah, right . . . 'David, I'm not being funny, but Lucy's only just out of labour and I've got a houseful of friends and family here celebrating. Is it absolutely necessary for us to do another no-notice exercise tonight?'

There's a momentary silence at the other end of the line.

'This isn't an exercise.'

I race over to the troop garages where the boys are hurriedly loading our kit onto the wagons. We've spent months training for a task like this, hoping that we'd get a chance to put our well-honed skills to the test, but now that the time has come, we don't know whether to be nervous, excited or scared.

'Have you told your missus?' Andy asks one of the bleeps.

'You're joking. She'd be terrified if she knew!'

We discover that none of us have told our wives. Not that any of us would be foolish enough to do so. Lucy's going to go nuclear when she finds out.

The boys are busy carrying out the last-minute modifications to their equipment and the Det is crackling with tension. Phil walks in with a mug of hot coffee.

'Is that a Jack brew I see before me?' Duffy says, never missing an opportunity to have a dig at his best mate. 'If you were any kind of good bloke you'd have made a brew for all of us. Or didn't you realize there's no "I" in "team"?'

'I know, Duffy, you're quite right.' Phil is immediately apologetic. 'But there are two in "sanctimonious cunt"!'

The mood lightens.

'You know what?' Duffy retorts. 'You remind me of a dyslexic dwarf: you're not big and you're not clever.'

I love listening to these two. If ever we need an injection of morale, Phil and Duffy can always be relied on to come up with the goods.

By the time we reach the police mounting base, the mood is very different. Dozens of firearms cops and hundreds of uniformed police are sitting quietly in the briefing room, waiting for their inspector to deliver his set of orders. It's a long way from the indifference we've experienced on some exercise briefings. You could cut through the atmosphere here with a knife.

'Ladies and gentlemen,' the inspector begins, 'at exactly 0300 hours we're going to be carrying out simultaneous raids on two properties in St James Street and Barton Street.

'You'll all be familiar with Richard Reid, the Al Qaeda operative who attempted to blow up an American Airlines flight in December 2001 with explosives hidden in his shoe. Well, our primary suspect is twenty-four-year-old Sajid Badat, a co-conspirator of Reid's who prayed with him at the Finsbury Park mosque and who we believe intends to attack a football ground, aircraft or tube train.'

He gives us a detailed description of Badat, who lives with his parents in St James Street.

'Our intelligence suggests Badat is supported by a team of *jihad*ists resident in a flat above an electronics shop in Barton Street.'

He gives us chapter and verse on these suspects and shows us imagery of them and the target buildings.

'The threat from Badat is assessed as low,' he continues. 'He'll be arrested by detectives from SO15, supported by our own uniformed officers.

'The second target, however, is thought to contain the explosive device or devices, and for that reason the initial entry will be made by our firearms team, supported by EOD specialists from Alpha Troop.'

He goes through the orders in detail. I'm relieved to hear that the raids are being conducted simultaneously and, more importantly, using speed, aggression and surprise. History has shown that if jihadists have time to prepare IEDs, they'll almost always use them against security forces.

Before he wraps us the orders, the inspector asks me to brief everybody on what behavioural indicators to consider when trying to identify a suicide bomber.

I explain that nervous glances or other common signs of being ill at ease are among the most recognizable features. 'This may include sweating, tunnel vision and repeated praying or muttering.' I tell them to pay particular attention to suspects who have their hands in their pockets or who are cupping them. They may be holding a triggering device. 'Suicide bombers also tend to pat themselves repeatedly, to keep verifying that the bomb vest or belt is still in place.'

After a brief introduction to our respective firearms teams and a quick set of rehearsals of our actions on target, we grab the rest of our kit and hurry outside to the waiting vans. The boys are shrugging on their body armour and Kevlar helmets in the glare of the head-lights. The firearms cops are fitting magazines to their weapons while the bleeps are checking our radios and testing the ECM. We pack ourselves and our kit into the wagons, adrenalin pumping, bombed up and ready to go.

As we scream through the lamp-lit streets of Gloucester, thundering past shops and houses, people rush to their windows in disbelief. I can feel my stomach performing somersaults. I think about Lucy, lying asleep with our newborn baby in her hospital bed, and Sophie at home with my friends and family. Her little face crumpled when I told her I had to go. It's the first night she's ever spent without one of us putting her to bed.

The radio crackles into life. 'Hello, all stations, this is Control, stand by, stand by . . .' Then: 'Five, four, three, two, one – go, go, go!'

We screech to a halt and debus from the unmarked vans before stacking up on the edge of the street. I'm going to be the first man through the front door. Phil will lead the assault through the rear. Andy, Duffy and the bleeps will remain in the vans as a reserve in case Phil and I are taken down in the first wave.

'Prepare to move,' the team leader says. Fingers on triggers, his guys are covering every arc.

'Move.'

My heart is pounding against the inside of my ribcage as we lurch forwards at breakneck speed. My breathing is rapid and shallow. Speed, aggression and surprise are crucial now.

We move low and fast, hugging the walls as we run towards the front of the target building. The TL reaches the door first and the assault team form up on either side. I shine my torch systematically along all four sides of the door, looking for evidence of booby-traps – *absence of the normal, presence of the abnormal.*

It's clear.

The entry man checks it isn't unlocked, then swings the battering ram into action. The clash of steel on steel reverberates into the cold, dark night. Two stun-grenades are tossed into the front of the electronics shop. There are two ear-splitting explosions and bright flashes of light. We burst in, each man covering a different firing lane. We make our way through the smoke and into the living area behind the shop.

A man in a *dish-dasha* lies quivering on the floor. He's surrounded by a widening puddle of his own piss.

The rear door collapses and Phil and his assault team come surging through. Their shouts are mixed with the screams of the terrified men in the flat above.

Outside, scores of uniformed police officers have begun evacuating families from their homes as others seal off the surrounding streets.

So far so good.

As Phil and his team hurtle up the stairs to the second floor, they toss another two grenades onto the landing. The hallway fills with smoke as the suspects are momentarily disoriented by the intense noise and light.

There are more shouts and screams as the firearms officers bark commands at the suspects. Moments later, each of them has his hands plasti-cuffed in front of him.

The guy in the pool of piss is on his knees now. His hands are sealed into a clear plastic bag to preserve any explosive or weapon residue on his skin.

'How many of you are there?' one of the cops asks.

The man just flashes them an uneasy smile. His teeth are like a row of condemned houses.

'How many?'

He's either deaf from the flashbangs or, more likely, doesn't speak a word of English.

I check the suspect for IEDs and carry out a cursory search of the ground floor. Then I go upstairs to RV with Phil. There are about a dozen cops going through drawers, cupboards, shelves and cabinets, emptying out the contents of each onto the floor. They've already unearthed a mountain of *jihad*ist literature along with a shed-load of DVDs, which, judging by their covers, appear to be of Coalition forces being attacked in Iraq and Afghanistan. But so far there's still no device.

I call in Andy and the rest of the team to assist us with the search. Phil and Duffy focus on everything upstairs while Andy and I crack on with the shop and the kitchen.

Now that the suspects no longer present a threat, the detectives from SO15 have begun filtering into the building. Some are questioning the suspects while others are photographing and bagging up the evidence. The senior investigating officer is on the phone. When he ends the call he lets out a jubilant cheer. They've struck gold at Sajid Badat's house. The heels of his trainers have been hollowed out and they've found enough explosives to blow off a lot more than his foot. It sounds like an action replay of Richard Reid.

As I continue searching through myriad drawers, cabinets and shelves containing every type of electronic component imaginable, the senior investigating officer reappears. 'Is there anything in here that could be made into a bomb?'

I turn and face him, and try my best not to sound terminally sarcastic. 'Erm . . . we're in an electronics shop.'

We drive back to Didcot, the adrenalin still surging. We're all feeling pretty chuffed to have been part of one of the most significant counter-terrorism operations ever undertaken by members of the Regiment. A newsreader begins reporting the incident over the radio.

'The continuing threat to Britain from Al Qaeda terrorists was once again underlined after police made a series of raids in Gloucester last night. One of those arrested was twenty-four-year-old Sajid Badat, who is charged with handling explosives. He is accused of conspiring with the Al Qaeda shoe-bomber, Richard Reid. Reid, twenty-eight, was the Al Qaeda agent who attempted to blow up an American Airlines flight from Paris to Miami in December 2001.'

The lads are beginning to drift off in the cab. I sit quietly and reflect on the day. I think of Badat and his shoe bomb and I think of my family and wonder how many similar families would have perished if he'd succeeded in his quest for immortality.

Luck was on our side this time, but we're not going to be lucky every time. The only way to ensure our loved ones' safety is to completely defeat these guys. But in order to defeat your enemy you need to understand him, and right now I'm afraid we never really will.

29

Some of us think holding on makes us strong; but sometimes it is letting go.

Hermann Hesse

11 March 2004

The CCTV camera whirrs as it tracks my progress to the front entrance of Headquarters Building. I swipe my card and punch in my PIN and the doors buzz open. Decades of anti-terrorist operations – including the provision of vital evidence in court to secure convictions – have made the members of 11 EOD Regiment RLC a very attractive target. A successful hit against this place would be like winning the Al Qaeda lottery, so it's better protected than Fort Knox.

I walk into the CO's office, wish him good morning and snap him a salute.

There's an ominous expression on his face. I rack my brains as to why.

'I've had a letter from the Chief Constable of Gloucestershire Police thanking you and your troop for your work on the shoe-bomber operations. He followed his letter with a phone call this morning. So well done – and please pass on my thanks to the boys.'

I'm a bit puzzled. A bollocking pretty much always follows a set format. First the recipient is ripped apart, then he has his sterling qualities reinforced ('This is obviously out of character . . . I know this was a one-off . . . We both know you're capable of better . . .'). So maybe he's just softening me up for some bad news. There's a six-month tour in the Falklands coming up, and predictably enough nobody wants it.

'I know you've been extremely busy during your time with Alpha Troop – it's the nature of the beast since 9/11 – and I know you're coming up to the end of your time with us . . .'

Where is he going with this?

'You're probably aware of the Falklands posting . . .'

Here we go. I fucking knew it . . .

' . . . but I've put a stop to that. I've arranged for you to hand over command of your troop in April, as planned, and then you'll be posted into Regimental Head-quarters as the training officer until you start at Staff College in September. It'll give you plenty of opportunity to prepare yourself for the course and you'll also be able to spend some time with your family.'

This is fantastic news, but where is the catch? There has to be a catch . . .

'There is one thing I need you to do for me, though . . .'

Here it comes. I knew this was too good to be true.

'I've been reading through your file and understand that you considered a career in counter-narcotics at one time.'

Wow, the CO's really done his homework. I didn't even know this stuff was on my file. 'That's right, Colonel.' I take a deep breath. 'My brother killed himself while I was at Sandhurst . . .'

He sits there silently, taking in every word.

'I'm really sorry to hear that,' he says. 'But having done so, I suspect this task will be even more up your street.' He tells me he wants me to go to Colombia. 'It won't be for long – a month or so. Essentially, you'll be training Colombian security forces in the methodology required to defeat IRA IED techniques. The IRA have been selling their bomb-making skills to FARC in exchange for weapons and narcotics.'

This sounds fascinating. I can't believe my luck. FARC, one of the most capable terrorist groups in the world, are largely funded by drug-trafficking, and Colombia is somewhere I've always wanted to go; I've heard from friends that it's one of the most breath-takingly beautiful places on earth.

To do battle with terrorism and the narcotics industry simultaneously is something I never thought I'd be able to achieve in the Army. I feel like all my Christmases have come at once. I just wish I could convince myself that Lucy will feel the same way . . .

'I'd really love to, Colonel. But my wife has recently given birth to our second child, and . . .'

His face remains completely expressionless. 'Go on . . .'

'Are you saying it's this or the Falklands?'

'I'm afraid that's exactly what I'm saying.'

I don't normally care where I go or for how long – as long as it's for a good reason; as long as I feel I'm making a difference. But I absolutely hate the thought of being needlessly away from my family. If I go to the Falklands I'll be sitting on my arse doing nothing.

I head back home and prepare to break the news to Lucy. This isn't going to be an easy conversation.

She's sitting in front of the television news with Ella asleep on her lap.

'Lucy, there's something—'

'Sssh . . . You'll wake the baby . . . Come and sit with me . . .'

'At just after six thirty a.m., four bombs exploded on a train entering Madrid's Atocha station, killing and injuring dozens of people. Three more destroyed a second train alongside a platform inside the station. There have also been two explosions at El Pozo and another at Santa Eugenia station. Eyewitnesses have described pieces of train flying into the air and bodies trapped in the wreckage. Over a hundred people have been killed and at least a thousand injured in the blasts . . .'

The camera pans across a series of gaping holes torn through the carriages by the blasts. Dead bodies are scattered over the railway tracks. The walking wounded, covered with blood, step over them as they attempt to flee to safety. Smoke billows into the sky.

I switch off the set and turn to her. 'Lucy . . . I've got to go away for a few weeks . . .'

She looks angry, sad and vulnerable all at once.

'Oh, God, no . . . not to Madrid!' She bursts into tears.

'No, darling . . .' I know what I'm about to say won't comfort her. 'I'm going to Colombia.'

'Colombia?' For a moment, her face appears to soften. But it's with mystification, not relief. 'Tell me you're joking, Chris . . . You've been away for so much of our relationship already – and now you're telling me you're heading off to one of the most dangerous countries in the world . . . How am I supposed to cope with two young children on my own?'

It's a fair one. I wish I had an answer.

'Anyway,' she says, wiping away her tears, 'when are you going?'

I gnaw on my lower lip. 'Today.'

'Today? Jesus, Chris, why today? And why you? It's always you, isn't it? Can't you just say no?' She stares at me, her eyes red, her expression raw. 'I really can't take much more of this . . .'

I try to reassure her that everything will be OK, that we're finally going to have a normal life. I explain how I had to accept the Colombia job – otherwise I'd have been sent to the Falklands for six months – and I tell her I've been promised a staff officer's posting as soon as I get back. I don't know what else I can do.

'We'll be able to enjoy some real quality time together . . . like a normal family . . . Please, darling . . . just hang in there a bit longer . . .'

Later that afternoon, I throw my bags into the Golf and head up to the school in Warwickshire where I'm meeting the other instructors. There are five of us and we've all served as operators on high-threat EOD tours in Northern Ireland.

Keith, the officer in charge of the Short Term Training Team, has just returned from his recce to Colombia. He does the introductions and then goes straight into it. 'Gentlemen, many of you will be familiar with media reports about the Colombia Three.

James Monaghan, Martin McCauley and Niall Connolly – a.k.a. David Bracken – are currently awaiting trial in the El Modelo prison in Bogotá. They're alleged to have trained FARC guerrillas in the use of explosives, the manufacture of car bombs and the construction of other devices including improvised mortars. Tests conducted on their clothing apparently turned up traces of four different kinds of explosives as well as cocaine and amphetamines. If convicted they'll get fifteen to twenty years.'

On 11 August 2001 the Colombia Three were asked a few routine questions at the Air France check-in desk at Bogotá airport. 'The Customs guys realized they were travelling on false passports. Despite claiming to be innocent eco-tourists, they were arrested and given the full treatment.

'According to Sinn Fein, Monaghan is a wise old Republican, McCauley his trusted aide and Connolly their guide, fluent in the language and culture. They claim the boyos were on a mission to preach conflict resolution among their Marxist comrades in Colombia – oh, and a spot of nature watching.'

But that isn't how their prosecutors see it. The Colombians believe Monaghan is an expert bomb-maker, McCauley is his second-in-command, and Connolly is allegedly head of training and commissary for the Provisional IRA, strategically placed in Cuba to facilitate contacts with international guerrilla groups.

Whatever the truth, two incidents since they've been in custody have done them no favours. The first was the mortar attack on President Ulribe's palace in August 2002. The second took place during a battle between FARC rebels and right-wing guerrillas in the town of Bellavista.

About three hundred women and children were seeking refuge from the fighting in the church of St Paul the Apostle when an improvised mortar struck the roof of the building. It caved in, killing 117 people – including forty-six children. The homemade mortar was fired by FARC but once again it was identical to those used by PIRA in the UK. The three Irishmen are seen by the majority of the population as being ulti- mately responsible for both attacks. They are hated by the Colombians and have received hundreds of death threats as a result.

'For what it's worth, my gut feeling is that the Colombian authorities are absolutely spot on.'

Connolly became Sinn Fein's official representative in Cuba in 1996. Nobody really knows what he did there. But weeks before his arrest in Colombia, he was in Dublin searching for a suitable building for the Cubans to house an envoy. Gerry Adams, the Sinn Fein leader, initially disowned Connolly after his arrest, but two months later he was forced to admit that he had been appointed – 'without my knowledge', of course.

'We know that Monaghan – the Donegal-born, Dublin-raised son of a Republican family – is definitely no angel.'

James 'Mortar' Monaghan conducted IRA weapons training at camps all over the Republic of Ireland during the sixties. He was also highly active in the IRA in the seventies, gaining notoriety as the IRA's senior bomb-making expert. He was arrested on explosives charges in 1976 and escaped from the Special Criminal Court in Dublin following a double bomb blast. He smuggled in explosives and blew a hole in his cell without hurting himself or damaging the getaway car. He was caught later when a newspaper van blocked his escape route.

'And that leaves McCauley,' Keith says. 'Monaghan's lieutenant.'

McCauley was shot in 1982 by an RUC undercover unit while inspecting the contents of an IRA weapons dump. He subsequently won an undisclosed compensation settlement for his injuries.

'Guilty or not, we do know that since the Colombia Three arrived in country, FARC have carried out a more intense and indiscriminate urban bombing campaign than has ever been seen before. Their technology and tactics bear all the PIRA hallmarks, and the Colombian EOD operators are being killed at a fearsome rate. The powers that be have ordered us to teach the Colombian EOD teams everything we know – and help redress the balance.'

He pauses, and looks around the room.

'Gentlemen, we leave in five hours.'

30

*Excellence is in the details. Give attention to the details
and excellence will come.*

Perry Paxton

30 March 2004

I'm feeling particularly vulnerable – like an animal
that's ventured too far from its lair and ended up in
unfamiliar surroundings, uncertain whether it's
predator or prey. We're travelling through the heart of
militia territory and we've been refused permission to
carry firearms – the Colombian government's excuse
being that armed police have been assigned to escort us
for the duration of our mission here.

That's all fine in theory, but if the shit hits the fan and
the policeman sitting next to me gets slotted or we're
ambushed and the two of us are separated, he's going to
be about as much use as tits on a fish. To top it all,
Freddie, our full-time driver and bodyguard, is over-
weight, wears beer-bottle glasses and is barely five feet

tall. It's a miracle he can see over the steering-wheel, let alone drive us out of danger. He insists on playing chicken with all the oncoming traffic and I've had more near-death experiences in the last half-hour than I've had in my entire career to date. It's probably just as well the Colombians haven't let us travel armed – otherwise I'd probably top the crazy bastard myself.

We cross the last bridge, the river glinting beneath us as it meanders through the milky-white gorge, and drive onto the training area. Our bone-rattling, death-defying journey is at an end.

The training area is about two hundred kilometres south-west of Bogotá, in the foothills of the Andes. My mates were bang on when they said it's the most beautiful place on earth. We're surrounded by lush rainforests and snow-capped mountains.

Colombia is Kidnap and Car Bomb Central. Forty-five per cent of the kidnappings in the world occur here – an average of one every two hours – and at least one in ten results in the death of the hostage. We've been told never to move around on our own and to remain situationally aware at all times. But in spite of the danger, it's an amazing country and I love the way the locals are always able to find a reason to smile and take everything in their stride.

While we're out here, we're working directly for the defence attaché. As a former ATO himself, he's taken a very active role in this particular task. The US Drug Enforcement Agency has presented the Colombians with some extremely high-tech equipment, including millions of dollars' worth of EOD robots, disrupters and bomb suits. Under the Plan Colombia initiative – the brainchild of Presidents Bill Clinton and Andrés Pastrana – the US has funded the kit and the Brits, as financially astute as ever, have agreed to provide the instruction.

We've run the training in two phases. We put the Colombian operators under some pressure, giving each man scores of devices to deal with so that we could assess their base-line level of competency. Then we began taking them through all the skills that had become second nature to us in Northern Ireland, but which were completely alien to them.

Although they're now over the moon to be on the course, they weren't so keen to begin with. There was more than a hint of 'We don't need you, what the fuck can you teach us that we don't already know?' in their attitude. We were in a *Catch-22* situation. The students resented us because they're all experienced operators who've dealt with numerous IEDs, and their superiors resented us because they saw our presence as a challenge to their authority.

We've had to tread very carefully. These guys are operationally hardened veterans of a major counter-insurgency, many of whom have had to deal with devices the hard way – up close and personal. They're incredibly brave men who are good at what they do. But, in truth, if we'd left them to carry on dealing with devices the way they had in the past – by muttering a few prayers and ripping them apart with their bare hands – they wouldn't be alive for much longer. The new IRA tactics and technology being adopted by FARC would guarantee that.

And so we've tried to be friendly and approachable, without being too familiar, and we've shown respect to both the operators and their superiors, so that neither has felt the desire to turn against us. Thankfully our strategy has paid off.

For the past three weeks, each of us has been training a dedicated five-man syndicate. I've worked my guys hard, and as we've progressed through the course I've made sure the tasks have become more and more demanding. Every time they've reached a certain level of competency I've ramped up the pressure and it's worked a treat. They've stopped making foolish mistakes and they've stopped allowing themselves to be channelled into the most obvious courses of action. They're finally thinking outside the box. Whenever they've allowed themselves to get a little over-confident I've thrown in another little funny – a learning point that brings them back to earth – and they're really starting to get it.

Most importantly, we've taught them how to operate in a high-threat environment – where they're being specifically targeted by terrorists. Not only do they now know how to neutralize IRA devices, they also know how to protect themselves and their teams from a range of complex secondary threats – ambushes, sniper fire and booby-traps.

But there's still one lesson I want to teach them. Years ago, a colleague of mine was operating in Crossmaglen – the most dangerous town in Northern Ireland at the time. He was tasked to clear a device inside a vehicle, which had been called-in by the IRA. He sent the robot down the road, managed to gain access to the vehicle and disrupted the device. While he was doing his follow-up manual approach the police and Army cordon came under attack and he was subsequently ordered to finish off the task from the relative safety of a nearby barracks.

Confident that he'd already neutralized the IED, he did so. But the IRA had planned the attack in minute detail. They knew that if they attacked the cordon once the first device had been neutralized, the operator would very probably be forced to move the vehicle. The vehicle contained a second timed device hidden in the dashboard. As my mate drove the vehicle into Crossmaglen Barracks, it exploded. Amazingly he survived, but he now has a glass eye and a shed-load of scars.

I set up a similar task for each of the Colombians to illustrate the point that once a vehicle has been in terrorist hands it has to be treated as though it's a bomb. Every inch of the structure has to be cleared before it goes back into the forensic chain. Up until now my guys have just been paying lip service to the drill.

I decide to give the first task to Jimmy Menezes, one of the superstars in my syndicate. He's a tough guy with an incredibly kind heart. As soon as he was old enough, Jimmy joined the police and quickly became one of the legendary Jungla Comandos. Having spent four years seeking out and destroying narcotics laboratories deep inside the Colombian jungles, he decided on a change of career and became a police EOD operator instead. Since then he's neutralized at least a hundred IEDs and been decorated for bravery four times. He's an exceptional man.

I brief him on a similar scenario to the Crossmaglen job. I tell him I'll act as the witness if he's got any questions and leave him and the boys to get on with it.

Just then, as the boys are preparing the equipment for the task, the defence attaché (DA) comes over for a chat. Colonel Williams loves the Colombians and, having only recently learnt Spanish, relishes every opportunity he gets to chat with them. As he stands there holding court, I can see the boys are in complete awe of him. They truly admire his extensive operational experience and they love the fact that he's taken the trouble to speak to them in their native tongue.

After a few minutes of banter he turns and congratulates me. I know he means it: there's a tear in his eye. He works very closely with the Colombian EOD community and has seen many brave men killed. Knowing he's responsible for them receiving training that's going to keep them alive means a great deal to him.

'I've got another piece of news for you,' he says. 'Hot off the UK press. This morning the Met arrested a suspected Al Qaeda cell who were planning to attack a series of UK targets. Another member of their cell was picked up in Ottawa yesterday.'

The Canadian was an expert in the design and construction of radio-controlled IEDs and the Met recovered 600 kilograms of ammonium nitrate from a lock-up in West London. They searched a number of other properties and also found a biscuit tin filled with aluminium powder.

'Ammonium nitrate and aluminium. So they were going to be making a big bomb . . .

'According to the police, the terrorists were going to attack Bluewater shopping centre, the Ministry of Sound nightclub, the Houses of Parliament and a football stadium. But the real coup is that almost as soon as the cell delivered the ammonium nitrate fertilizer to the storage unit in Hanwell, the security services installed covert cameras in there and switched the ammonium nitrate with an inert substitute.'

'Pure genius, Colonel,' I reply, trying not to give away the fact that I'm intimately aware of the operation.

'Anyway, just thought you'd like to know,' he says. 'I'll leave you and your boys to it.'

While his team are carrying out their search of the area Jimmy goes straight into the detailed questioning. He quickly ascertains when and where the device was found and at what time the area was secured. He identifies which parts of the route have been walked by the security forces and whether or not the vehicle has been accessed. So far so good.

While he's firing questions at me, his number two – another likeable young operator called Galeano – tells him he's found a device in the ICP.

Jimmy calmly orders the team to withdraw a hundred metres back along the track. The robot trundles down the road and points a disrupter at the device. Jimmy orders everybody to get under hard cover. After taking the shot he makes a manual approach to confirm that the secondary device is explosively safe, then cracks on with the vehicle. Until now this has been a textbook performance.

Having neutralized the device in the ICP, he carries on and renders safe the first device in the car but he only completes a cursory search of the vehicle, presumably because he thinks that's all he's going to be tested on.

I ask him to talk me through the rest of the task. He tells me that having searched the vehicle he'd ensure the device components are made safe before unloading the EOD weapons and handing over the crime scene to a forensics officer.

'Are you sure?' I ask him.

'*Sí, Capitán*,' he replies, as confident as ever.

'OK, come with me.'

Sure enough, as I lead him down to the vehicle the timer runs down and there's a small bang as the sound unit explodes. His team-mates think it's hilarious but Jimmy is devastated.

He's a complete perfectionist and, like most good operators, he's always relied heavily on his intuition. That intuition told him the car was safe. He feels he'll never be able to trust his judgement again.

'Don't beat yourself up about it, Jimmy. We've all been there.'

Thankfully, when I tell him all the operators from all the other syndicates have made exactly the same mistake, he finally manages to force a smile.

'That's it, gentlemen,' I say, turning to the group. 'You're ready. One final word of advice, though: if you're out on the ground and the hairs on the back of your neck start standing on end, just remember that if it *feels* wrong, it *is* wrong. Remember *absence of the normal* and *presence of the abnormal* and, most importantly, always remember you're the expert. Don't ever allow anyone to bully you into doing something that doesn't feel right. It's better to be tried by twelve than carried by six.'

31

The future depends on what we do in the present.

Mahatma Gandhi

21 August 2004

Our convoy pulls out of the Basra Palace HQ and into the bustling city. The stench of shit and rotting garbage catches in the back of my throat and makes me want to gag. Even after all this time I still can't get used to it. The sewers have been blocked since the war started.

When I got back from Colombia I promised Lucy I wouldn't be going away again. But instead of going straight on leave, I made the schoolboy error of nipping into the squadron to drop off some kit, and ended up getting spammed to come out here.

I was convinced Lucy would leave me when I told her: our marriage is hanging by a thread.

It's been a hell of a tour. But nothing I've ever done has given me the exhilaration of the past three months. It's been one of the most powerful and defining periods of my life. I finally feel I'm doing something that's making a difference.

We're up against some of the most hardened and technically advanced terrorists in the world. We've faced the daily threat of snipers and roadside bombs and been constantly on the receiving end of enemy rocket and mortar attacks. We and the insurgents have climbed the same deadly learning curve, and the line between killer and innocent bystander has become increasingly hard to draw.

Four days into the tour we were ambushed on the way back from an IED task. Two of us were shot and wounded; I still don't know how we managed to fight our way out. It was the most terrifying experience of my life – and the first time I've seen the head of another human being in my rifle sight and squeezed the trigger. I still haven't come to terms with it yet – but I know this tour has changed my life for ever.

In the first eight weeks, we attended forty-five IED incidents. And as we became more skilled at disabling their crude, unstable devices, the bombers also became increasingly sophisticated and determined. We started coming up against devices that were specifically designed for us; I ended up with a price on my head and was taken off counter-terrorist bomb-disposal duties. I'm now a weapons intelligence officer charged with identifying and targeting the bomber networks.

I was absolutely gutted to leave my team. Over the two months we worked together, those men had become my family. I don't think I fully appreciated it at the time. We lived in each other's pockets twenty-four hours a day, seven days a week, enduring fearsome amounts of stress and tension, yet not one of them ever put himself before the others. Our comradeship was forged in the fieriest of furnaces; we lived together, fought together and were prepared to die together. I miss them like mad.

But since then, my new team of intelligence specialists has succeeded in taking down the entire Sunni bomber capability in Basra. We've brought an end to the Sunni RCIED attacks. Unfortunately the same can't be said for the Mahdi Army's Shia bombers. They've gone from strength to strength; the bastards seem to be completely untouchable – not least because they've penetrated the highest echelons of the national infrastructure, including the police and the army.

In short, it's also been one of the most emotional tours I've ever experienced. I've seen destruction on an unprecedented scale. I've experienced an extreme range of intense emotions on a day-to-day basis.

Predictably enough, it's taken its toll. How could it not? One minute I'm standing at the cliff edge, just me and the bomb, pushing it to the max, the next I'm racked with guilt, falling short on my responsibilities to

Lucy and the girls, trying to come down to earth and be normal again. And I know that if I spend long enough living on the edge, I'm eventually going to fall off.

Out here the switch continues to flick rapidly and repeatedly from full off to full on. The team's mood changes the moment we leave the safety of the camp. Every one of us is completely focused, poised, weapons in the aim and ready to react. We're now weaving our way through the back-streets, screaming past the sprawling mass of flat, sand-coloured homes, public monuments and seventies-style concrete apartment blocks.

We hit a left onto the Red Route – IED Alley – a kilometre further on. The six-mile stretch of pot-holed tarmac is teeming with donkey carts, trucks and taxis. Rows of two-storey, flat-roofed buildings line each edge of the dusty wasteland that borders the road. The nearest are at least a hundred metres away and provide perfect cover for snipers and RCIED triggermen. It feels like the world's longest bombing range. Dozens of Coalition patrols have been hit here in the last few months.

I'm on top cover. It's fifty degrees in the shade and my face feels like I'm standing a few feet behind a jet engine. Corporal Townsend, my infantry escort commander, gives us a blow-by-blow commentary on the radio. He's covering the likely threats as well as alerting us to any other potential dramas – including the Iraqi kamikaze drivers screaming towards us on the wrong side of the road.

Whoever designed the Basra traffic system must have been banged off their heads. Junctions appear randomly out of nowhere and every few seconds another car travelling in the opposite direction veers straight into our path. It's as if they're goading us, challenging us to a game of chicken.

We leave IED Alley with some relief and follow the Green Route to the western part of the city. It's simmering with uneasiness. Life among the shops and houses appears normal but millimetres below the surface the place is bristling with anger and tension. We're taking no chances: our safety catches are off, all the doors are open and we're ready to lay down fire the moment things kick off. We scrutinize every single person we pass and scan houses, donkey carts, piles of rubbish and parked cars for IEDs and shooters.

Children are playing in piles of sand at the side of the road; they smile and wave as our vehicles whiz past them. We respond with frosty, impassive glares. No wonder we're perceived as arrogant Westerners who don't give a shit about their country – but at times like this we're left with no choice.

As the lead vehicle of a Warrior patrol drove through a Shia area on the opposite side of the city nine days ago, it was hit by a huge, improvised claymore mine. The explosion engulfed the heavily armoured vehicle in flames and peppered it with hundreds of steel ball-bearings. The commander survived; by sheer chance he'd dropped down into the turret moments before. But the driver never stood a chance. Marc Ferns was killed instantly. The WIS team didn't find a single bomb component at the scene. All that remained was a colossal smoking crater.

Now we're slap-bang in the middle of the Shia heart-land and our intelligence tells us that the guys in this neighbourhood are actively supporting the bombers. In my heart I want to reach out and connect with the Shias, but the fact is, we don't know which, if any, of them we can trust. If we drop our guard – we die.

As we scream down the road, using the rubbish-strewn hard shoulder to weave in and out of packets of congested traffic, we can finally see friendlies: we're approaching the cordon.

At the ICP I'm met by Tony Gibbs, one of my WIS operators. He was one of my instructors on the ATO course; after leaving the Army at the end of his twenty-two years he was invited back into the trade as a reservist. And he absolutely loves it. For him it's a vocation, a way of life. He's completely – intellectually and spiritually – absorbed by what he does and, being the wise old man of the unit, his level of technical knowledge is unsurpassed. But he's come up against a set-up he hasn't seen before. 'Sorry to call you out, mate,' he says, 'but I wanted a second opinion. I'm thinking Lebanese Hezbollah. Can you come over to my wagon and check it out?'

Tony opens the rear door of his Snatch Land Rover and removes two large forensic sacks, each containing an explosive charge. 'A search team operating on the Green Route found this improvised claymore mine this morning.' He points at the first bag. 'It was hard-wired to the explosively formed projectile in that other bag.'

When I led the technical investigation into the Marc Ferns killing nine days ago, I realized there was something very familiar about the attack. I'd seen the MO somewhere before. Not in Iraq: there had never been an attack like it in Iraq. Certainly not something so advanced, where the claymore was specifically designed to vaporize all the firing circuit's componentry and thus destroy the forensics. No. That MO had only ever been seen in southern Lebanon. The attack on Private Ferns's Warrior was a classic Hezbollah strike, and I'd had a feeling then that if Hezbollah and the Iranians were providing the Mahdi Army with improvised claymores, it would only be a matter of time before they started cooking up their other signature dish – the explosively formed projectile.

The EFP – once famously used by the Red Army

Faction in the assassination of Alfred Herrhausen, the former head of Deutsche Bank – is a cylindrical, dish-shaped charge designed to penetrate armoured vehicles. A particularly lethal version was used by Lebanese Hezbollah against the Israelis; when detonated, it projects the dish forwards, causing it to form an armour-piercing slug travelling at well over a thousand metres a second. Worse still, they're armed remotely and initiated when a vehicle passes a passive infra-red trigger, which makes them extremely difficult to detect or defeat.

He tells me he's done some back-of-a-fag-packet calculations and worked out that the foam-covered claymore mine – which isn't much bigger than a briefcase – contains around ten thousand ball-bearings and more than twenty kilos of high explosive.

Jesus. That's enough to sink a battleship . . .

I slip on my nitrile gloves. The presence of the second charge, the EFP, is more ominous still. We remove the plaster-of-paris-covered projectile from the bag and lay it on a forensic drop-sheet.

There have been mutterings about Lebanese Hezbollah and Iranian bombmakers being in Basra for some time now, but the discovery of EFP-linked claymores has just confirmed it.

'Look at the workmanship that's gone into it,' Tony says, with the kind of passionate admiration you normally expect to see during an episode of *Antiques Roadshow*.

These are the most sophisticated and lethal bombs ever seen in Iraq. They're clearly being field tested against the British, and right now we're completely powerless to do anything about them.

The battle against IEDs has just been taken to the next level, and unless we find a counter-measure quickly, things are going to get a whole lot worse.

32

The West will be crying north, south, east and west.
London will burn in these four quarters . . .

Al Qaeda in Europe website, June 2005

7 July 2005

My feet beat rhythmically against the pavement as I pound my way along the tree-lined banks of the river Thames. The rising sun warms my face as I pick up the pace and sprint towards Wandsworth Bridge.

According to the shrinks, my running addiction is 'almost certainly' linked to a deep inner need to feel strong and empowered – in defiance of circumstances that would otherwise leave me feeling weak and powerless. There might be something in that, but I still think it's more strongly linked to a deep inner need to get to work without having to rely on the London Underground.

Perhaps it's a bit of both. I'm certainly struggling at HQ at the moment. I've served in the Army for almost

316

fifteen years, and for the first time in my career I'm reporting to someone who seems to want to turn every day into an obstacle course. I've spent all these years alongside the best of the best, trying to find a real sense of purpose in what I'm doing, and now that I'm in a job where I know I really can make a difference, my efforts are being hampered by a guy who's so universally admired that you have to buy a case of champagne if you mention his name in the Mess.

The man known affectionately as Voldemort (of *Harry Potter* fame) seems determined to make my life even more difficult than it is already, with my rapidly failing marriage and my team working every minute of the day in our mission to identify and interdict bombers all over the world.

I pass a block of swanky riverside apartments, then head east through Chelsea and onto the Embankment. I run pretty much the same route every day. It takes me about an hour, and it's probably the only thing that keeps me sane. It also gives me a chance to mentally prioritize my day.

For the last few weeks I've been trying to find out what Hezbollah and the Iranians are up to in Iraq. Their EFP-linked claymores are killing and injuring five times the number of Coalition forces than previous devices, and we've been tasked to identify who's building them and how they're getting into Iraq.

A source from the Iranian Revolutionary Guard's Special Forces has told the London daily *Al Sharq al Awsat* the location of three insurgent training camps on the Iran-Iraq border. He estimates that between 800 and 1200 members of Muqtada al-Sadr's Mahdi Army have already received training there in guerrilla warfare, the production of bombs and explosives, the use of small arms, reconnaissance and espionage. It seems only natural to me that the three camps – in Qasr Shireen, 'Ilam and Hami – would also be used as cross-border smuggling points, so I'm supposed to be heading back out to southern Iraq any day to investigate it further.

I'm looking forward to going back, despite everything. After my IEDD team returned from our Iraq tour last year, three of the lads were redeployed with the Black Watch battle group. They'd just finished a massive route-clearance task when a suicide bomber drove through the prematurely collapsed cordon and detonated his car bomb right next to their Warrior. Mick Brennan and Neil Heritage both lost their legs above the knee, and Dan, my number two, was blown thirty feet into a field but, by some complete miracle, escaped physical injury. I don't think he's been as lucky with the psychological scars, though. I suspect they're going to stay with him for life.

My pounding leg and arm muscles send blood rushing through my veins, which clears my mind of all the recondite shit I've been building up in it. I feel good. I make the final dash past the Palace of Westminster to my office. I like getting in early, before the rest of my team arrives. It gives me a chance to make a bit of headway before the phones start ringing and it all goes crazy. I switch on the computer and grab a quick shower while it's firing up.

I take out a notebook when I get back to my desk and begin scouring the databases for int about the Iranians. I want to get a better understanding of who their bomb-makers are. I'm looking for information about the components they're using, their infrastructure, their support mechanisms and the tactics, techniques and procedures they've been employing. When I've established those key components, my team and I can start to drill down and predict when and where they're going to strike next.

As we put the jigsaw pieces together we'll be able to fuse that prediction with technical and tactical intelligence. Then we'll be in a position to produce detailed targeting information packs containing, among other things, high-definition satellite imagery of the camps and smuggling routes and digital mug-shots of the terrorists.

If we can build up a decent enough picture it might even be possible to identify and recruit somebody on the inside; and if we can run somebody on the inside, we'll be able to disrupt their logistics capability and perhaps even bring down the entire network. In theory, we could get in the way of the whole chain of events before the next IED is even emplaced.

I'm scribbling notes when my phone beeps twice. It's a text message from Robbie, one of my team: *I parked in a disabled space the other day and this traffic warden shouts, 'Oi what's your disability?' 'Tourette's!' I said. 'Now fuck off, you cunt!'*

Robbie's a sergeant in the Intelligence Corps and one of the funniest int operators I've ever come across. He also never stops working. He's like Zippy on speed, never able to sit still – and nothing's ever too much trouble. Very much the golden boy of his infantry battalion, he was one of the youngest colour sergeants in the Army.

He was absolutely flying until he went out for a drink one night with his girlfriend and a couple of RMP NCOs started gobbing off at him. He took exception to it and dropped them. When their back-up arrived, he dropped them too, and ended up doing a six-month stretch in the glasshouse in Colchester. He was busted down to private, but when he got out of the clink he joined the Intelligence Corps and has made it back in the space of four years.

Seconds after the text he calls me. 'Chris, we're in Caffè Nero, next to Embankment tube. Where are you?'

Fuck. I'd forgotten it was Thursday. It's the day our

team normally meets up for a brew before work. 'On my way. Be with you in five.'

As I walk into the crowded coffee joint, Robbie waves me over to a table in the corner where Nick and Jo, the other two members of our team, are busy tucking into a small mountain of croissants. Nick's a WO1 and the other ATO on the team. We have a global remit, but he's focusing predominantly on IEDs in Afghanistan while I concentrate on those in Iraq. Nick and I have known each other for years. We both served in the same squadron at 11 EOD – he was the troop warrant officer at Aldershot Troop when I was the Shorncliffe Troop commander – then attended the same STT course and deployed to Northern Ireland as high-threat operators together.

We spend the next few minutes shooting the shit and generally ripping the piss out of each other, and then it all gets serious. Each of us gives the rest of the group an update on what we've been doing.

Robbie kicks off with the work he's doing on Iranian and Hezbollah front companies who are procuring seemingly innocuous components from companies all over the world, piecing them together as bomb kits, then smuggling them into Iran and Iraq.

Nick tells us about a new type of radio-controlled IED that's flooding into Afghanistan. It's been introduced by foreign *jihad*ists who've used it successfully against Russian forces in Chechnya.

Jo is the only non-military member of the team. As a career civil servant who has specialized until now in submarine warfare, she's had a steep learning curve, but is the youngest and brightest of us all. She's looking at the possible proliferation of Qassam rockets and centring her efforts on a former Palestinian bombmaker who, we think, is the general commander of the Izz ad-Din al-Qassam Brigades, the military wing of Hamas.

Once the briefs are over, we finish our designer brews and prepare to head into the office.

'Can I borrow your phone, mate?' Robbie asks. 'Mine's got bugger-all signal.'

I hand it over, fully expecting a repeat of the Tourette's gag.

'Bollocks . . . yours doesn't either.'

Nick and Jo check theirs and shake their heads. Suddenly it seems like everybody inside and outside the café is juggling mobile phones.

Jo turns to a couple on the table next to us. 'Excuse me . . . have you got a phone signal?'

'No . . . sorry!'

The four of us exchange knowing glances. Something's happening.

Jo switches on the television as soon as we get back into the office. Sky News is reporting a massive power surge on the Underground system that's caused a series of minor explosions in the power circuits. For the next half-hour there's a parade of images of people being evacuated from a series of tube stations, some suffering from burns and smoke inhalation.

None of us is convinced.

Voldemort strolls into the office, looking even more pissed off than usual. 'Three bombs have exploded on the London Underground within fifty seconds of each other. I don't know why, but the COBRA assessment staff have specifically asked for you to be seconded to them. And that means immediately.'

The Cabinet Office Briefing Room is a government coordination facility that's activated in cases of national or regional emergency. It's situated in an underground bunker deep in the heart of Whitehall. As I enter the secure suite, dozens of engineers are busy installing banks of telephone lines; representatives from the Metropolitan Police and the intelligence agencies are hurriedly setting up fax machines, computer terminals, video conference facilities, and other state-of-the-art communication equipment. Everybody's in their own world. The place is absolutely frenetic.

I feel a tap on my shoulder and turn to find myself re-acquainted with another blast from the past. It's Duncan Stone, my old pal from Sandhurst. He's working for MI6. Why am I not surprised?

Just when I think things can't get any more surreal another voice booms out from the corner of the room. 'Mr Fucking Hunter! I thought you'd be dead or in prison by now!'

Suddenly everybody's stopped what they're doing and all eyes have focused on me. I feel my face instantly redden.

It's Colonel Kemp, the CO of the Royal Anglian battle group I served with in Northern Ireland. He's now the head of the COBRA assessment staff.

He gathers everybody round and explains why we're here.

'Ladies and gentlemen, this morning three bombs detonated simultaneously on the London Underground. The first exploded on eastbound Circle Line sub-surface Underground train number 204, travelling between Liverpool Street and Aldgate, about eight minutes after it had left King's Cross St Pancras. At the time of the explosion, the third carriage of the train was approximately a hundred yards down the tunnel from Liverpool Street. The parallel Hammersmith and City Line track from Liverpool Street to Aldgate East was also damaged.'

He tells us that the second bomb exploded in the second carriage of a westbound Circle Line train, which had just left platform four at Edgware Road heading for Paddington, having left King's Cross St

Pancras about eight minutes earlier. There were several other trains nearby, one of which was also damaged in the blast.

The third bomb was on a southbound Piccadilly Line train en route to Russell Square. 'It detonated about one minute after leaving King's Cross, by which time it had travelled about five hundred yards. The blast ripped through the rear of the first carriage of the train, causing severe damage to the front of the second carriage as well, and to the tunnel.'

I look around the room. You could have heard a pin drop. These people are all seasoned veterans of a number of crises, but nothing as devastatingly close to home.

'Our purpose today is to enable the Prime Minister – who is currently on his way back from the G8 summit in Gleneagles – and his senior ministers and key government officials to have real-time information about the bombings and provide him with an assessment of who the bombers are and where they might—'

Before he's finished his sentence one of his staff announces a fourth explosion in Tavistock Square on a number 30 double-decker bus travelling from Marble Arch to Hackney Wick.

I can't believe this is happening. London is under siege – and this series of blasts could be a prelude to an even more catastrophic event. I feel a knot form in the pit of my stomach, and think of Lucy and the girls.

When I call her, the first thing she asks is if I've seen the news.

'Yes, darling,' I reply.

'Is it true?' she asks. 'Are we really being attacked by terrorists?'

'It seems so,' I say. Then I explain that I can't talk for long, don't know when I'm going to be home, or even if I'll be able to call again today. I tell her I love her, not to go out unless she absolutely has to . . . and definitely not to use any public transport. She doesn't need me to say it twice.

As I walk back into the briefing room, the TV screens are playing yet more sequences of bomb victims carried out on stretchers. The BBC are showing pictures of a bus that looks as though its roof has been peeled back by a giant can opener. Sky zooms in on an M25 warning sign, which reads: *AVOID LONDON. AREA CLOSED. TURN ON RADIO.*

Everybody in the room is scanning intelligence reports, speaking to witnesses on the ground or searching through databases looking for even the slightest of clues that might help us identify who's behind the attacks and where they might strike next.

There have been a mass of conflicting news reports. The origin, method and even the number of explosions seems to have been misrepresented. The Met originally announced that there had been six explosions on the Underground rather than three and the bus bombing brought that total up to seven. I can see why they leapt to that conclusion: because the blasts were initiated between stops, the injured were brought out from the stations both ahead of and behind each targeted train.

A voice blares out over the Tannoy: 'Can all heads of department meet in the main briefing room?'

I look at my watch. It's already 11 a.m. 'Do you think that includes me?' I ask Duncan.

'I'm not sure, mate. Is anybody else here from Defence Intelligence?'

'Don't think so.'

'There's your answer.'

Inside the main briefing room there's a large oak table with embedded laptop ports and several large plasma screens mounted on the walls. About twenty senior intelligence officers from all the main agencies are seated around it, with the imposing figure of Colonel Kemp at the head. He waves me in and we crack on.

'OK. This is what we know so far . . .

'One: A Code Amber alert was declared at 0919 by Transport for London, and the Underground immediately began shutting down the network, bringing trains into stations and suspending all services.

'Two: There have been four confirmed bombings,

the first three of which exploded within fifty seconds of each other, suggesting that a timing device or remote activation was used.

'Three: The capital's hospitals are now full.

'We still don't know exactly what happened, how many casualties there are, and who might have been responsible.'

A series of separate exchanges sparks up. Rather than concentrating on what we don't know, it seems a large number of the people in the room are more concerned with trying to justify why they failed to identify these attacks before they occurred.

Five weeks ago, the Joint Terrorism Analysis Centre, which reports to the head of MI5 and is responsible for assessing the threat from international terrorism to the UK, lowered the national alert state from 'Severe General' to 'Substantial' with the words, 'At present there is not a group with both the current intent and the capability to attack the UK.'

This is definitely not the time to start arse-covering and Colonel Kemp diplomatically but firmly takes control of the situation.

'OK. Is there anything else we know that we can add to the Prime Minister's briefing?'

'Yes,' one of the intelligence officers replies. 'This is the first bombing of a London bus.'

As the colonel scribbles that down, I feel it's time to

pipe up. I know I'm going to sound like the class swot. 'Actually, Colonel, that's not entirely accurate. On the eighteenth of February 1996 there was a bombing at Wellington Street near the Aldwych, which killed the IRA operative transporting the device. Admittedly, though, it was thought to have been the result of an accidental detonation of a device that he intended to plant elsewhere, rather than a suicide attack.'

'Who said anything about a suicide attack?' The question comes from another of the intelligence officers, a middle-aged lady who, if looks could kill, would probably have done for me a thousand times over.

'Actually, that was going to be my second point. The colonel mentioned that the first three bombs exploded within fifty seconds of each other, suggesting that a timing device or remote activation was used. I don't currently subscribe to that view.'

'Really, Major Hunter? Then what do you think?'

'I think this is an Al Qaeda suicide attack.'

The female officer now treats me to the kind of expression that used to be the preserve of Victorian maiden aunts. I can feel the indignation coming off her in waves. She asks me who I am and what could possibly qualify me to come out with such a bold statement.

Colonel Kemp introduces me as a suicide-terrorism specialist.

'The reason I *believe* this to be a suicide attack is because the explosions were simultaneous, on a major transport hub, targeting civilians, and because so far no explosive residue has been discovered . . .'

'Go on,' the colonel says.

'Because it's so difficult to acquire plastic explosives in this country, I would reasonably expect a terrorist group to use organic peroxide, such as that used by Palestinian groups in the occupied territories. Organic peroxide explosives leave very little residue when they detonate, while plastic explosive residue can be detected immediately. Also, there was mention of the possible use of a remote-controlled initiation system such as a mobile phone . . . and it's not currently possible to use mobile phones on the London Underground network.'

Kemp nods. 'I'll get that amended. Now, has anybody got anything further to add?'

Nobody has.

'Right. Keep up the good work. We'll reconvene in an hour.'

As I make for the door, the colonel grabs me and takes me to one side. 'Chris, they're good people around that table, but they're well outside their comfort zones. I need you to get over to New Scotland Yard and get me some hard facts.'

* * *

I ask one of the security guards the quickest way to the Yard and he leads me through a maze of underground corridors and up to street level. 'Go through that door, turn right and a constable will direct you from there.'

I make my way into St James's Park and a few minutes later I'm standing in the foyer of New Scotland Yard waiting to be met by Detective Sergeant Max Chapman, the head of the Metropolitan Police Bomb Data Centre. He looks absolutely exhausted.

'OK, Chris, here's what we know so far. First the bus – it started its return route from Marble Arch to Hackney Wick at nine a.m. and arrived at Euston bus station five minutes later. Crowds of people who had been evacuated from the tube were leaping onto buses, and the driver had to deviate from his normal route because of road closures in the King's Cross area – due to the earlier tube bombings. At the time of the explosion he was travelling through Tavistock Square – just on the corner, where it joins Upper Woburn Place.'

He tells me the explosion ripped off the roof and destroyed the back of the double-decker.

'Most of the passengers at the front of the bus survived, but those at the top and lower rear took the brunt of the explosion. A number of passers-by were also injured, and surrounding buildings suffered fragmentation damage.'

The bomber also appears to have died in the blast.

He was on the top deck, at the back. The only reason more people weren't killed was that Upper Woburn Place is the home of the British Medical Association, and a number of doctors in or near the building were able to provide immediate emergency assistance. 'What's even more heartbreaking is that some of those injured were people who'd been evacuated from the Underground blast. That's all I can tell you, I'm afraid. I'll give you a bell when I hear back from the boys at the Underground blast scenes.'

By the time we reconvene in the COBRA briefing room, more information has flooded in. The police investigation has been conducted with unprecedented speed.

We've learnt that each of the Underground bombs exploded as two trains passed one another, further evidence of human triggers. And the police confirmed as much a few moments ago when they revealed the identities of four men whom they believe were responsible. It's still not clear why they were carrying items capable of identifying them, but a number of ID and bank cards have been recovered.

'OK. Has anybody got anything else to add?' the colonel asks.

'Yes, Richard,' one of the int officers replies. 'The BBC *News* has just reported the discovery of a website known to be operated by associates of Al Qaeda. On it is a two-hundred-word statement claiming responsibility for the attacks. The announcement claims they were in response to the British involvement in the 2003 invasion of Iraq.'

'I don't know if it's the same site,' another says, 'but a message was posted on the Al Qaeda in Europe website last month too, stating that "The West will be crying north, south, east and west, and London will burn in these four quarters."'

The jigsaw is falling into place. It looks like the terror- ists intended to carry out four explosions on the Underground forming a cross of fire with an arm in each of the cardinal directions, symbolically centred at King's Cross. The Northern Line was suspended today due to technical difficulties, which might explain why the fourth bomber detonated his device on a bus almost an hour later.

'Anything else?'

'Yes,' one of the policemen responds. 'Two more suspicious packages have been found on Underground trains and were destroyed by the Met Explosives Section – but they turned out to be false. In the meantime, you should know that this is the first suicide bombing in Western Europe.'

The room goes silent again. The significance of this statement has not been lost on any of us.

As the rest of the day unfolds, more int about the bombers comes to light. On 3 February 1993 Sidique Khan was arrested and cautioned for a Section 47 assault committed on 26 December 1992. In keeping with normal procedure, a police record was created and his photograph was taken. The incident was not related to national security, however, so the information was not passed by West Yorkshire Police to MI5. Then, on 14 April of the same year, West Yorkshire Police conducting 'pattern of life' surveillance of a known extremist, as part of an investigation with MI5, saw him leaving a mosque in Beeston, Leeds, with four or five others, getting into a BMW and being given a lift towards the city centre. On 16 April 2003 West Yorkshire Police checks on the PNC revealed that the keeper of the BMW was Sidique Khan. The contact lasted only three minutes, and was also assessed not to have had any national security significance, or relevance to the subject of the investigation.

It appears the bombers were all 'clean skins'.

I glance at my watch. It's 7 p.m. I know that everybody in the room is utterly drained. It's been a profoundly stressful and emotional day and we're all feeling the strain.

'OK. To sum up, then . . .' the colonel says. 'The police have managed to grab a still from security-camera footage of the bombers entering Luton station at 7.22 a.m. It appears that all four travelled to Luton by car, then on to London by train. They were recorded on CCTV arriving at King's Cross station at about 0830, after which they went their separate ways.

'In all, fifty-two people were killed in the attacks and about seven hundred more were injured, of whom about a hundred are still in hospital. The incident is the deadliest single act of terrorism in the United Kingdom since Lockerbie, and the deadliest bombing in London since the Second World War.

'Thank you for all your hard work today. You've done an exceptional job. Now I suggest you go home and spend some time with the people who really deserve it.'

As I walk back along the Embankment, desperate to get home to my family, I think of the images that flashed across the TV screens throughout the course of the day, and I think of those people who aren't going to make it home tonight.

I think of the bravery, humility and selflessness of all those passers-by who stopped to help and comfort the injured as they lay bleeding and dying, and I think of the millions of calm, resigned Londoners who got on with their lives as four twisted fanatics tried to rob them of everything they cherish.

Across the capital, thousands of Londoners are probably thinking and doing the same, walking slightly more slowly than usual, and talking once more on their phones. Despite their sadness, I don't think I've ever seen so many people smile. And I've never heard so many people say, 'I love you.'

33

The strength of the British people has always been that of a free people who take their own decisions and are ready for the greatest sacrifices to defend their freedom . . .

President Nicolas Sarkozy

1 September 2005

When I was a young lieutenant I could never understand why essays were deemed an 'essential' part of our officer career development; it's only now I'm an intelligence officer that I've got it. I seem to spend my life writing reports and briefings, and since the Iraq forty-five-minute WMD débâcle, accuracy is everything.

Voldemort has just come into the office and given me an hour to put together a briefing he's going to be delivering later today about IEDs in Afghanistan. I have a sneaking suspicion he's known about this for weeks.

As the lead on all IED activity in Afghanistan, Nick's agreed to share some of his wealth of knowledge while

I try to craft a written brief. He's terminally busy, though, and really does have far more important things to do right now.

'OK, let's begin with what we know,' he says.

He tells me that IED activity in southern Afghanistan is up 50 per cent on this time last year and that there's been an increase in radio-controlled attacks using stacked anti-tank mines, which rely on blast to over-match Coalition force vehicles. 'The only problem they're having at the moment is synchronizing the explosion with the exact moment the vehicle travels over the top of it, but they're learning pretty damn quickly.'

Bombings have become a major threat in the city of Kandahar since June this year; most have been hastily laid surface IEDs, though there have been more sophisticated devices hidden in roadside street furniture.

I scribble furiously as Nick fires another barrage of information at me.

'We've also seen an increasing prevalence of daisy-chained IEDs.' He's referring to a series of shells or mortars, linked together with the aim of causing maximum attrition to large convoys. There's also been extensive use of choke points – a spot where a vehicle is forced to reduce speed and thus present a softer target.

'In virtually every case IED attacks have been

followed up with small-arms fire, with between four and twelve aggressors.'

'And are the IEDs camouflaged?' I ask.

'Absolutely. They're using everyday items – such as large cooking pots stacked outside those stalls that line the road. Pressure cookers are a real favourite too – because you see them everywhere you go.'

He believes that Pakistani militants are the most skilled bombmakers in the region and reckons they're largely responsible for the supply of RCIEDs. According to his reports, they use the same smuggling routes to bring in IEDs from Pakistan as they do to smuggle opiates back out again.

He describes a new type of radio-controlled IED that's been flooding into Afghanistan. 'The firing device is housed in a commercially bought Sega games console cartridge. Although it looks perfectly normal, the cartridge is actually an RCIED. These devices are known as dual-tone multi-frequency, or DTMF, and we know they've been used against the Russians in Chechnya, but not much more than that.'

True to form, Voldemort strolls into the office just as I'm grappling with the final paragraph and tells me the brief's not needed any more.

That's strike one. But, from the look on his face, I'm guessing there's more to follow.

'I understand you speak Russian, Chris. We've got a

Russian diplomatic delegation arriving tonight and have been asked to provide some hosts. I'd like you to be one of them.'

Fucking hell. Of all the evenings. I tell him I'm planning to spend a rare evening at home looking after the girls while Lucy treats herself to an art class.

He stares at me coldly for several seconds, then tells me I'll need to get a babysitter.

Before he disappears down the corridor he glances back over his shoulder. 'Oh, and you need to phone the DA in Colombia. He wants to have a word.'

As he leaves, Robbie says, 'Some cause happiness wherever they go; others, whenever they go.'

'But on the plus side,' Nick says, 'you can always get the Russians pissed and ask them to give you the low-down on those DTMF devices . . .'

I dial up the number for the DA in Bogotá, and find myself slightly thrown by an unfamiliar voice: 'Colonel Mark Vaughan here.'

He thanks me for getting back to him, and apologizes for calling out of the blue – but beneath the courtesy something tells me he's about to deliver some bad news. 'I understand you taught an IED defeat course here last year . . . and that one of your students was Officer Jimmy Menezes . . . and another was Officer Galeano?'

This conversation definitely isn't going to have a happy ending.

'I'm sorry to have to tell you they've both been killed.'

I knew that was what he was going to say, but I still can't believe it.

He tells me they were both in the jungle, tasked to deal with separate vehicle-borne IED incidents on the highway. Much like Alpha Troop, the Jungla Comandos have to carry everything they need – to operate and survive – on their backs, and therefore don't generally have ECM or deploy with robots.

I listen intently to the DA, focusing on every word, but I still don't get it. From what he tells me, the boys carried out textbook arrival procedures; they asked for witnesses; they asked for cordoning and evacuation to take place, and they also requested the presence of roving army patrols for perimeter security. Just like I'd taught them on the course.

'So what went wrong, Colonel?'

All their requests were refused by the incident commanders, and when they argued the toss, each was accused of cowardice. 'And as I'm sure you know, Chris, Colombian men don't take kindly to being called cowards.'

I think back to the pep talk I gave them at the end of their course. *Always remember you're the expert. It's better to be tried by twelve than carried by six . . .*

Fucking hell. What a terrible waste.

I sit quietly at my desk and begin ploughing through the reports. At times like this it's probably better not to dwell on it. Then Robbie reappears and switches the TV to the Al Jazeera news channel.

The martyrdom video of Mohammad Sidique Khan is being given its first airing.

'I and thousands like me are forsaking everything for what we believe. Our drive and motivation doesn't come from tangible commodities that this world has to offer. Our religion is Islam, obedience to the one true God and following the footsteps of the final Prophet messenger. Your democratically elected governments continuously perpetuate atrocities against my people all over the world. And your support of them makes you directly responsible, just as I am directly responsible for protecting and avenging my Muslim brothers and sisters. Until we feel security you will be our targets, and until you stop the bombing, gassing, imprison- ment and torture of my people, we will not stop this fight. We are at war and I am a soldier. Now you too will taste the reality of this situation.'

It's impossible, after that, for us not to revisit the 7/7 bombings. Robbie, who was away at the time of the 21/7 follow-up, asks me why the second set of devices failed.

In fact, partial explosions occurred at Shepherd's Bush, Warren Street and Oval Underground stations, as well as on a bus in Shoreditch, and it was only by sheer luck that the bombers got the mix wrong and only triggered the detonators. All the suspects legged it after their devices failed and a fifth bomber dumped his without attempting to detonate it.

I was dispatched straight back to work with Colonel Kemp and his team at COBRA. The CCTV images of four suspects wanted in connection with the bombings were released the following day.

One of the reasons for this was because a member of the public witnessed what must have been a rehearsal for the 7/7 bombings. She saw Sidique Khan and his fellow conspirators behaving suspiciously 'military like', but didn't realize its significance at the time. She only reported her sighting after seeing the attacks on the television. The Met didn't want to miss another opportunity to catch the failed bombers.

But then tragedy struck.

Following the release of the CCTV images on 22 July, the police mounted a huge anti-terror operation – hoping to catch the perpetrators before they escaped abroad. Evidence obtained from the unexploded IEDs led them to an apartment block in Tulse Hill. Security forces kept watch on the building until a young man fitting the description of one of the suspects emerged.

But Jean Charles de Menezes was not a *jihad*ist. The Brazilian electrician was entirely unconnected to terrorism of any kind. He had come to London to earn money, hoping to return home one day and invest in a farm.

As Menezes made his way to a job in Kilburn later that day, he was followed by several plainclothes policemen. He caught a bus to Stockwell tube station, then sat waiting for his train to move off. Before it did so, the firearms cops rushed into his carriage, grabbed him and shot him dead. A total of eleven shots into his head and shoulder, in full view of the other passengers.

The Met initially messed up big-time by claiming that Menezes was trying to resist arrest, but eventually came clean and admitted this was not the case – and that they had made a tragic error. The Commissioner issued a full apology.

The public remains divided. I'm surprised by the tactics used, and can't help thinking that had the drills been carried out more thoroughly, he might still be alive. But then again, following the events of 7 and 21 July, the Met received 761 calls reporting suspected suicide bombers, and dealt with every single one.

Ultimately, as tragic as Jean Charles de Menezes' death unquestionably was, those firearms cops walked up to a person they suspected of being a suicide bomber and shot him at point-blank range, having seen the effects of suicide attacks at first hand. If he'd been carrying a device, they'd have been hailed as national heroes. I think back to my time in Alpha Troop and wonder if I'd have done anything differently.

Robbie tells me he's busier than a one-armed Baghdad bricklayer but his interest is piqued when I ask him to check out if there's any more int on Abu Ubaida al-Masri.

'The Al Qaeda bombmaker?'

'That's the one. Also known as Midhat Mursi al-Sayid Umar and Abu Khabab al-Masri.'

'What have we got on him already?' he asks, pencil at the ready.

I know he's a chemist and part of Osama bin Laden's inner circle. He was born in Egypt and was among a contingent of Egyptians who fought the Soviets in Afghanistan and was then sighted in Bosnia and Chechnya before his arrival in Britain. He also travelled under an alias to Munich in 1995 and requested asylum. His suit was rejected; he was jailed pending deportation and then released.

He returned to Afghanistan in 2000 where, according to the Americans, he ran the infamous Derunta training camp and used dogs and other animals for a series of chemical experiments. As an expert in IED design, he personally trained Richard Reid, the shoe bomber, and

Zacarias Moussaoui. He is also the author of the official Al Qaeda explosives manual.

Robbie pulls him up on his computer screen. 'Al-Masri ... late forties, five foot seven, muscular, greying black hair and beard. Missing two fingers, probably as the result of an explosion in Chechnya during the 1990s. Now suspected of being AQ's top bombmaker ... Oh, and the United States has a five-million-dollar bounty on his head, so—'

'No, Robbie, we don't get to trouser the five mil.'

'So if we're not in this for the money . . .' he grins '. . . why are we interested in him?'

There's been chatter about him coming up with a new breed of homemade detonator. And it's got me thinking. Why would he need to design a new detonator?

'Because he's devised a new type of IED?'

My thinking precisely. But I've got to head up to Warwickshire to meet the Russians.

We're sitting in a swanky restaurant and I'm feeling particularly vulnerable. The UK is one of Russia's major espionage targets and there are many agents working here.

Russia has an estimated eighty-eight thousand millionaires and Putin is determined to return her to superpower status by building a strong economy, winning international respect and restoring foreign influence. 'There's no such thing as a former intelligence officer,' he once said. And don't I know it. They haven't stopped trying to grill me all night. And, typically, they're giving us fuck-all in return. They're also angry that Britain is providing sanctuary to Boris Berezovsky, the exiled oligarch – not that any of us here tonight can do much about it.

As the diplomatic small-talk eventually subsides into drunken revelry, the Russians start to open up. This is intelligence work in its rawest form: getting pissed and remaining in control.

I decide it's time to up the ante.

'So, Major, what you can share with us today?' the general asks, for the umpteenth time.

I offer him my empty vodka glass for a refill. 'Well, I suppose there is one thing . . .'

I mention the Black Widows, and can see his interest is piqued. They're a group of mainly Chechen female suicide bombers whose soubriquet is down to the fact that the majority of them lost male members of their families when Chechnya went head to head with Putin.

'They're dressed from head to toe in black and wear the so-called "martyr's belt", filled with explosives. The first Black Widow was Khava Barayeva, who blew herself up at a military base in Chechnya in June 2000.'

He waves a hand dismissively. 'We know all this already.'

'I'm sure you do, General, but what do you know of their recruiter?'

His eyes gleam like a James Bond villain's at a poker table. I'm about to give him some serious int that is going to win him a Putin-sized pat on the back. In fact, it's not secret intelligence, it's intelligence that we've gleaned from the internet – but, at his level, he won't know that.

'The main recruiter is a mysterious, dark-eyed, middle-aged woman known as Black Fatima.' I give him a description of her hooked nose and dark hair, and explain that she's been spotted in virtually every location where a Black Widow bombing has taken place.

'We know that a resident in Grozny, Medna Bayrakova, can identify her – she vividly remembers her showing up at her front door.' Apparently she asked if she could speak to Bayrakova's twenty-six-year-old daughter Zareta, and, unaware that anything was amiss, Bayrakova let the visitor into her house.

'The daughter and Black Fatima spent half an hour in the bedroom. When they left, she told her mother she was walking the woman to the bus stop. She still hadn't returned an hour later. Then several men in camouflage uniform came to the door and told

Bayrakova they'd taken her daughter away – told her she'd agreed to marry one of their members.'

Unsurprisingly, Bayrakova protested violently, not least because her daughter had been suffering from tuberculosis. The men in combats told her that they would give her medication and make sure she was well looked after.

'Bayrakova and her husband next saw their daughter twenty-four days later, when Chechen rebels seized the Dubrovka Theatre in Moscow. Apparently her dark eyes were unmistakable, even though they were only visible above a black veil on the television screen. Her hands were clasped firmly below a martyr's belt. She'd joined the Black Widows.'

He's lapping it up.

'I remember the incident like it was yesterday.' He recounts how on 3 October 2002 fifty heavily armed Chechen terrorists besieged a theatre in Moscow, taking more than eight hundred hostages and terrorizing them for several days with hostage-, suicide- and command-initiated IEDs. They then seized a school in Beslan near the Russia-Georgia border in September 2004 and threatened to kill more than a thousand hostages with IEDs and small arms. By the end of the siege, 339 students, teachers and parents had been killed, and at least seven hundred injured.

'The Moscow theatre siege ended when OSNAZ

forces pumped a chemical agent into the building's ventilation system – all but two of the terrorists died from it. But when the Chechens seized the school in Beslan, they deployed suicide bombers with dead man's switches, and dogs to provide early warning of the gas. They also wore body armour and gas masks.'

Now that we're new best mates, I spend the rest of the evening plying him with vodka and pumping him for information.

He tells me about the DTMF radio-controlled bombs being used in Chechnya, and that wires, charges and other explosive components used in a series of IEDs in Afghanistan originate from two factories in Pakistan. I make a mental note of their names – I'll have to write them up later.

'What do you know about Maximus?' the general asks. Apparently Maximus is a nineteen-year-old European Muslim, living on the outskirts of Sarajevo, who plans to carry out a suicide attack on a European embassy in Bosnia.

As we polish off the rest of the bottle, I glance at my watch. It's 4 a.m. My Jekyll and Hyde performance is over. At least for now.

34

Depth of friendship does not depend on length of acquaintance.

Rabindranath Tagore

8 September 2005

As we drive along this long stretch of dusty road, the warm desert breeze gently blowing through our hair, I can't help but feel captivated by the magic of this place. Robbie and I sit in companionable silence for a few moments as I think ruefully of the promise I made to Lucy last year. I told her I'd never go back to Iraq. And I'm sure I meant it at the time. But the problem is I feel exhilarated, truly alive, every time I find myself in a warzone. We're still together – by the skin of our teeth – but I don't know how long it's going to last. When I look into her eyes these days, the warmth that used to radiate from them seems to have been replaced by the kind of wildness I associate with cornered animals. I wish I could suppress my adolescent desire for danger and uncertainty, but I guess we sometimes just have to accept what we are.

A soldier watches us, hawk-like, through the sights of his machine-gun as we turn beneath the sangar's fortified watchtower. We roll on through the centre of the air station, past a series of tented sites, a Pizza Hut and a huge, well-stocked Naafi until we finally arrive at the entrance to a compound of green two-man Portakabins.

Robbie and I report to the gatehouse, where a young infantry NCO hands us the keys to our hut. It's twenty metres or so along a covered walkway several rows to our left and comes fitted with two bunk beds, a locker, a table and chairs, and air-conditioning. It's completely devoid of character, but that's fine by us: we're not going to be spending much time in it. We dump our kit and make our way across to Divisional Headquarters, the former airport hotel.

Scores of soldiers are lugging their weapons and Bergens into the huge terminal building. Some are going home. Others are heading north. A large sign hangs above the entrance: *Headquarters Multi-National Force Division South East welcomes you*.

We push open the huge smoked-glass doors into the air-conditioned foyer.

'Do you know where you're going, sir?' asks the young airman behind the desk as he hands us our passes.

'Yes, thanks,' I reply. 'I used to work here.' I spent the

last two months of my Iraq tour planning counter-bomber operations from this building.

We navigate our way through a series of interconnecting corridors until we finally reach the operations centre. The hotel's erstwhile dining room is filled with banks of desktop computers. Scores of staff officers of all nationalities are working alongside their British counterparts, tapping away diligently at their keyboards as radio traffic booms out of the speakers and live news feeds play continually across plasma screens.

Nothing's changed except the faces. Everything's done at breakneck speed. People are shouting; the phones are ringing. It's just like the old days.

'Who the fuck are you?' asks an arrogant-looking infantry major. 'Robocop?'

It's a fair one, I suppose. I'm wearing an assault vest with eight magazines of ammunition; I've got a Heckler & Koch G3 assault rifle hanging from my shoulder, a fighting knife strapped to my vest and a Sig Sauer semi-automatic pistol in my drop holster.

'When were you last ambushed, sir?' Robbie echoes my thoughts precisely. The last time I was here my team and I were caught out by a group of Shia militia on the way back from an IED incident. It was the most terrifying thing I've ever experienced. We had the bare minimum of weapons and ammunition and were heavily outnumbered. I promised myself afterwards that I'd never put myself in that position again.

The major responds with a curl of the lip and strides away.

A young corporal from the Intelligence Corps spots us standing vacantly at the edge of the room. 'Major Hunter and Sergeant Lawford? The boss is expecting you next door.'

The room he guides us to is equally large, but deathly silent.

We're met by a stocky, affable major. At first glance, Mark Holland, the deputy head of Joint Intelligence appears older than his thirty-something years. 'So you're the guys from Whitehall? Welcome to Basra, fellas. How was your journey?'

I tell him we've actually been down in Shaibetha for a couple of days with the Joint Force EOD Group. 'We thought they'd be able to give us a pretty comprehensive understanding of the current battle-picture.'

He nods sagely and gestures in the direction of a small mountain of crates of bottled water stacked in the corner of the room. 'What can I offer you – water or coffee?'

We go for the second option. So does he. He's survived on a diet of strong coffee and no sleep for weeks. Now he's just looking forward to going home. He's engaged to an NCO in the Royal Military Police and all he wants to do is get back to her. They're getting married soon and are looking forward to starting a family.

He puts down his mug and cracks on: 'The reason I've asked you guys to come over is that since the beginning of last month over a dozen servicemen have been killed by EFPs. We believe the IEDs are being smuggled in from Iran, but we can't say for sure whether the Iranian government is involved or if it's a splinter element using Iran for their own purposes.'

It's virtually impossible to stop anything being smuggled across the long and very porous border.

'According to US intelligence, the Iranian Islamic Revolutionary Guard Corps and their LH bombmakers have been providing the hardware, which has obviously encouraged the Mahdi Army to up the ante and kill as many British soldiers as possible.'

I ask him to take us through the 'What do we know?' and 'What do we think we know?' routine.

His team thinks Iran is providing material support for attacks on British and American troops, and that the Iranian Revolutionary Guard Corps (IRGC) Qods Force is the primary vehicle for this activity in Iraq.

'The Qods Force is the IRGC's Special Forces. We believe their role is to train extremists and insurgents in terrorist tactics and guerrilla warfare. They're providing advice, training and weapons to insurgents and terrorist groups.'

'You're not wrong,' Robbie says. 'These guys are about as much fun as a group hug at a burns centre.'

'Last month we seized a weapons shipment close to the Iranian border containing triggering devices and other IED components – and an Iran-produced Misagh-1 Man Portable Air Defence System missile was recovered following a failed attack near Baghdad International Airport on the sixteenth of August.'

That also ties in with what we've uncovered. 'We've been told by both Iranian and Iraqi detainees that the Qods Force supports any extremist group engaged in anti-Coalition targeting.'

Money, weapons, training – they provide whatever it takes.

'According to our reports,' Robbie says, 'the money and weapons are escorted across the border using a range of different vehicles that only travel at night. Much of the weaponry comes via the Mehran crossing point, which is also used by Mahdi Army personnel heading the other way for training.' He pauses. 'OK, so where does that leave us?'

Mark refills our mugs. 'We need to know where the bombs are being made. We think we know the source of the technological know-how and we've got a pretty good idea where the parts are coming from, but we're still not certain where the actual manufacturing is taking place.'

Robbie brings out his notebook.

'OK. What else do you know?' I gulp a mouthful of coffee. 'What else is happening here in theatre?'

Suicide bombings are clearly top of his list. Since 2003 there have been more of them in Iraq than Hamas have racked up in Israel, Hezbollah in Lebanon, and the Tamil Tigers in Sri Lanka combined.

'Many if not most of the perpetrators are foreign fighters. In the main, they belong to Al Qaeda, and are spawned by second-generation *jihad*ists trained in Afghanistan during the 1990s. The overwhelming majority target Iraqi security forces and Shiite civilians rather than Coalition forces – with ATOs and WIS teams as the notable exceptions.'

'Yeah, the boss was targeted by both the Shias and the Sunnis when he was here in 2004,' Robbie says.

'Well, they've definitely not let up any.' He tells us about Captain Pete Norton, who was the 2i/c of the Combined Explosives Exploitation Cell. On 24 July, a vehicle patrol from the Georgia National Guard was hit by a huge device in the Al Bayaa district of Baghdad. The explosion completely destroyed a Hummer and killed four US personnel. Pete and his team were tasked to the scene. As they were carrying out their arrival drills, he was alerted to the presence of a command wire IED.

Being an ATO, and knowing that insurgents in the area used secondary devices, Pete instructed his team and the US forces in the immediate vicinity to remain with their vehicles while he went forward to confirm the sighting.

Moments later, there was another huge explosion. Pete sustained a traumatic amputation of the left leg and serious blast and fragmentation injuries to his right leg, arms and lower abdomen. He was still conscious when his team came forward to give him life-saving first aid, and his only concern was for their safety. He realized he'd activated a VO and was concerned about the presence of further devices. Before he would allow anybody to give him first aid he insisted on telling his team which areas were safe and where they could move, and coolly directed all follow-up actions in spite of his horrific injuries.

I'm stunned. I had no idea Pete had been hit – but his behaviour doesn't surprise me at all. We served in the same squadron when I first joined 11 EOD. He was an inspiration even then. 'He's known in the trade as Perfect Pete . . .'

'As it turned out,' Mark says quietly, 'there was a tertiary device less than ten metres away. He saved a lot of lives that day.'

It takes us a moment or two to compose ourselves. With a visible effort, Mark shifts his attention to current operations. 'We're just putting together the targeting packs for a raid on the Office of the Matyr Sadr (OMS) offices in Basra. We're expecting to find an Aladdin's cave of weapons and explosives in there. And seeing as the place doubles as the Mahdi Army HQ, it wouldn't surprise me if we found a shit-load of EFP devices in there too.'

It certainly sounds as if they're taking the fight to the enemy. Part of me wishes I could be there with them. 'I was targeted by those fuckers last year. The cheeky sods even filmed me neutralizing a device outside their building.'

My sandbag stories feel distinctly out of place after Pete Norton's story, so I just ask Mark what Robbie and I can do for him at the strategic level.

He asks for as much historical data as we can supply on all previous IED events to help them start to identify patterns of activity. 'We'd also like to know who the key individuals are in the EFP procurement chain and, more specifically, how they operate. Is the purchaser a front company, an individual or an intermediary? Do they conduct company visits? Do they employ any counter-intelligence measures? All that sort of stuff . . .'

Robbie's scribbling away like a man possessed.

'And we want to know everything we can about their manufacturing processes, transport modes and assembly nodes. Are they made in Iran or Iraq? Do they carry out any R and D? Any pre-deployment testing before they bring them across the border?'

'Getting all this, Robbie?'

'Every word, Boss,' he says, pausing to tug his forelock.

I tell Mark we're going to focus our efforts on identifying the components in the IED chain, along with all previous incidents. That way we'll be able to assist him with the pattern identification piece. 'We'll obviously action all the intelligence requirements you've listed, but in addition to that, we'll look closely at the manufacturers of those components, and drill right down into the detail. We'll get batch numbers, date stamps, the lot, and wherever possible we'll also do a complete audit of the manufacturers' sales records.'

I explain that most of the firms involved in the sale and manufacture of IED components are based in North America or East Asia, so enforcement authorities in pro-Western states such as Japan and Taiwan should be on-side when it comes to tackling their illicit trade.

'The only problem area will probably be China. In my experience, the Chinese authorities will only act on specific, incontrovertible evidence, and that might pose some challenges. But, fuck it, we'll cross that particular bridge when we come to it.'

'That sounds like a plan.'

Mark asks if there's anything else we need from him.

'Actually, sir, there is one thing,' Robbie says. 'Since many of our Coalition partners only have a few years of experience in this field, the reports coming out of theatre sometimes lack detail. Anything you can do to improve the recording of IED incidents would be very welcome.'

I pick up the baton. 'The other thing is that from 1979 to the mid-eighties the Iraqi government allegedly sponsored the 15 May Organization, led by a Palestinian called Muhammad al-Umari, a.k.a. Abu Ibrahim. Ibrahim is widely believed to have been an expert bombmaker who specialized in the manufacture of unusual variants of plastic explosive and was also highly skilled at the concealment of sophisticated explosive devices.

'Four years ago, Israeli security forces raided two refugee camps, and while under interrogation, a number of the detainees stated that they had received military training – including how to manufacture IEDs – in Iraq. We believe the trainer was Ibrahim, and that with the assistance of Iraqi intelligence, he carried out numerous attacks and assassinations in London, Rome and Athens. A baby was killed and twenty-four people were wounded when one of his bombs detonated at an Israeli-owned restaurant in West Berlin. He also bombed a Pan Am airliner.'

An Iraqi in possession of bomb-making equipment

was arrested at Heathrow in December 1979, and a year later a further attempt – with explosives concealed in a shaving-foam container – was foiled by alert security staff.

The Iraqi embassy in London was rocked by a suspected explosion in June 1981, but police officers on the scene were not allowed to investigate. Kurdish protesters managed to gain access to the Iraqi embassy in 1991 and discovered ammunition and bomb-making accessories. 'It looks like Ibrahim has been a very busy boy – and while he's presumed dead by some, we believe he's still very much alive and possibly living in the Al Mansour district of Baghdad.'

'And you want us to find out if he's still there? Leave it with me. I'll do what I can.'

The warm desert air is heavily perfumed with the stench of shit and decaying rubbish. Some things never change in Iraq. But as we're about to jump on the transport over to the terminal building I realize that others do – considerably. A convoy is parked at the side of the road, preparing to depart, and four Gurkhas are arguing about who should be in the front vehicle.

'What's all that about?' Robbie asks.

'None of them wants to travel in the front vehicle. I'm guessing it's because of the EFP threat.'

The Gurkhas are some of the bravest and most

fearless soldiers in the world. If they're scared, it speaks volumes about the impact EFP are already having on our soldiers' morale. We need to do something about this, and quickly.

Back on the aircraft, Robbie snores away happily. I look around the cabin and find myself staring at the two hundred or so soldiers around me. They seem completely exhausted: their gaunt faces and weather-beaten combats tell an all too familiar story.

I'd read something on the internet recently that summed it up perfectly.

The average age of the British soldier is nineteen. At home he'd still be considered wet behind the ears and barely old enough to buy a round of drinks. Yet here he's old enough to die for his country. Like most boys their age, our young soldiers aren't particularly keen on hard work, but they'd definitely prefer to be grafting in Iraq than signing on the dole back in the UK.

The average squaddie left comprehensive school as a modest student, played some form of sport, drove a crap car, and in all probability had a girlfriend who broke up with him while he was out here. When he returns home he'll be about a stone lighter than he was when he left – because he's been fighting from dawn to dusk and beyond. He may have trouble spelling, so letter-writing is a pain, but he can strip and reassemble his rifle in less than a minute, even in the dark. He can recite every detail of a machine-gun or grenade launcher and use either if he has to. He digs trenches and toilets without the aid of machines and can apply first aid like a professional paramedic. He can march until he is told to stop, or stand perfectly still until he is told to move.

The British soldier obeys orders instantly and without hesitation, but he's certainly not without a rebellious spirit or a sense of personal dignity. He's proudly self-sufficient. He always has two sets of uniform with him: he washes one and wears the other. And he keeps his water bottle full and his feet dry. Sometimes he forgets to brush his teeth, but he never forgets to clean his rifle. He cooks his own meals, mends his own clothes and fixes his own hurts. If you're thirsty, he'll share his water with you; if you're hungry, his food. He'll even share his life-saving ammunition in the heat of a fire-fight if you run low.

He has learnt to use his hands like weapons and regards his weapon as an extension of his hands. He can save your life or he can take it, because that is his job – it's what a soldier does. He often works twice as long and hard as a civilian, for half the pay. And he has nowhere much to spend it.

He's seen more suffering and death than he should have in his short lifetime, and has wept in private and in public for friends who have fallen in combat. While standing rigidly to attention, he feels every chord of the National Anthem vibrate through his body. He'd kick off with anyone who showed disrespect to his regiment or his country, while vigorously defending their right to be an individual.

He's prepared to risk his life daily in order to protect ours, and he asks for nothing in return – except our respect, friendship and understanding. We may not like what he does, but sometimes he doesn't either – he does it because he has to.

I'm not sure who wrote it, but he's said it all.

35

Life is not about what you've gained, but what you've done.

Wong Ka Kui

12 September 2005

The tantalizing aroma of freshly ground coffee and warmed croissants is too much to bear. 'Am I too late to change my mind?'

'I knew it . . .' Robbie passes me one of the delicious pastries. 'You're rubbish. I knew you'd break.'

Robbie had been looking into Iranian and Hezbollah front companies for several months before we deployed to Iraq, but we've both been working on them flat out since we got back. There are many ways to attack an IED network – identifying their support elements, locating their training facilities, recruiters, financiers and trainers – but targeting their logistic network is without doubt the most effective. It's the same as conventional warfare.

I remove a lever-arch box file marked *Iranian IEDs* from the cabinet and pile the intelligence reports on my desk. I work through them one by one, scanning every page. My brain has gone into Google mode, searching for similarities in the components being used. I promised Mark Holland we'd focus our investigations on the IED procurement chain, looking to identify the manufacturers. Then, by auditing their sales records, we should be able to identify the front companies. But they won't be handing this stuff to us on a plate: we'll need to drill right down into the detail.

I look at the number of devices used in each attack: whether they are single or multiple charges; whether the charges are artillery shells, mines, improvised explosives or EFPs. I examine the source of the ordnance, the insurgents' favoured types of explosive – and ask myself the question why. I knock back cup after cup of strong coffee, taking copious notes on the anomalies. And finally I strike gold.

Earlier this year an unexploded IED in Iraq – similar to those being used against British forces – was found to contain an American-made computer circuit. According to the report, the serial numbers and sales records show that the circuit was purchased from a company in California and subsequently made its way through to Mayrow General Trading, a company in Dubai.

I fire up the computer and begin sifting through the various databases. They appear to have shipped a number of components from Dubai to Iran, after which they've ended up in IEDs. The presence of particular circuit boards and timers in those devices suggests the US as the country of origin – and they've had a trade embargo with Iran for decades. The Iranians are using Mayrow as a facilitator to get around it – which means they're using American components in bombs that are killing American servicemen. That's really taking the piss.

I know we're getting closer. But the jigsaw is far from complete. 'Robbie?'

He doesn't respond.

I glance across the room. He's just sitting there in stunned silence.

'What's wrong?'

He looks up from his screen, his face a mask of anguish. 'You'd better come over here, Chris . . .'

The press release in front of him reads:

With great sadness and regret, the Ministry of Defence has confirmed the name of the British Army officer killed in an attack in Iraq on 11 September 2005.

My stomach sinks as I scroll down the page. The name jumps out at me.

At approximately 1100hrs local time, an armoured Snatch Land Rover was attacked in Basra City by an improvised explosive device. Major Mark Holland was killed in the explosion.

Three other British soldiers also travelling in the vehicle were seriously injured. The casualties were taken to the UK Field Hospital at Shaiba Logistics Base and are now in a stable condition. An Iraqi civilian was also injured in the attack and was taken to an Iraqi hospital for treatment.

Major Holland was thirty-four years old, single, and came from the London area. He joined the Army in 1988 and served with the Intelligence Corps. At the time of his death, he was serving as a staff officer with the headquarters of Multi-national Division (South East).

Major Holland's death brings the number of UK soldiers killed in Iraq to 95.

Fucking hell. I can't believe it. Every time a soldier is hit by an IED it feels personal. But when it's somebody you know, somebody you've worked with, somebody you've shared a brew and a laugh with . . .

I feel completely numb.

We were only with him for a matter of hours, but even in that short time it was obvious that he was a brilliant officer who genuinely gave a shit. Robbie and I were completely energized by his unquenchable enthusiasm.

'What a fucking waste . . .' They're the only words Robbie seems able to muster right now, but they're straight from the heart.

We stand there in silence, but I know he can hear Mark's voice as clearly in his head as I can in mine.

We'd also like to know who the key individuals are in the EFP procurement chain and, more specifically, how they operate. Is the purchaser a front company, an individual or an intermediary? Do they conduct company visits? Do they employ any counter-intelligence measures? All that sort of stuff . . .

Mark knew the answers to those questions would save soldiers' lives. Perhaps they might have saved his own.

We go back to work with heavy hearts but a newly strengthened resolve, and prepare to finish what we've started.

As Robbie continues with the internet and database searches, I break open another lever-arch file and continue going through the hard-copy reports. Before long we're bouncing information back and forth, and I'm surrounded by scraps of paper on which I've scribbled names, dates, locations and details of suppliers and distributors. I stick them on the wall and link them with pencil lines whenever I can find a correlation. Before long it looks like a giant spider's web.

'OK,' Robbie says. 'According to the records, Mayrow is the hub of a procurement network that's been operating since the early part of this decade. Dubai seems to be a bit of a centre for shell companies seeking to buy weapons parts and technology for countries that can't import them legally.'

As we trawl through the databases and files, a clearer picture of Mayrow's activities begins to emerge. It seems they've been working in tandem with three other outfits that place alternate orders with US firms for thousands of electronic parts. On paper they appear to be separate and legitimate trading companies seeking parts for a variety of industrial uses, yet all four share the same business address and the same principals.

'Right, I've got the names of the other three companies: Atlinx Electronics, Madjico Micro Electronics and Micatic General Trading. And Mr Ali Akbar Yahya, a forty-eight-year-old businessman, appears to be running or, at the very least, operating all four.'

The Mayrow network has acquired thousands of sensitive parts from manufacturers in California, Florida, Georgia and New Jersey. It looks as though they've created a wall between the Iranian entities and the US suppliers, and succeeded in camouflaging the true end-users.

Jo, our civvies analyst, appears as I pour us another

couple of coffees from the percolator. 'Another soldier's been killed in Iraq . . .' She hands me a printout.

I piece together Mark's final moments. He'd just finished a meeting at Basra Palace and was waiting for a helicopter. But the heli had a mechanical fault and the pick-up was cancelled. Mark needed to get back to the office, so he hitched a lift with a patrol that was heading to Basra air station.

Mark was in the passenger seat, to the left of the rear door – presumably because the Snatch vehicles were fully manned – and as the Land Rovers passed through Basra City, his was struck by an EFP device. The fist-sized copper slug punched straight through the armour beside him at about two kilometres a second. It would have killed him instantly. The three others were evacuated by helicopter and are now being treated in the UK.

Mark was declared dead on arrival at the medical facility in Shaiba Log Base.

As I hand the report to Robbie, a dark cloud suddenly looms over us. Voldemort has walked in.

'Chris, Major Holland's parents have been on the phone to MoD Main Building. They'd like to speak to an IED specialist about the death of their son. I know it's not a very pleasant thing to have to do, but I'd very much appreciate you going to talk to them this afternoon.'

I'm completely thrown. It seems he does have a compassionate side after all.

The Hollands' flat is a short walk from Liverpool Street station. Photographs of Mark seem to adorn every wall, table and mantelpiece. They're everywhere – as a child, as a teenager and as a proud soldier in his ceremonial uniform. One thing seems not to have changed over the years: they all show the same happy, smiling face. The face of a son secure in the love of his immediate family.

Mrs Holland's eyes are raw with tears shed and unshed. She's clutching a framed photo of Mark in exactly the same way my mother did after she was told of Tim's death.

'Thank you so much for coming, Chris . . .' Beneath Mr Holland's quiet dignity I can see him struggling to endure the unendurable. 'I know this is going to be very difficult for you, but we'd like you to tell us honestly – and candidly – exactly how Mark died. We know he was killed instantly, but we want to know more about the bomb and what it would have done to him . . .'

I'm tortured by the thought of causing them more pain, but they genuinely want to know what happened to their son. It's the very least I can do for them.

'I know this will offer you little in the way of comfort, but before I go into the detail, I want you to know that Mark wouldn't have felt a thing . . .'

36

An eye for an eye will only make the whole world blind.

Mahatma Gandhi

31 August 2006

As the plane touches down on the airport runway, I'm still reeling from Sophie's comment this morning. She overheard a conversation Lucy and I were having about the night I was ambushed in Basra back in 2004. As I gave her a kiss and picked up my case, she asked me where I was going. I gave her my stock answer: 'I'm going to speak to some goodies who want to stop some baddies from doing bad things.'

What she said next hit me for six: 'Are you going to have to kill anybody this time, Daddy?'

I'm absolutely gutted. No four-year-old should have to deal with something like that.

As I pass through the third baggage search in a long line of security checks, it strikes me that if a single bead of sweat appears during questioning – which is pretty much inevitable in the middle of a Mediterranean summer – my underwear, wash-bag and pretty much anything else that could cause embarrassment will be turned out in full view of the two hundred people behind me.

The overzealous official picks his way through each item in my luggage, barking, 'What is this?' and 'What is this?' This part of the process isn't celebrated in their tourist commercials. 'What are you doing in our country?'

I tell him I'm giving a presentation at a counter-IED conference.

'And what is this?' he asks, removing a green spherical object from my hand luggage.

I do my best to keep an entirely straight face. 'It's an apple.'

These guys are clearly on edge. The whole place is simmering. But that's hardly surprising. Last month a terrorist group launched a major operation against them. They began with a diversionary rocket and mortar shell attack on the settlements and military camps closest to the border, then crossed into the country and attacked an army patrol, killing three soldiers and capturing two others. The prisoners were spirited back across the border to be used as bargaining counters by the terrorists.

An IED killed all four crew of a main battle tank as it

tried to follow them. Another soldier was killed when he attempted to rescue his mates from the burning tank.

Their government immediately ordered air, naval and ground attacks against terrorist targets across the border, and the terrorists responded by launching hundreds of rockets back at them. The conflict has resulted in the deaths of hundreds of people, mostly civilians. More than a million and a half civilians have been displaced, and a warship was damaged off the coast when an unmanned drone rammed into it, exploding on impact.

The UN Security Council approved a resolution on 11 August in an effort to end the hostilities. A few days later a tentative ceasefire was agreed, and tentative it seems to have remained.

Having survived the security checks and a hair-raising taxi-ride through the teeming streets of the capital, I check in at the oak-panelled reception desk of my water-front hotel and am handed the keys to 1205. No surprises there. It's my third visit and they've put me in the same room every time.

The receptionist tells me it's 6 p.m. local. My meeting's in half an hour.

I head upstairs to drop off my kit, but slip my laptop, phone and memory-stick into my day-sack. I'm definitely not leaving those in my room tonight.

This city is one of the most cosmopolitan places in

the Middle East. I walk past the salt-water pool and marina, then along the boardwalk. Music blasts out of the balls-achingly trendy bars and cafés that line the beach, and slim, tanned bodies laze in the sun or strut their stuff on the volleyball courts.

Elderly Russian ladies stroll arm in arm along the sand. Arab women bathe in the warm waters fully clothed, next to their scantily clad westernized counterparts.

Even though I'm ten minutes early Adam is already sitting at the far end of the bar – where he can see everybody entering and leaving. He's a freelance counter-IED consultant and we've known each other for years. I'm pretty sure he's a former member of their intelligence services, but he's never admitted it. Once again I find myself thinking of Putin's assertion that there's no such thing.

I feel ill at ease as soon as I walk inside. Dozens of pairs of eyes are burning into the back of my neck. Maybe I'm just being paranoid.

Adam greets me like a long-lost brother. We exchange pleasantries, grab a couple of beers and get straight down to business. I need to know about the IEDs Hezbollah are using against his fellow country-men, and their most effective counter-measures.

He asks what I'm able to tell him about Afghanistan.

'Only what I've read in the papers . . .'

'Of course!' His smile broadens. 'So tell me what you've read in the papers.'

I admire his style.

I tell him that ten US and four Canadian soldiers were killed by IEDs in the first four months of 2006. Oh, and a senior Canadian diplomat perished in a suicide vehicle-borne IED attack. 'During the same period in 2005, one US soldier was killed by a roadside bomb.'

'That's all?'

The only other information I have to share with him is that explosive remnants seem to be forming the basis of the majority of IEDs used in Afghanistan. By March this year, nearly 31,000 tonnes of munitions had been found in about 800 caches.

'And what sort of caches were they?'

'Everything from small shipping containers to large bunkers.' I remind him that I need his take on Hezbollah.

He tells me that they pioneered the use of IEDs against military forces after the 1982 invasion of Lebanon. His countrymen withdrew to a buffer zone in the south in 1985 and Hezbollah continued their IED attacks on their vehicles right up until their withdrawal in May 2000. 'One such bomb killed one of our generals in early 1999. He was our highest-ranking officer to die in Lebanon.'

Adam gives me some more details on the tank hit.

Iran has been supplying Iraqi insurgents with the technological know-how to make shaped charges, which focus the blast upwards and can pierce even the most heavily armed vehicle. 'But you already know this. The British government has publicly accused Iran of such things, yes?'

His own country's forces have recently been attacked with platter charges, rectangular or circular pieces of flat metal with plastic explosives pressed onto one side. 'The explosive is usually the same weight as the platter, enabling it to be fired into the target at a range of about fifty metres. Both types of device are triggered with a passive infra-red sensor.'

I ask what he can tell me about the Iran connection.

'I've read that Iran sent ninety of its fighters across the border shortly after the fall of the Saddam regime – in order to neutralize any attempt by your Coalition forces to activate opposition from within Iraq.' He goes on to say that elements of the IRGC are leading many of the operations directed against the Coalition forces.

'So how do you counter these devices, Adam?'

Once again, he deliberately ignores my question, asking me what I know about the airline bomb plot and Rashid Rauf. And once again I tell him I can only talk about what I've read in the papers and seen on the internet. I'm not sanctioned to share classified intelligence.

Undercover police officers reportedly witnessed two young Muslims filming what appeared to be a martyrdom video three weeks ago in a small apartment in the East End of London. 'As you bomb, you will be bombed; as you kill, you will be killed,' one of them said. And as he warmed to his theme he said he hoped God would give them some serious Brownie points.

'According to the papers, the surveillance operation began as a result of information received from the July the seventh bombings last year.' Flats were apparently bugged, phones tapped, emails monitored and cash transactions checked. Later that day Scotland Yard made the decision to arrest them, and in doing so got in the way of a plot to detonate liquid explosives on board a number of commercial airliners travelling from the UK to the United States.

'Around twenty-four suspects were arrested. They appeared to have been aiming to destroy ten aircraft in mid-flight. The liquid explosives would have been smuggled on board in the suspects' hand luggage.'

'So which airlines were going to be targeted?' he asks. 'And where were they flying from and to?'

According to the media, the airlines included American Airlines, British Airways, Continental Airlines, and United Airlines flights from London Heathrow and London Gatwick airports to Chicago, Illinois; Los Angeles, California; Miami, Florida;

Orlando, Florida; Boston, Massachusetts; Newark, New Jersey; New York City; San Francisco, California; Cleveland, Ohio, and Washington DC.

'And what about the bomb?'

I explain that the police found a plastic bin filled with liquid at a London address, along with batteries, nearly a dozen empty Lucozade bottles, rubber gloves, digital scales and a disposable camera. 'One theory is that the camera was going to be the firing device, and a hollowed-out battery would be filled with explosive and used as an improvised detonator. The main charge would be secreted in the bottles, modified to facilitate the introduction of liquid organic peroxide dyed with orange food colouring.' Peroxide-based liquid explosives are sensitive to heat, shock and friction, so they can be initiated simply by fire or by an electrical charge.

'That makes sense. But what prompted the arrests?'

Rashid Rauf was alleged to have been one of the ring-leaders of the plot, sanctioned by Al Qaeda's 2i/c, Ayman al-Zawahri. 'I guess they were triggered by fears that his arrest in Pakistan might force his accomplices' hand – that they might have felt the need to carry out the attacks sooner than they'd originally intended.'

'So liquids of any kind have now been banned on flights between Britain and the US, nearly half a million passengers were affected and twenty thousand bags were misplaced at Heathrow . . .' Adam's implication is clear, even without the raised eyebrow.

I feel my face redden, because there is no excuse. It's no secret that Al Qaeda considers an attack on aviation assets one of its highest priorities, and everybody within the security community knows that they try to repeat a failed or aborted attack – which means the security services either failed to ensure that Heathrow had adequate contingency plans or to spot the connection between what Rashid Rauf and his mates were up to and 1995's Project Bojinka.

In January of that year a suspicious fire broke out in a Manila apartment. Its three occupants – Ramsi Ahmed Yousef, Abdul Hakim Murad and Wali Khan Amin Shah – were suspected of Al Qaeda affiliations and had attended pilot training schools in the Philippines. The resulting police search unearthed plans to destroy a dozen aircraft over the Pacific Ocean, along with a number of devices containing liquid chemicals. Yousef and Murad had developed a new breed of highly sophisticated and virtually undetectable nitro-glycerine bombs hidden in contact-lens solution bottles.

Yousef and Shah managed to escape, but Murad was arrested when he came back to retrieve his laptop computer and allegedly had a discussion with his captors about a plot to fly aircraft into the headquarters of the Central Intelligence Agency in Langley, Virginia.

The details of Project Bojinka were extracted from Murad's hard drive: to sabotage up to twelve civilian aircraft simultaneously and blow them up in mid-air as they crossed the west coast of the United States – or hijack and crash several commercial passenger jets into civilian and government buildings . . .

Adam has a point. We should have seen this coming.

He frightens up a couple of perfectly chilled Peronis and starts – albeit circuitously – to fulfil his side of the bargain. 'What do you know about al-Masri, Chris?'

'We were talking about counter-measures for Hezbollah EFP devices . . .'

He smiles. 'Actually, we were talking about the airline bomb plot – which is why I mention al-Masri. What do you know about him?'

'I've read that the CIA believes he had hepatitis C and died from it earlier this year.'

'You mean the same CIA that claimed he was killed in an attack in January 2006, then admitted they'd got it wrong?'

Where's he going with this?

'I can't say for sure,' he continues, 'but al-Masri is reputed to be a top Al Qaeda bombmaker who is particularly expert at designing IEDs that can be concealed in everyday items. I've heard rumours that he's still very much alive, and that he's been working on a new concealable detonator. Now this may be a long shot, but have you given any consideration to the possibility of him being the designer of the detonator for your airline liquid bomb?'

I tell him I'll certainly do that – then try once more to get him to answer my original question. 'Counter-measures?'

'OK, but first . . . what have you heard about the Hariri assassination?'

Rafik Hariri was a Lebanese politician and outspoken critic of Syria. The available evidence suggests he was most probably killed by a single suicide bomber driving a vehicle-borne IED containing up to a tonne of high explosive. 'I'm told the bomber parked up in front of the St George Hotel and detonated the device just as Hariri's convoy was passing. The sheer weight of explosive seems to me to tell us two things: as a former prime minister, Hariri would probably have had ECM and an armoured vehicle to overmatch – and whoever's responsible obviously didn't give a shit about how many other people were killed.'

'Which brings us neatly back to counter-measures . . .' He pauses. 'As a military man, you'll be aware that the best form of defence is attack. It sounds to me like your main focus should be on targeting the bombmakers.'

'Adam, we do things differently where I come from. Assassination isn't really our style.'

Posing with the Alpha Troop team.

Left: An Alpha Troop operator deals with an 'access denial device' outside a stronghold.

Below: An operator carefully positions a disruptor behind an IED.

Left: A member of the troop neutralizes a suicide IED during a training exercise. When the CO first tasked us with the development of counter-suicide-bomber tactics, some dyed-in-the-wool Northern Ireland veterans believed we were wasting valuable time and resources. But it wasn't raining when Noah started work on the Ark.

Below: Members of Alpha Troop fast-roping onto a target during a police training exercise.

Above: Soldiers first, operators second. I (*centre*) and my team of Assault IEDD personnel practise close-quarter combat skills.

Left and below: A police firearms team engage a suicide bomber at close range during a training exercise. Alpha Troop was instrumental in devising the procedures for countering a suicide-bomb attack on the British mainland – should such an attack ever occur.

Left: Alpha Troop warrant officer and I manually neutralize a car bomb during a counter-suicide-bomber exercise.

Left: March 2004. Two of the Colombian EOD operators from my syndicate control their robot from a remote monitor unit as they prepare to neutralize a car bomb.

Right: Having disrupted the device using the robot, one of the Colombian EOD operators begins the search for bomb components.

Below: Me (*centre*) with my syndicate of Colombian EOD operators. The two operators on the front row were later murdered by Revolutionary Armed Forces of Colombia (FARC) terrorists in separate IED attacks.

Left: We frequently travelled through the heart of militia territory, but were refused permission to carry firearms. Instead, armed police were assigned to escort us for the duration of our mission. We felt very vulnerable.

Below: CCTV footage aired on national television during the Operation Crevice (fertilizer bomb plot) court case. Almost as soon as the terrorist cell delivered the ammonium nitrate fertilizer to the storage unit in Hanwell, the security services installed covert cameras and replaced the ammonium nitrate with an inert substitute.

Below: A photofit image showing the similarity between one of the 21/7 bomber suspects (*left*) and Jean Charles de Menezes (*right*), who fatefully lived in the same apartment block and was killed by undercover policemen in a case of mistaken identity.

Below: An explosively formed projectile IED. When the device is detonated a dish is projected which forms an armour-piercing slug travelling at well over a thousand metres a second. These devices are armed remotely and are initiated when a vehicle passes a passive infra-red trigger.

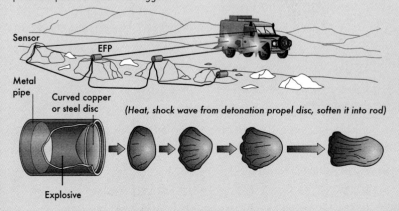

Sensor

EFP

Metal pipe

Curved copper or steel disc

(Heat, shock wave from detonation propel disc, soften it into rod)

Explosive

Left: Author neutralizing an IED by hand.

Below: 2007. Brummie left the Army and immediately became a hostile-environment close-protection operator in Iraq. Like many former soldiers who leave and are thrust into civilian life, he quickly became bored and was desperate to get back into the thick of the action.

Above: A miniature EOD robot used by the US Marine Corps EOD team who lived with us at Garmsir.

Below: Me and a team of private military contractors on the ranges, grouping and zeroing our secondary weapons – Glock 17 9mm pistols. We went on the ranges at least once a week to ensure there was no risk of 'skill-fade'.

Above: In 2008 I too was operating as a hostile-environment close-protection operator, in Helmand Province, Afghanistan. I had left the military to become a writer, but, like Brummie, I wasn't quite ready for civilian life.

Above: Two of the coalition students on the covert operators course Andy and I began teaching when we left the Army.

Above: September 2008. The Taliban spent the day forming up on the opposite side of the bridge, preparing for a mass attack. Their intention was to cross the heavily defended southern bridge. Within easy reach of it are the governor's compound, the police HQ, the intelligence services building and the prison – where dozens of their mates are holed up.

Left: About to deploy on a task in Lashkar Gah, Helmand's provincial capital. There was a constant threat of ambush, rocket attacks and suicide bombings.

Above: Driving through Lashkar Gah. Beyond the camp gates, the maze of city streets was crammed with potentially hostile forces; we had to scan every face, every building and vehicle, searching for signs of an ambush, a sniper or a roadside IED.

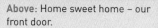

Above: Home sweet home – our front door.

Right: Inside the accommodation block we shared with a platoon of Jocks from the Scottish Regiment at the Forward Operating Base (FOB) in Garmsir, Helmand Province.

'Bigger than life and as brave as a lion.' WO2 Gary O'Donnell was the first person in twenty-six years to be awarded the George Medal twice.

'Oh, really?' he says. 'So how do you explain the Ahwaz bombings?'

In January this year eight people died and dozens were injured when two bombs exploded at a bank and a government building in the Iranian city of Ahwaz. Iran's foreign minister told reporters that Britain had to be held to account for its role in the atrocity. There was a third bombing the following month and the Intelligence Ministry arrested a number of suspects they claimed had ties with London. A government spokesman said, 'The mother of all corruption, Britain, has become an opponent of Iran. Our opponents are supported and empowered in London.'

'It's total nonsense,' I say. 'And, besides, targeted killings just don't work.'

'Well, I think you need to be tougher.' He leans towards me. 'Are you acquainted with *Lex Tallionis*?'

'An eye for an eye,' I say. 'A tooth for a tooth. But it's not one of our laws.'

'Perhaps it should be. If people don't want to share this world with us, then we don't have to share it with them. And if they want to bomb our women and children and destroy our way of life, then we have no choice but to destroy them first.' There is no longer a hint of warmth in his expression. 'It's like my gardener used to say: when dealing with hornets, first you find the nest and then you burn it.'

I think of Mark and Gaz and Jimmy, and find myself sorely tempted to agree, but deep down I still believe it's wrong. And it only escalates the conflict.

Ten years ago, the chief bombmaker of Hamas, Yehiya Ayyash, was assassinated by a state intelligence service. Also known as 'The Engineer', he was an expert in suicide-bomb construction and was wanted for the murder of scores of civilians. He had been on the run for two years.

On 5 January 1996 he received a telephone call from his father on a mobile phone belonging to the owner of the house in which he was then hiding. The phone exploded as he identified himself, killing him instantly. It had been a gift from a relative, who subsequently disappeared. I suspect that a glass or two were raised by his victims' families that night.

But retribution was swift. A month after Ayyash's death, a Hamas suicide bomber boarded a bus in the centre of a Middle Eastern city and killed twenty-two people. Within an hour, another rammed his car into a bus queue. There were eighty more casualties. Ayyash's successor, a Palestinian electrician called Muhi a-Din Sherif, was apparently responsible.

'Don't you see, Adam? Every hornet you kill is replaced by a whole lot more even angrier hornets.'

'I'm sorry, Chris, but I disagree. It's like saying, "Why cut my fingernails when they'll only grow back again?"'

'But don't you care about the way your country is perceived by the rest of the world – especially when you get it wrong?'

In July 1972 a state intelligence service targeted the well-known Palestinian writer Ghassan Kanafani. His car was booby-trapped and his nine-year-old niece was killed in the blast.

Elie Hobeika, a key witness in a war-crimes case being pursued in a Belgian court against a Middle Eastern prime minister, was blown up outside his house in Beirut two days after he agreed to give evidence. Three bodyguards and a civilian bystander were also killed in the blast.

And in 1997 an attempt was made on the life of Khaled Meshal, a Hamas leader. Two men walked past him as he was about to enter his office in Amman and sprayed poison into his ear. They were subsequently arrested by the Jordanian police and found to be foreign intelligence agents posing as Canadian tourists. In order to prevent Jordan breaking off diplomatic relations, the country responsible was forced to release Hamas's founder and spiritual leader, Sheikh Ahmad Yassin. To add insult to injury, Khaled Meshal recovered from the attack after the Crown Prince of Jordan obtained the antidote for the poison.

Adam isn't in the mood for a debate. 'Of course it works,' he says indignantly. He cites the example of

Mohamed Tahir, known as 'Engineer Number 5'. A leading Hamas bombmaker, he also planned numerous suicide attacks. One of his devices, detonated outside a Middle Eastern nightclub, killed twenty-one civilians, most of them teenagers. Another killed nineteen passengers on a bus. In total, he was believed to have been responsible for the deaths of 120 civilians. He was killed in 2002 when foreign Special Forces soldiers raked his house with gunfire. 'And, besides,' he says, 'everybody else is doing it.'

'Like who?'

'The Americans, the Russians, you name them. Who do you think took out Shamil Basayev?' The Chechen warlord – who was responsible for both the Beslan school and the Kizlyar hospital sieges – was driving a truck packed full of explosives last month in the village of Ekazhevo, Ingushetia. 'The Russians actually admitted to planting the bomb that killed him and I don't see anybody in deep mourning . . .'

I shake my head. 'I just think it's wrong, Adam. That's all.'

'Well, before you start judging us, perhaps you should get your own house in order.'

That hurts. I know exactly what he's referring to. Three years ago, two second-generation Pakistani immigrants walked into the very bar we're sitting in and attempted to detonate their suicide devices. Only one succeeded. The other was later found dead on a beach near by. Both the bombers held UK passports.

I buy him a beer and have one last crack. 'So . . .'

'Counter-measures are off-limits, Chris. You know how it works. We don't share that stuff with anybody – and, more importantly, nor do you!'

'Well, you can't blame me for trying, Adam.'

'No, I can't,' he says. 'But I . . . What's that phrase you used? I read something in the paper . . . about high-power microwave devices. And I'm pretty sure if you ask your other allies about them, you'll find exactly what you're looking for.'

37

The world is a dangerous place to live in not because of the people who do evil, but because of the people who sit by and let it happen.

Albert Einstein

12 December 2006

'You'd better take a look at this.'

Robbie's just handed me a report about a shipment of IED components heading for Dubai.

'Do we know where the vessel is now?'

'Yeah, in the Arabian Sea, about three hundred miles off the west coast of India.'

'Nice work, Robbie. I'll run it straight through to the boss.'

I feel a rush of excitement as I make my way along the corridor. I love moments like this. We spend weeks and weeks going through reports, writing assessments, putting together a fund of information that may or may not be used by the men on the ground. Then every now and again we come up with a piece of actionable intelligence.

Today is one of those days.

This will give us the perfect opportunity to hit the bad guys where it hurts – their supply chain. When IED components are in transit, they're out of the direct control of both manufacturers and bombmakers, and that means they're particularly vulnerable.

'Morning, sir. Robbie's just pulled this off the system.'

He flicks it into his in-tray and asks if I've finished the brief he asked me to produce this morning.

I take a deep breath. 'Very nearly, Colonel. But I wanted to bring that report to your attention now, because it needs your urgent attention. There's a shipment—'

'Thanks.' He turns back to his computer screen. 'I'll look at it later.'

I have a strong sense of deference towards my seniors. There are so many good people in the military – people who believe in duty, honour and self-sacrifice; people who work their bollocks off for the greater good and ask for nothing in return. But I'm really struggling to come to terms with where I am right now. I've served in the Army for seventeen years, and until I came here I worked for and alongside some of the best officers and soldiers it had to offer. All I ever wanted was to find a sense of purpose, to make a real difference; I'd thought that having a brilliant team who are prepared to devote every minute of every day in their quest to identify and interdict bombers around the world would achieve that.

And we've had our fair share of successes. Over the last year we've arrested some bad people, we've interdicted shipments of their IEDs and explosives, and we've acquired and exploited a number of new IEDs, enabling us to provide the technical information that's led to the introduction of life-saving counter-measures.

But we could be doing so much more.

The real problem is resources, and people in positions of power who are too arrogant or ignorant to see it.

The 9/11 attacks cost the perpetrators about $500,000, but the cost to America to date has been in excess of $105 billion. The Madrid train bombings cost the terrorists less than €10,000, yet they cost Spain an estimated €212 million. And the combined cost of the 7/7 bombings and the airline bomb plot was less than £20,000, but so far those two incidents alone have cost the British economy well over £600 million.

No amount of spin can hide the reality that under Gordon Brown's chancellorship, the British defence community has been starved of funds and treated with complete contempt.

There always seems to be plenty of cash for pen-pushing civil servants and new government quangos, yet the regular Army is the smallest it has been since the Battle of Waterloo, and the Royal Navy is at its smallest since the Battle of Trafalgar.

Today we're fighting a global war on terror and our forces are deployed on two fronts, yet the defence budget is around two per cent of our gross national product – the lowest it's been since the 1930s. At the end of the Cold War it was almost double that figure.

It's insane. We're fighting a completely different enemy, requiring far more operational resources, yet we still seem to be configured for Cold War operations – and on half the budget. Our troops are at massive risk because they're overstretched and under-equipped and, to add insult to injury, many fully trained soldiers are paid less than a traffic warden.

I wish I could be more objective, but I can't help blaming it on the politicians. We now have more than four million people of working age living on benefits and 180,000 men and women in the armed forces. It doesn't take a genius to spot where the lion's share of your votes is coming from.

'What did the boss say, Chris?'

'He didn't, Robbie. He just put it straight into his in-tray.'

'Fucking hell. Sometimes I wish we could just book

a flight, go over to whatever country they're operating in and pay some locals to top the fuckers. It would be so much quicker.'

'Fair one, Robbie, but I'm still not convinced that's the way ahead.'

I tell him about the Beirut bombing in 1995. The director of the CIA at the time is said to have colluded with a Saudi Arabian ambassador in an assassination attempt against Sheikh Mohammed Hussein Fadlallah, the head of Hezbollah.

The media reported that the sheikh, a radical Shiite cleric and founder of Hezbollah, was linked to several terrorist attacks against Americans, including a massive suicide-bomb attack against the US Marine Corps HQ in Beirut. The same year, Hezbollah carried out a separate suicide bombing against the US Embassy, killing the entire CIA team in country.

Funded with $3 million donated by the Saudi Arabian government, a former member of the SAS was apparently hired to kill the sheikh. On 8 March 1995 a huge car bomb exploded about fifty yards from Fadlallah's Beirut apartment. The blast completely destroyed the building, killing eighty civilians and wounding 200 more, but Fadlallah emerged unhurt. 'It's hard to see how you can describe an attack like that as anything other than terrorism.'

Since we're grappling with the big questions, we

move on to the torture of suspects. 'I don't think that works either . . .'

I was shot in Iraq two years ago, as a result of an ambush that stemmed from Piers Morgan publishing photographs of alleged prisoner abuse when he was the editor of the *Daily Mirror*. The photos were faked, but the effect they had on the local population was catastrophic. At Friday prayers in the Al-Hawi Mosque, Sheikh Abdul-Sattar al-Behadli told three thousand worshippers that a $350 reward would be given for the capture of every British soldier, and $150 for each one killed. Anyone capturing a female British soldier could keep her as a slave. He also called on them to launch *jihad* against us.

'I think it can be counter-productive.'

'But what about when we're complicit in it? You can't tell me that of all the thousands of reports we receive each month not a single one contains at least some information that hasn't been squeezed out of a terrorist the hard way. Interrogators in Pakistan aren't exactly famed for doing the whole Fair Trade thing.'

He's right. The difficulty we have is that following 9/11, when we woke up to the fact that the threat posed by Al Qaeda and its affiliates was global and substantial, we swiftly realized we didn't have a thorough under-standing of their capabilities: we were only in a position to *assess* that attacks were being planned – and in all possibility, they could occur imminently. Our intelligence resources weren't configured for the threat we now faced, so we had to rely on others who had experience of working against Al Qaeda on their own turf. And some of them deal with potential terrorists rather differently, using techniques that we wouldn't condone.

And that's our problem: if we refuse to deal with them on ethical grounds, we're potentially denying ourselves vital information that could prevent attacks on our own doorstep. But should we turn a blind eye and gain access to intelligence that could safeguard this country from attack?

It's a no-brainer. Foreign intelligence is critical to our success. Virtually every serious plot to attack the UK this decade has had international links, so we need to grit our teeth and harden up.

'Nobody really seems to appreciate precisely what we're up against. The primary reason for Western failure in the War on Terror is our fundamental inability to truly understand our enemy.'

In the UK there are believed to be around thirty *jihadist* sleeper cells at present, and more than two thousand operators. We've had some successes: the 21 July 2005 London suicide-bomb attack failed, and our domestic intelligence organizations foiled the transatlantic airline bomb plot, attacks on shopping centres and nightclubs, dirty bomb attacks, a kidnap and beheading plot and a possible chemical attack.

But they still miss some of the basics – like Al Qaeda's determination to return to a failed or aborted mission.

In 1993 Ramsi Yousef attempted to blow up the World Trade Center with a vehicle-borne IED. He calculated the exact amount of explosive and the optimum position for the device to bring down one tower and topple it into the other. Thankfully, he overlooked the fact that if you're depending on a particular space in an underground car park for the location of your bomb, you need to ensure that that space is reserved. By sheer fluke it was taken on the day of the attack, and he had to park on a different level at the opposite side of the building. The blast destroyed five floors, but failed to bring it down.

Al Qaeda reassessed the plan and flew two aircraft into the Twin Towers eight years later.

On 12 October 2000 Al Qaeda operatives rammed a boat full of explosive into the side of the USS *Cole* in the port at Aden. Seventeen US servicemen were killed. Al Qaeda had attempted – and failed – to do exactly the same thing to USS *The Sullivans* while it was in the same port nine months earlier. The boat used in that attack was so over-laden with explosives that it sank before it reached its target.

Project Bojinka failed, and the subsequent airline liquid peroxide and shoe bomb plots did too. But in the aftermath of Richard Reid and Sajid Badat it will only be a matter of time before another lone male attempts to blow up an aircraft with a device hidden on his body.

'And that's the problem,' Robbie says. 'Our enemy is quick-thinking, agile and unconventional, and we're not configured to match him.'

'That's why I don't think fighting terror with terror is the way ahead. Look at the Israel-Palestine conflict. There's no military benefit whatsoever in a suicide bomber slaughtering people at a bus stop or in a café. The benefit to the Palestinian terror groups comes from the highly predictable Israeli response. When the Israelis go in to get the perpetrators, they invariably end up killing the innocent along with the guilty, bull-dozing homes and farms and creating economic hardship for the masses of innocent Palestinians who would probably rather live in peace with Israel. The impact of the Israeli retaliation to a suicide attack is to foment hatred against themselves.'

It's exactly the way the other *jihad*ist groups work. They provoke their victims into becoming the perceived aggressors, resulting in them winning over the support of the local population. And the same thing is happening in Iraq and Afghanistan too. Insurgents strike US troops, resulting in a level of retaliation and collateral damage that erodes trust in America and inflames the hatred of the local populace.

'Retaliation isn't the answer. We need good enough intelligence to detect and prevent terrorist acts, and we need to be patient and disciplined in our efforts to win the hearts and minds of the local population. It's classic day-one, week-one counterinsurgency. We need to remove the support base from the terrorists, and killing civilians – whether by design or by accident – will never achieve that in a million years.' The alternative is a world of perpetual conflict where innocent people are caught in the crossfire as we continue to help the *jihad*ists increase their membership.

And the final problem is that half the time the British public doesn't believe these plots are real because the government treats them like morons and never tells them anything. They need to know that the extremist elements we're facing want a state of conflict around the world where every infidel is either converted or dead.

'Chris, I'd better stop you there,' Robbie says. 'There's been another incident in Baghdad.'

He hands me the report of a suicide bomber who lured a crowd of labourers to his vehicle in Tayran Square with the promise of work. Seventy people have been killed and at least 236 injured. Last month six car bombs exploded in different parts of the Sadr City area of Baghdad, killing 202 people and injuring 250.

It's the straw that breaks this camel's back.

What the fuck am I doing here?

Every day I arrive home after my children have gone to bed and leave before they wake. Despite our best efforts, the number of attacks in Iraq and Afghanistan seems to be increasing day by day. In the last year I've been to Iraq, Afghanistan, Colombia, Israel. I've spent more nights out of my bed than in it.

Lucy sent me an email recently: a poem written by a terminally ill young girl in her hospital bed.

Have you ever watched kids on a merry-go-round?
Or listened to the rain slapping on the ground?
Ever followed a butterfly's erratic flight,
Or gazed at the sun into the fading night?
You'd better slow down. Don't dance so fast.
Time is short. The music won't last.
Do you run through each day, on the fly?
When you ask, 'How are you?' do you hear the reply?
When the day is done, do you lie in your bed
With the next hundred chores running through your
*   head?*
You'd better slow down. Don't dance so fast.
Time is short. The music won't last.
Ever told your child, we'll do it tomorrow?
And in your haste not seen his sorrow?
Ever lost touch, let a good friendship die
'Cause you never had time to call and say, 'Hi'?
You'd better slow down. Don't dance so fast.

Time is short. The music won't last.
When you run so fast to get somewhere,
You miss half the fun of getting there.
When you worry and hurry through your day,
It's like an unopened gift just thrown away.
Life is not a race. Do take it slower.
Hear the music. Before the song is over . . .

This job is costing me dearly. I never see my family. Ella, my youngest daughter, has started calling the telephone 'Daddy'. It's affected my relationship with Lucy too. Whenever I see her now she seems utterly detached, lost in a world of her own.

I know why she sent me that email. It wasn't just because she felt I needed to slow down. She's telling me something much more important. I'm losing them. Throwing away the most important gift of all.

I need to do something about it. I need to change.

I don't want to be one of those soldiers who leaves the Army at the end of a long career only to realize he's failed in every other aspect of his life. I don't want to leave and realize I've missed my children growing up and that my wife and I have become complete strangers.

I wanted to save the world – or, at least, make some sense of it. But I'm wondering now whose benefit I was doing that for. I want to be a better husband and father.

I have two wonderful daughters and a beautiful, long-suffering wife, and I've spent too much of my life focused on my career instead of on them.

'Does it ever get to you, Robbie?'

We've lived in each other's pockets for so long now that he knows what I'm thinking without me having to explain.

'Everything does,' he says. 'All the time.'

I think back to that conversation with Major Hudson. *I totally respect your decision. But if you really want to make a difference, if you genuinely want to have an impact on the global drugs trade, then stay in the Army and fight terrorism . . .*

I'm not sure I'm making that much difference any more.

I need to speak to Lucy.

I dial the number and she picks up immediately.

'I'm thinking of resigning my commission.'

'What will you do?' she asks. 'Where will we live?' And her questions speak not of panic and uncertainty but of delight and infinite possibility.

38

Show me a thoroughly satisfied man and I will show you a failure.

Thomas Edison

29 June 2007

> In the surreal, high-stakes, high-pressure world I was living in, where every decision could have been my last, I learnt that fear can be your friend. Confucius once said, 'Our greatest glory is not in never failing, but in rising each time we fail.' He was spot-on. Instead of allowing fear to curtail success, if you let it be your friend, it will give you the decisive edge . . .

The monitor glows in front of me. I'm writing the concluding paragraphs of a piece for *GQ* magazine: 'Keeping Your Cool Under Pressure'.

I resigned my commission on 12 December 2006 –

the day I walked into Voldemort's office to tell him about the shipment of IED components heading to Dubai – and within four months was effectively out of the Green Machine. I took Lucy's advice: I set up a counter-IED consultancy and wrote a book about my Iraq experiences. *Eight Lives Down* is a bestseller and the consultancy is going from strength to strength. If I looked over our garden fence, I'd be tempted to throw up; we really do seem to be living the dream.

I take a slurp of coffee, get up from my desk and walk across my study to the window that overlooks our back garden. Sophie and Ella are running around on the perfectly manicured lawn, laughing and giggling as they play throw and catch with Ralph, our perpetually obliging black Labrador. Their faces shine with happiness.

Lucy sits on a picnic rug beside her immaculately sculpted flowerbed, sipping green tea and flicking through a glossy magazine. This is the happiest I've ever seen her. The picture-perfect scene beneath me could double as a television commercial.

It's the life we've always dreamt of; our rural idyll. We live in a chocolate-box cottage on the edge of Hay-on-Wye. We spend dreamy mornings walking along the river, idle away afternoons in quaint cafés and book-shops and throw impromptu dinner parties for old friends. It feels like we have everything we could wish for – an access-all-areas pass to the Garden of Eden. Not a day goes by without one or other of us waking up and feeling the need to pinch ourselves.

Our lives have changed beyond recognition. I've become a regular contributor to several major TV and radio news stations and we've been spoiled rotten, rubbing shoulders with real writers and enjoying swanky publishing dinners in Michelin-starred London restaurants. I still can't get used to appearing at literary festivals, being asked to sign copies of my book and being treated like a minor celebrity.

Sophie looks up and catches sight of me standing at the window. She waves, and I wave back. And, for a fleeting moment, I realize I'm still on the outside, looking in. I realize I've never felt that any of this is real; or, perhaps more truthfully, that I'm really part of it.

On the surface, the transition from military life to Civvy Street has been seamless – but inside I'm a man who's still at war. Maybe it's because I don't believe I quite fit in; maybe it's because, deep down, I don't actually feel I deserve it.

'When I look at you sometimes,' Lucy said, this morning, 'I get confused. I used to hate every minute of every day when you were away on ops; any time the phone rang or there was a knock on the door my head filled with images of you being blown to pieces in some godforsaken back alley an awfully long way from home.

But now it's almost worse. I know you're physically here . . . I see a familiar silhouette . . . but part of you, a really important part of you, is still somewhere else.'

It's become Lucy's mantra. And the terrible thing is that I know she's right. I've tried my best not to bring my wars home with me, but I'm increasingly aware that I've left part of myself behind – the part that still wishes I was fighting the bombmakers.

Maybe it's a result of leaving the Army so suddenly, or maybe I've always been this way. For years we moved from shitty married quarter to shitty married quarter; I was catapulted from one war-zone to the next. First Bosnia, then Northern Ireland, then Colombia, Afghanistan, Iraq . . . Even working for Voldemort was a battleground of sorts. I've not drawn breath, not paused for thought, for as long as I can remember. Even when we were living in a four-bedroom flat in one of the coolest parts of London and Lucy and I should have been having the time of our lives, we didn't, because I never had the space.

I spent years being desperate to deal with my first IED – constantly primed, forever handcuffed to a ten-minute pager, waiting for the call that never came. I was bored off my tits and incredibly frustrated. But then I started to get into it; I became more accomplished, and the tempo of operations increased – until it suddenly reached critical mass. After 9/11 it seems as if I've never had a spare moment to myself.

Not so now; for the first time I can remember I'm in a place where my weekly timetable has given me room to reflect in a way I've never had the opportunity – or perhaps the inclination – to do before. And that's the problem. I have this perfect life, but it has forced me to address all the difficult issues that still need to be resolved. I'm back at square one. At the centre of it all, a war continues to rage inside my head.

The day I walked into Voldemort's office and told him I was leaving, I thought I'd never been more certain of anything. I thought I was ready to move on. I thought I was ready for something different. But, as unreasonable as I know it must seem, I'm just not yet.

I know I'm being selfish. I also know that we always lie loudest when we lie to ourselves. I need to admit it. I've made a mistake.

I need to get my head together. I need to get up into the hills.

By the time Ralph and I are within reach of the summit of Hay Bluff, the warm summer breeze has become a howling gale. As the wind pounds the side of the mountain and batters my exposed body, I think of my brother Tim and feel his ashes still swirling around the hillside above me.

The last time I saw him we were in some shit-hole of

a council estate in East Sussex. I remember the day the two of us went on his drug rounds: half-a-dozen starry-eyed junkies stirred from various stages of intoxication and began mauling him like zoo animals at feeding time.

I can still taste the shock and revulsion I felt as I saw one of his female dealers and several of her junkie mates preparing foil and a tooting tube. I'd never seen anybody chasing the dragon before. And I'm still haunted by the circumstances of his death.

The tension crackled between us all the way back to Lewes. It wasn't until the newsreader announced that a massive bomb had exploded beneath New York's World Trade Center that I looked into his sensitive, intelligent face and realized his eyes had started to fill with tears.

I wish I'd listened more closely when he told me he just wanted out. But I was too wrapped up in my own frustration and anger to hear his cry for help.

As I sit looking out over the Golden Valley I realize I was in exactly the same state of mind the last time I was up here. Once again, I'm in absolute turmoil.

My mind swings back to the Thiepval Barracks bombing, and on through a procession of the other horrors I've witnessed over the years.

As I try to make sense of those senseless killings, try to establish whether anything I've done in my career has had even the slightest impact, I find myself fighting for air, submerged once again amongst the bodies in the lake at Rumboci; standing alongside the mothers holding their babies with nooses around their necks; staring down into the mass graves in Srebrenica . . .

I think about Brummie's pep talk after I lost it in the Bicester Sergeants' Mess. He told me he thought I was a man in search of meaning. Someone who was still trying to make sense of his brother's death; who was determined to do the right thing by him, by his parents and by the world at large. He said I had a burning desire to solve the problems of the world.

He was right. And there's still so much unfinished business.

I think about Mark Holland in Iraq and the super-sonic copper slug that smashed straight through his armour and killed him as he sat in the rear of the Snatch Land Rover.

I think of Jimmy Menezes, taking the Long Walk up to that car in the Colombian jungle, knowing it almost certainly contained a radio-controlled bomb – but being forced onwards by fear of being branded a coward. I think of him moments later, his life violently snatched away in a whirlwind of cacophonous sound and flame. And all because his superior officer was too arrogant to accept Jimmy might be right.

It strikes a depressingly familiar chord. It's exactly the reason I left.

*　*　*

As my faithful black Labrador and I begin weaving our way down the rocky mountain path, he suddenly shoots off into the distance.

I make the long walk towards the distant car park alone. But in my head I'm back on the sun-baked streets of Basra. I'm crawling on my belt-buckle, scanning the ground for any hint of disturbed earth, the tip of a bomb canister, the glimmer of a tripwire. I slide my feeler forwards. I move the telescopic rod close to the earth, but not touching it. I focus on its tip. Everything else is a blur. I raise it an inch, then two, and now I'm standing. I'm totally oblivious to outside sounds now. I move the feeler left . . . agonizingly slowly . . . then right . . .

No tripwires.

Sweat is pouring off me, stinging my eyes. My pulse is racing. I search with my fingertips, stone by stone, inch by inch, before crawling forward half a metre and then repeating the whole process.

The crowd behind the cordon is getting more and more hostile; their low murmurs have become shouts and threats. The insurgents are getting ready to attack. We've got to get off the ground.

But not yet . . .

My eyes are drawn to the mechanical timer on top of the fourteen-volt motorcycle battery, attached to four rockets by a series of interconnecting red and white wires. Beads of sweat crawl across the back of my neck. I swallow hard. The timer is on its final graticule. There's one minute left.

But it's stuck fast.

Decision time . . .

As I reach the car, Ralph's welcoming bark snaps me firmly back to the present.

I love what I have, immensely, but I know it's not going to last. My life in Hay is a gift; I know I should be grateful beyond measure for what I have. But the truth is: standing in a bookshop just isn't the same as taking apart a bomb, or taking down a bomber network. Sometimes, when you're crouched over a device, the hardest thing you face is yourself. And I'm scared I'll never find something as viscerally challenging elsewhere.

If only I hadn't rushed the decision to leave. If only I'd been astute enough to realize how things would really pan out. If only this . . . if only that . . .

I jump into the 4×4 and gun the engine. As I make the short drive back to the cottage, a breaking news report announces another terror attack on the UK. 'Last night, a suspected *jihad*ist group smuggled two car bombs into the heart of the capital. Fortunately, both devices were located and disabled before they could be detonated. The first device was left near the Tiger Tiger nightclub in Haymarket at around one thirty a.m.; the second was in Cockspur Street. The cars and their triggering mechanisms were recovered intact for forensic examination and both vehicles were found to contain petrol cans, gas canisters and a quantity of nails, with a mobile-phone-based trigger . . .'

It feels so strange hearing about an incident on the radio and not having a clue about the background details. I'm no longer the man in the loop.

I switch off the radio as I pull into our driveway and walk into the house.

Lucy pours me a glass of wine. When she hands it to me I can see she's been crying.

'Are you OK?' I ask.

'I am,' she says. 'But I'm not so sure about you.' She hesitates, unsure perhaps about peeling open this particular can of worms. 'Chris . . . is this really what you want?' She stares deep into my eyes, her expression torn between desperation and love.

'I'm . . . I'm so sorry . . . I . . .' It's pathetically in-adequate, but I realize I have absolutely no idea what to say.

'I'm not sure where you are right now, Chris. But I do know it's not here, with me and the girls.'

She's not completely right. A part of me *is* somewhere else, and I hate myself for that, but a big part of me is still here too. I adore them. I'm just not ready for this.

She's not expecting an answer. She knows it won't make any more sense to her than it does to me. The pain in her face tells me everything.

'I'll respect whatever you decide to do, even though I can't say I'll really understand it. But please . . . come back to us one day.'

39

A man who has been in danger,
When he comes out of it forgets his fears,
And sometimes he forgets his promises.

Euripides

28 February 2008

The wind shrieks and the freezing rain beats a tattoo against the side of the lock-up. The number one cocks his head sideways and listens, tuning in to our new environment.

We've just arrived on target. The four of us stand perfectly still. Not a flicker of movement. We need to make sure nobody has seen or heard us infiltrating the area. Even sleepers can be sensitive to the slightest changes in sound, the slightest adjustments to the molecules of air in their immediate vicinity. We wait a little longer, giving ourselves a chance to let our pulse rates settle down before we enter the bomb factory.

The number one gives us the thumbs-up. Good: still

no movement, no have-a-go heroes or late-night dog walkers.

The number two slides our forensic over-boots from his day-sack and hands a pair to the team leader, then gives me and Andy ours. One at a time, we holster our pistols and ease them on. We pull on our balaclavas too and each of us taps the man in front to let him know we're good to go. If anybody compromises us now, we'll just pretend we're burglars. The over-boots will save us leaving behind any trace of the shit we've just accumulated walking across the muddy field.

The number one deftly and assiduously picks the padlock. Moments later we're in.

We close the door carefully behind us then stop, look and listen. Each of us instinctively allows our jaws to drop open so that all the internal noises – like breathing and swallowing – don't compromise our ability to hear an approaching threat.

'Oscar One One, this is Echo One Zero. That's us made entry into Alpha 1, over.'

In our ear-pieces, we hear the instantaneous response of the sniper who's hiding out in the OP, covering our arses. 'Oscar One One, roger that. All quiet . . .'

The lock-up is completely silent; no ticking clocks, no creaking beams, just the patter of rain on the corrugated-metal roof.

As the number one begins photographing the bomb

components with his infra-red camera, the number two gets to work on the laptop. He plugs in his data lead and fires up the remote hard-drive. Seconds later the laptop's memory has been completely duplicated.

Next he deals with the mobile.

He lifts it from the workbench, makes a note of the IMEI and Sim card numbers, then replaces it in exactly the same position relative to the laptop and bomb-making manuals on the worktop in front of him.

During the Second World War, a group of specially selected US servicemen from the Office of Strategic Services joined members of the British Special Operations Executive at a stately home in the heart of rural England to be trained in the black arts of clandestine warfare. The Operation Jedburgh teams each comprised three men who were then parachuted into Nazi-occupied France by night to conduct sabotage and guerrilla operations and lead French Resistance forces against the Germans.

Now, sixty-five years on, a group of former British Special Forces soldiers and two former SF bomb-disposal operators are once again teaching our Coalition allies covert operations skills.

Having marked the students on their ability to make a covert entry into the target, Andy and I step outside to discuss the next phase of their assessment. We're part of the growing number of former soldiers who've become private military consultants. He used to be my warrant officer in Alpha Troop and we've been working together on this training contract for several months now.

'Did you see that piece in today's newspaper about the soldier getting charged for ABH when he was pissed? Why is it that if a civvy does something wrong, his profession is never mentioned, but when it's one of us the article always kicks off, "A former soldier was today remanded . . ."?'

'I hope it's because society has certain expectations of them,' I reply. 'The difference between a soldier and a civilian is that the soldier accepts personal responsibility for the safety of his tribe, and most civilians never have to.'

'Mmmm . . . I'm not sure society puts soldiers on pedestals any more.'

I admire Andy immensely. He's an outstanding bloke and, considering all the minefields he's crossed in his career – several tours of Northern Ireland, Afghanistan, Iraq and Colombia – he's one of the most together guys I know. He and the characters sitting behind us show no outward sign of the fact that not too long ago they were risking their lives in countless war-zones. They killed for their country, took bullets and watched their best friends die painful deaths, but recount their experiences as if they were on nothing more than a series of impromptu camping trips where things occasionally got a bit out of hand and some of the guys got bruised.

We're driving back to the country estate with our students when Andy asks how things are with Lucy.

I tell him I have a feeling we're probably going to go our separate ways.

'Jesus, Chris . . . I thought you two were totally loved-up.' He goes into a rant about the difficulty of spending a career in the military and then coming back into Civvy Street and realizing you and your missus live on different planets. 'I guess there's no such thing as "happily ever after" in our neck of the woods.' He's been through a divorce and a string of failed relationships.

'You can't blame her, though,' he says. 'It can't have been easy with you away all the time, even when you were in that intelligence job. It must have done her head in, not knowing where you were or when you were coming home.'

I don't need to be reminded.

'Then again, life is always a mixture of good and bad. Beyond it all, life goes on. And so must we.' He's become quite the philosopher now that he's no longer constrained by the uniform.

But he's absolutely right. The back-to-back tours had a hugely detrimental effect on our relationship. I'm more addicted to a life in conflict than I'd ever realized, and the price Lucy's paid for it is more or less constant loneliness. There's a limit to how much any of us can cope with that before things reach critical mass, and I didn't realize how much our marriage had deteriorated, or how permanent the damage was.

'I suppose I'd got it into my head that love is supposed to last for ever, whatever the circs. But maybe all relationships are on a ticking clock.'

I think wistfully about Lucy and remember a line I once heard in a film: 'The saddest thing in the world is loving someone who *used* to love you.'

'I think I've been a pretty crap husband and dad . . . But, whatever happens, I'm really glad we had the time we had together, and that we've got two beautiful daughters as a result.'

'Here, take a look at this.' He switches on the map light and digs a sheet of paper out of the glove compartment. 'One of the lads emailed it today and I printed a copy off for you. I thought it would make you laugh.'

RE-CREATING GARRISON LIFE AT HOME

- *Surround yourself with people who smoke like chimneys, drink like fish, bitch/whine/complain about EVERYTHING, and use the kind of foul language that would make a biker blush.*
- *Wear only military uniforms. Even though nobody cares, clean and press one ceremonial uniform and wear it for twenty minutes on the whim of some crusty old guy who yells at you.*

- Ask for equipment or articles of clothing you really need, have somebody tell you that you're not entitled to it. Walk away without recourse.
- Have your spouse whine about how you're always on deployment. Get her to put on 20kg and wear your PT army shorts around in public. Take away her makeup and leg-waxing strips.
- Whenever you're bored, get drunk. Get bored as often as possible.
- Study the owner's manual for all household appliances. Routinely take an appliance apart, clean it and put it back together, even though it hasn't been used.
- Start a project, any project. Have somebody continually stop by and make stupid suggestions to make the job 'easier'. Say, 'Yes, sir,' and do it the way they told you to do it. After they leave, go back to doing it the right way.
- Repaint your car every month, whether it needs it or not.
- Move every two years. Whether you want to or not. When you get to a place you really hate, stay there for fifteen years or until your wife leaves you and you lose everything. Have your application for re-posting accepted a year after she leaves.
- Replace all your appliances and furniture with others that are outdated, in need of constant repair or

dangerous to use. Do more with them than you would if they were new.

- If you have nothing to do, clean something that doesn't need cleaning.

INTERACTION WITH CIVILIANS

- Leave behind anyone who smokes like a chimney, drinks like a fish, bitches/whines/complains about EVERYTHING, and uses foul language that would make a biker blush.

- Whenever civilians say or do anything stupid (and it happens a lot) shake your head and mutter, in your most contemptuous/condescending tone, 'Fuckin' civvies'.

- Use copious amounts of acronyms but NEVER explain them. When asked to explain shake your head and mutter, in your most contemptuous/ condescending tone, 'Fuckin' civvies.'

- Have other people say stupid things to you like: 'You don't pay taxes, do you?'; 'You get free housing,'; and, 'Man, you must get paid a lot.' Shake your head and mutter, in your most contemptuous/condescending tone, 'Fuckin' civvies'.

- Demand that everyone never thanks you for anything you do for them, looks at you in a condescending manner and calls you names like 'G.I. Joe' and 'soldier boy'. Shake your head and mutter, in your

*most contemptuous/condescending tone, 'Fuckin'
civvies.'*

I know it's meant to be funny, but it's alarmingly close
to the truth. I probably could have done with reading it
before I left the Army.

It's almost 4 a.m. by the time I arrive home. I switch on
one of the twenty-four-hour news channels and images
of Iraq blaze across the screen. Some things never
change. The next item makes me sit up sharply.

'Details have emerged of the alleged assassination of
Imad Mughniyeh, a leading figure in Lebanese
Hezbollah. He was killed in a bomb blast in the Kfar
Sousa district of Damascus earlier this month when a
booby-trapped headrest in his 4×4 exploded.'

Mughniyeh had been a target for Israel and America
for as long as I can remember. He was believed to have
been one of those responsible for bombing the US
Marines barracks and the embassy in Beirut in 1983, in
which more than 350 died, and was rumoured to have
masterminded an attack on the Israeli embassy in
Buenos Aires in 1992, which killed twenty-nine.

I can suddenly feel every single nerve-ending. I'm
overwhelmed by the need to be back in the thick of it. I
miss my old life. It's a million miles away from what I'm
doing now. I spent my whole career working as part of a

close-knit team; my new occupation is at the opposite end of the spectrum. Being a writer is about as solitary as it gets. I really love it, but I also miss the buzz of operations. And I do feel I've failed as a husband and father. Perhaps that's why I still need to try to find some meaning elsewhere.

I think about the heartfelt words I wrote at the end of *Eight Lives Down*:

> There is a limit to how much any of us can cope before things reach critical mass. We came dangerously close; we were in a bad place, and I don't want us to be there ever again.
>
> Was it all for the greater good? I hope so. 'Fight what is wrong, believe what is true and do what is right.' It's a difficult path to tread, but I keep trying. I also try to be a better husband and father. There's one phrase muttered more than any other by soldiers dying on the battlefield: 'Tell my wife I love her.'
>
> By the time I found my way home, I'd used up eight of my nine lives. I had two wonderful daughters and a beautiful, loving wife, and spent too much of my life focused on my career instead of them.
>
> What happens in the future, only time will tell. I'm eight lives down. I'm not going to waste my last.

I meant every word, but I guess some poems don't

rhyme and perhaps my story has no clear beginning, middle or end.

For the first time, I realize why so many soldiers are reluctant to leave the Army, even when they want to. Because when it comes to the crunch, it's often scarier being out than in.

Someone at my publisher's once asked me if I believed in angels. I told her I was open-minded about most things. She said she was convinced I had a guardian angel. I've always been convinced it's a whole lot simpler than that: you die when your time's up. So maybe I'm still around for a reason: to go and do something important.

I think I've given Civvy Street a fair shot – but perhaps I'm just not that good at it. And since life's not throwing up much in the way of excitement right now, what else is there to do?

The voice in my head tells me I'm going to Afghanistan.

40

There is but one way to be born, but a hundred ways to die.

Chinese proverb

18 April 2008

Another wave crashes against the shore, churning up the golden sand in a glorious mixture of emerald greens and frothy whites. For a moment I think I'm in paradise, but the spell is immediately broken.

'The strong live off the weak,' our instructor says. 'And the clever live off the strong.' We've been in Cape Town for three weeks on an intensive hostile-environment close-protection course. It was one of the prerequisites for my forthcoming contract in Afghanistan.

Over the past twenty-one days we've become adept in every aspect of close-quarters battle. Every morning we practise long- and short-range combat using a variety of armed and unarmed techniques. We've learnt how to fight with sniper rifles, assault rifles, pistols, batons and knives. And we've been taught how to incapacitate any type of aggressor in less than three seconds.

'OK, ladies and gentlemen, look in. I'm now going to demonstrate how to disarm and shoot an assailant with his own weapon. I'm going to need a volunteer.'

Predictably enough, there's an uncomfortable silence.

'I suggest one of you volunteers, gentlemen!'

I feel a beasting coming on.

But Shand steps forward and takes the proffered pistol. The six-foot-seven-inch giant is told to aim it at the instructor. He does so uneasily, gripping the weapon with both hands and aiming it straight between the instructor's eyes. Then with lightning speed the instructor slaps away the gun and simultaneously knees Shand in the groin, taking him completely by surprise. The giant loses his balance and feels himself beginning to fall. But before he hits the deck the instructor grips his wrists with one hand, forces the barrel of the pistol up and back with the other, and rams its foresight down into Shand's throat. The pain must be excruciating. But his ordeal isn't over yet.

The former South African Special Forces instructor thrusts another knee into Shand's groin for good measure, then slam-dunks the weapon between his arms, freeing it completely from his grip. Now in complete control, he cocks it and jabs the muzzle into Shand's eye, forcing him to crumple to the floor, momentarily blinded.

'Well done, Shand.' The instructor offers him his hand. 'You're a natural.' Turning back to the rest of us he continues, 'Had this been for real, I'd have finished the move by ensuring Shand's dexterity and mobility were completely removed – that way he wouldn't be able to come after me as I make my escape. Naturally I'd have achieved this by shooting him in the wrists and knees. Any questions?'

We're all rooted to the spot.

'Good. Now get into pairs and practise. This isn't a game, ladies and gentlemen. It's Big Boys' Rules out there, and only practice makes perfect. That way the drills will become lodged into your muscle memory. Then, when you do find yourself in a high-stress environment and you're unable to think clearly, you'll still be good to go. Believe me, it will happen completely instinctively.'

He concludes the lesson by explaining that the best form of defence is in fact avoiding conflict altogether – by talking your way out of it. 'The clever live off the strong . . .' But he stresses that if you have absolutely no choice, your attack must be hard, fast, unexpected and merciless. 'The key to success is visualization. Cortisol, adrenalin, testosterone, all those hormones will rush through your body and give you strength, but before you land the first blow, you have to visualize exactly what you're going to do to your opponent. And when you do, you'll fuck him up big-time.'

Shand and I have become good mates since we began the course. He's a big, hard South African who, like me, lost his father when he was younger – the only difference being that his was shot dead by bandits.

When the boys on the course – most of whom are former British infantry NCOs – realized I was the only ex-officer, they thought it would be hilarious to get the instructor to pair Shand and me up. But in spite of his terrifyingly imposing frame, he's an excellent fighting partner and we've stayed paired up for the rest of the course.

Our instructors are all former Special Forces operatives who've amassed a wealth of experience in pretty much every high-threat theatre on the planet. They're all big, hard fuckers, and although they're often miserable with it, their knowledge and instructional ability are second to none.

We've learnt every trick in the bodyguarding book, and these guys have taught us all sorts of proactive skills, such as threat and risk assessment, the law, operational planning, surveillance and counter-surveillance.

But by far the most interesting stuff has been the reactive training.

'If you learn exactly how the body works and how to fix it when it's broken, you'll not only be able to keep your client and your team alive, you'll also be able to end the life of your enemies far more efficiently.' Those chilling words opened the tactical paramedicine phase.

Since then, we've also learnt both defensive driving and tactical high-speed driving, including how to carry out J-turns and handbrake turns while under fire.

After an hour or so beating the crap out of one another, we all head back to the snazzy apartment block we've been billeted in and grab a quick shower before the next lesson – communication and verbal-conflict management. I'm sharing a room with an ex-Royal Marine called Connor, and we're sharing the flat with a couple of Kiwis.

I'd forgotten how easy it is to live with the military. You never have to worry about anyone being jack. If somebody finishes the milk in the fridge you know they'll go straight down to the shop and buy another couple of bottles. If they're using the shower and there's a queue of people waiting, they'll be in and out in two minutes flat. And if they're putting a load in the washing- machine, they'll always come round and ask if anyone wants to throw anything in.

I love being back in this environment.

Back in the classroom, Susanne teaches us

verbal-conflict management. Nobody knows her back-ground, but, like all the instructors, she is also a licensed paramedic – and an awesome one at that. At weekends, we go out regularly with them in their ambulances. I was on shift with her last weekend. She taught me more in a day than I learnt in my entire military career.

One of the reasons this particular course is so popular is because you get to practise giving live treatment to real patients. And because the majority of call-outs are to the townships – the slums, ruled by brutal armed gangs – the majority of incidents are shootings and stabbings, the majority of patients infected with HIV. As pre-deployment training it really doesn't get much better.

'More often than you might think,' Susanne says, 'we bodyguards have to use our charm, guile and wits to encourage someone to do something they may not want to do, or to get them to tell us things which perhaps they should not. Some would call it manipulation, but I prefer to think of it as persuasion.

'If you're not comfortable approaching people, all your emotions are going to try to get the better of you, especially when speaking to members of the opposite sex. When that happens, you'll feel shy and self-conscious – but you have to deal with it in the same way you'd deal, say, with a stone in your shoe. It's annoying, but you just have to get on with it.'

For the next twenty minutes or so she explains how to win over blokes and how to get angry ones to calm down by changing your body language and the tone of your voice. It's all pretty common-sense stuff.

Then she expands upon the principles of eye movement: how to tell when somebody is lying to you by the direction of their eye shift; and what constitutes an 'indication of interest'. 'If a female asks you what your name is, that's an IOI. If she asks you if you're single, that's an IOI. If you take her hands and squeeze them and she squeezes back, that's an IOI.'

This isn't so much a lesson in conflict management as one in seduction, and the lads are lapping it up. It's another in a long line of things we all wish we'd known when we first started our military careers.

She talks about the contrast between the male and female psyche. 'For men, it's all about pride, ego and esteem. For girls, it's about excitement. She wants an adventure . . . all girls do.'

Susanne teaches us how to speak and how to listen; how to identify the exact moment when a member of the opposite sex becomes attracted to us; how to know when to talk and when to shut up; when to push and when to pull; when to tease and when to be sincere.

If I'd known all this before now, I think ruefully, I might still be married.

She explains that winning somebody over – whether

they're a member of the opposite sex or not – is often about describing something with enthusiasm. That way, the object of your attention will want to try whatever you're suggesting, especially if you deny them the opportunity to say no.

She tutors us in non-verbal communication and ESP techniques. 'The latter are especially good for getting girls to take an interest in you,' she says.

She turns to two of the lads in the group.

'I'm going to write down a number between one and ten. I want you to trust your instincts, and don't think about what we're doing.'

She tells them there's no particular magic required to read minds. 'Just listen to your inner feelings.'

Susanne scribbles something on a piece of paper and hands it to the lads, face down.

'Now tell me the first number that you think of.'

'Three,' one says immediately.

'Five,' says the other.

'OK, now go ahead and turn over the paper.'

There's a boldly drawn number seven.

'That's rubbish,' one of the lads says.

'You think so?' she replies. 'Try it in the bar tonight.'

She tells us that obviously it's not about ESP or any other mind-reading technique: it's just one of those mysterious psychological tricks. If you ask a girl to choose a number randomly between one and ten,

80 per cent of the time – especially if she's rushed into a decision – the number will be seven.

'Unfortunately it doesn't work on guys.'

No shit.

Later that night, Shand drives a group of us into Cape Town. The Café Caprice is meant to be one of the coolest bars in South Africa.

Even before we've got the first round of drinks in, Connor is cracking straight into the two girls standing next to him.

'I'm going to write down a number between one and ten. What I want you to do is trust your instincts, just listen to your inner feelings . . .'

The girls are already mesmerized – and so are we.

He writes on a piece of paper and hands it to the girls, face down.

'Now tell me the first number you think of.'

'Seven,' they say in unison, then turn to one another, astonished by the coincidence.

'Good. Now go ahead and turn over the paper.'

One of the girls does so with agonizing slowness, until there's a big number seven staring right back at her.

'Oh my God,' she says. 'That's amazing!'

Looks like I'll have the room to myself tonight.

41

*What you are is what you have been, and what you will
be is what you do now.*

The Buddha

8 September 2008

The distinctive beat of the giant Sea King echoes
around the walls like cannon fire as it swoops down
onto the Garmsir HLS.

I drop to one knee, turning to avoid the clouds of dust
and grit being churned up by the heli. The thud of its
rotors resonates through my body. I pull on my Bergen
with one hand and grip my Heckler & Koch G36
assault rifle with the other. The loadmaster gives us the
thumbs-up and the principal and I run towards him.

The downdraught sears our faces as we scuttle inside.
I expect to be greeted by a bunch of weary-looking
soldiers, but the cabin is empty except for the crew. It's
been tasked exclusively for us.

One call to an ex-Army pal in London and within a

fortnight I was in South Africa. Minutes after the end of that course I'm in Helmand Province as a private military contractor attached to the Foreign and Commonwealth Office. It's been a fascinating experience, and my heart rate has started to quicken again.

My team leader, Derek, aimed me in the direction of the Sea King this morning. He doesn't know anything about the principal other than that he's a diplomat and we have to get him out of the country as quickly as possible. My job is to escort him as far as Bastion and baby-sit him in the FCO compound until his connecting flight leaves tonight. Then get back here, soon as.

It sounds simple enough. A former Coldstream Guardsman, Derek has been on the circuit for five years and here in 'Stan for the past three. I've only worked with him for two weeks, but I know he doesn't fuck around.

I buckle my passenger into the seat opposite me, then sit down myself and upturn my weapon so that its barrel is pointing to the floor. As we begin our rapid ascent the door-gunner swivels his gympie, taking in every detail of the farms and mud-roofed buildings beneath us, on constant alert for potential sources of incoming fire. We're at our maximum risk of being destroyed by enemy rockets during take-off and landing.

The pilot banks hard left, drops 100 feet and executes

a sharp ninety-degree turn. The airframe judders violently as he jinks right and left in a series of evasive manoeuvres.

I make eye contact with my principal and give him the thumbs-up. He does the same in response but I'm not convinced he's really OK – he's turning a very strange shade of green. Moments later, the loadmaster passes him a paper bag, which he immediately vomits into. Then he comes up for air, flashes me a smile and gives me the thumbs-up again.

'WHO ARE YOU WITH?' I shout above the roar of the rotors.

'Department for International Development. I've got a spot of compassionate leave . . .'

'Oh, I'm sorry to hear that.' And I would be normally, but he looked distinctly uncomfortable when I asked my question and his eyes shot up and to his right. I suspect he's talking bollocks. The compassionate-leave story is a perfect cover for a Brit, since we all tend to look immediately at our feet and avoid asking any more awkward questions. I'm cool with that. Either he's a spook or his granny really has just pegged it.

After the world's longest rollercoaster ride the pilot tweaks the cyclic, levels off the aircraft and powers over the desert, heading north to Camp Bastion. I look out of the port windows – to the west – and see a huge sand-storm billowing beneath us.

There's a sudden flurry of activity. The loadmaster has just held up three fingers. Three minutes to landing. My principal and I begin replacing our helmets and donning our kit. The pilot lowers the collective, pushes the cyclic forward and we plummet towards Bastion at breakneck speed.

I hear an explosion and see flashes of light beside the fuselage. It's nothing to worry about – just the pilot firing off some decoy flares. Then we're on the ground and striding across the HLS to a waiting FCO 4×4.

Instead of taking us across to the FCO compound the driver whisks us straight across to another waiting heli – the principal's connecting flight. This has been the shortest and simplest bodyguarding task in history. It's gone like clockwork.

Just when I thought it couldn't get any better, our FCO facilitator tells me there's an Army patrol driving back to Garmsir in an hour; I can either jump in with them or sit around getting bored, waiting for tomorrow's heli.

It's a no-brainer. Camp Bastion has fresh rations, shops and even a Pizza Hut. It's a million miles from the squalor of Garmsir. I'll stock up on goodies from the shop, then take the road option.

'*Major* Hunter . . .' Gaz O'Donnell beams me his trademark wide-toothed grin. I've not seen my old ATO buddy since we worked together on the counter-suicide-bomber stuff.

I tell him he looks sickeningly well and that it's not 'Major' any more, that I got out of the Army last year.

'No way!' His eyes widen. 'I thought you'd be in for the duration. Genuinely. Come on, let's get a brew – I want to hear what life's like on the outside.'

I give him the rundown on what I've been up to since leaving, and tell him about the split with Lucy. I'm relieved to hear that he and Toni are still going strong. 'She's just given birth to our youngest. He's nine weeks old.'

He glows with pride. He's always been a big-time family man. He's got two kids from his first marriage, another two from his second, and he absolutely adores them.

'Are you getting much down-time?' I ask.

'Not as much as I'd like.' He tells me that in the past four months the ATO teams have defused 120 roadside bombs and dealt with the aftermath of at least another eighty.

'But we don't call the Det Lash-Vegas for nothing.' He smiles. The guy's a legend – and not just for his singing and guitar playing, or the fact that he always manages to build a pool anywhere he's based so he and his boys can cool off in the heat.

We spend the next fifteen minutes shooting the shit and chatting about our plans for when we get back to the UK. Then we talk shop.

He's had an epic tour, and a fascinating career. He was awarded the George Medal – one short of the Victoria Cross – last year for repeatedly neutralizing bombs under fire in Iraq. Following an attack on Basra air station a bank of rockets were discovered on a timing device. In order to minimize the risk to the thousand-plus soldiers and civilians working at the base, he put himself in their direct line of fire and disabled them manually.

The rumour back in Lashkar Gar is that he's been written up for another GM, for 'repeated and sustained acts of immense bravery' during his time in Afghanistan. He's defused more than fifty bombs out here. During one incident, he stopped a device from going bang by jamming his finger into its clothes-peg detonator. If he does win another GM, it will be the first time in twenty-six years that it's been given to the same person twice.

An hour later, I'm steaming along in an open-sided WMIK Land Rover. How little things have moved on since my time in Iraq. The Main Supply Route here is known as 'The Gauntlet' or 'IED Alley' – which is why the lads stick to the sketchy desert roads that flank the irrigated fields along the Helmand river.

The constant threat of IEDs and suicide attacks has turned life into a never-ending game of Russian roulette

– but with five slugs in the barrel instead of one. Over 70 per cent of all our casualties are IED victims. Anyone can be hit – it's the enemy you can't see – and the psychological effect on our soldiers is more corrosive than you can imagine.

The boys know they can hold their own in a traditional one-on-one fire-fight – and they regularly do. But IEDs have claimed so many lives and caused so many casualties this year that our troops are suffering the worst attrition rate since the Falklands.

Only the growl of our diesel convoy breaks the sweltering midday silence as we thunder along these dirt tracks. The sun is high in the sky, bleaching the colour from everything in sight.

Derek strolls across to meet me as we sweep into the compound. 'You took your time. I thought you were coming back two days ago.' He raises an eyebrow. 'Too busy scoffing pizza up there in Slipper City?'

I shake my head. 'My six-hour road trip turned into a two-day epic.' We ended up spending two nights in the forward operating base at Gereshk because somebody reported IEDs on the route. 'It's the only place I've been to that's worse than this shit-hole.'

We're sharing an accommodation block with a platoon of Jocks from the Scottish Regiment. It doesn't take long to get there; the entire compound is only about 200 metres by 100. There's an HLS on one side of camp, a vehicle park on the other, and a volleyball court marked out in the sand alongside an outdoor gym. It's draped in a camouflage netting to keep it cool, and the weights are fashioned from old ammo boxes and fence pickets.

The toilet is basic – a tiny hut thrown together from wire and Hessian frames normally used for blast walls. Inside there's a wooden table with an oval hole above a small bin bag. It's infested with flies and the smell brings tears to your eyes. The bags are emptied every day by some poor squaddie and the shit is incinerated in the burn pit.

The urinal is a Desert Rose, a strangely romantic name for what is basically a piss-reeking plastic tube dug into the sand. The shower is just as basic, but absolutely luxurious. Black plastic bags full of well-water soak up the sun's heat during the day. By mid-afternoon they're too hot to use, but by late evening you can hoist one over the wooden scaffolding and scrub away at least some of the sweat and grime of the day.

Furniture shops are scarce in Helmand, so the boys have improvised. Cookhouse benches are fashioned from boxes that once housed Javelin heat-seeking anti-tank missiles. A few Hesco frames have been lashed together to create the shower cubicle – which provides a modicum of privacy, from the waist down at least.

I love it here. It feels good to be back.

Our block is about forty feet long and twenty wide, with a slanting roof and a hole cut at either end of the mud walls to let in the light. Aluminium cots, cocooned in giant mosquito nets, line each wall. I jettison my body-armour and peel off my sweat-soaked shirt. You never get used to the heat; you just learn to live with being constantly drenched.

I have a quick strip wash outside and make my way over to the cookhouse – another dilapidated, fly-infested mud hut. We all live on rations in Garmsir: cereal, bread and tinned sausage for breakfast, and whatever they can rustle up from the twelve-man ration-packs for lunch and dinner. Once a week, when the chefs are cleaning out the kitchen, they issue us with American 'Meals Ready to Eat'. The food is awful, but it's not the cooks' fault. The ingredients are limited, to say the least, and trying to feed 200 people on ration-packs alone is an almost impossible task.

As I join the queue, a medic yells, 'Don't take any lip off him, Chef. Go on ... make him have seconds ...'

The cookhouse fills with laughter.

But the outbreak of cheerfulness is short-lived. News comes through that Operation Minimize has been called. It means another British soldier has been killed and nobody can use the satellite phones or emails to contact their loved ones back home until the deceased's next of kin have been informed.

Derek and I grab our weapons and head across the sand to the ops room, where the Quick Response Force are waiting for the next imminent call-out.

There's a live radio feed booming out of the speakers, transmitting the battle group and company radio traffic. The signallers are scribbling frantically, trying to log the activity, while on an adjacent table the ops officer and his team pore over maps, planning the arrest of an insurgent commander who's using the proceeds from the poppy harvest to direct operations across the province.

Derek grabs the ops warrant officer and asks him about the fatality.

'Some EOD bloke,' he says.

'Do you have any details?' I ask him.

He opens up the brigade log on his computer screen and starts to read aloud.

A high-risk search team detected a confirmed IED while they were clearing a route for the Royal Scottish Regiment in and around the western side of Musa Qaleh.

'Looks like the ATO that was sorting it was hit by a secondary device.'

'Do you have a name?' I ask.

'Er . . . hang on . . . um . . . yep . . . it says here . . . WO2 O'Donnell.'

No. That can't be right. He's got four kids. I spoke to him only two days ago. There must be some mistake . . .

But, of course, there isn't.

My mate Gaz is dead.

I can't begin to count the number of people who owe their life to the bravery and skill of that one man.

How on earth did they get him?

I try to visualize what must have been going through his mind as he made that final walk. Gaz wouldn't have had a robot, but knowing that everyone depended on him, he would have cracked-on regardless.

He'd almost certainly have wanted to let the device soak – to leave it well alone until any timers had run down – but, given the tactical situation, it probably wouldn't have been an option. He wouldn't have wanted to risk the soldiers on the cordon by giving the Taliban the chance to organize an attack.

I know his every sense would have been on full alert as he briefed his team and prepared to face the task ahead. He'd have maintained a healthy measure of paranoia; it goes with the turf, and keeps you sharp. No matter how much faith an operator has in his equipment or skills, at some stage everyone's time – and luck – runs out.

His number two would have handed over Gaz's gear – nearly a 100lbs of equipment – as he prepared to take the Long Walk. The sun would already have started to fry his brain. Each footstep would have been laboured, the terrain difficult and uneven. Sweat would have poured off him as he shuffled towards the device. In those conditions, a hundred and fifty metres feels like a hundred and fifty miles.

I picture him finally crouching down on one knee – just short of the bomb – and examining it from a safe position, focusing on its circuitry, following the loop of wires through his binoculars.

He'd have dropped down onto his belt-buckle and taken out his metal detector and trip-wire feeler, then begun the fateful search. He'd have expected to find a secondary.

Fucking hell . . . That's it. The secondary.

An operator with Gaz's experience doesn't get caught out by a secondary, no matter how well concealed – not unless something's changed significantly. That's got to be it . . . The enemy must have been watching his every move, and modified their devices.

The bastards must have killed him with a new type of bomb.

Later that night, as I look out over the starlit desert, I sit and reflect on the life of that brilliant man and ask myself why he continued risking it day after day, in spite of the fact he had a loving wife and kids who needed and adored him.

And I know that if the cards had fallen in a different sequence, he would have been sitting here asking the same question of me.

Everybody in the trade is absolutely hooked. It doesn't just challenge and motivate us mentally; the fact that we get to save the lives of scores of people we don't know and will never meet is massively inspiring on every level. And each device we neutralize takes us one step closer to tracing and bringing down the bombmakers.

But make no mistake: it's about adrenalin as well as altruism. If he's honest, any operator, serving or retired, will tell you that the biggest, most powerful incentive is the buzz. It's living on the edge, in a world where everything is black and white; a world of truly elemental choices. It's not about paying council tax or remembering to put out the wheelie bins, it's about life and death. Rendering safe a terrorist bomb is not healthy, it's not normal, and it's probably the most dangerous thing we'll ever do. But it's also the most exciting.

I'm shooting the shit with the other FCO bodyguards in our Portakabin compound in Lashkar Gah. We're all ex-forces – mostly British infantry, airborne and commando forces, but with a smattering of Foreign Legion and firearms cops too. I love working with these guys. There are no big-timers, Walter Mittys or thugs-in-Oakleys here. Each one of them has been at the sharp end; each one of them has an extraordinary story to tell; each one of them has proved himself time and time again, both in his previous life and as a close-protection operator. They're quietly unassuming to a man, and as hard as fuck.

We've been out on tasks all day, travelling the length and breadth of the city. The Taliban have spent the day forming up on the opposite side of the Helmand river, preparing for a mass attack. Their intention must be to cross the heavily defended southern bridge. The governor's compound, the police HQ, the intelligence services building and the prison – where dozens of their mates are holed up – are all within easy reach of it.

Beyond the camp gates, the maze of city streets is crammed with potentially hostile forces; we have to scan every face, every building, every vehicle, searching for signs of an ambush, a sniper or a roadside IED.

Everywhere we go in our up-armoured Land Cruisers we're immediately surrounded by buzzing swarms of motorcycles. The intelligence cell has been telling us for days that cycle-borne suicide bombers are actively targeting Coalition patrols and private military contractors. We have to be fully alert at all times, primed, instantly ready to return fire.

Every time one of those bad boys gets too intimate, whichever BG is closest lowers his assault rifle deliberately enough to leave the rider in no doubt as to what's going to happen next, then brings it back into the shoulder, aims it straight at his face, and screams at him to stop.

It seems to work, but it's mentally and physically exhausting.

As we sit in the smoking area throwing back the coffee, a ripple of gunfire drifts towards us on the evening breeze. The Taliban have begun their night assault three kilometres away. For the next hour, all we can hear is the distant crump of RPG rounds striking the Afghan Army and British infantry positions – and the unmistakable roar of two Apache gunships opening up on the enemy with their 30mm cannons.

And then there's silence.

Moments later, one of the Army CMTs comes running into the compound. 'Any of you guys medic-trained?'

Three of us put up our hands.

'Good, we need your help. We've got five civvy casualties coming in by heli any minute. They've been hit by an IED.'

The three of us jump to our feet and sprint back after him.

We make the 200-metre dash to the sand-bagged medical centre just as the first of the Sea Kings touches down on the HLS and the doc starts barking instructions.

'We're from the Close Protection Team,' Rob says. 'Just let us know what you want us to do.' He's a former airborne-forces medic who trained as a bodyguard and then qualified as a paramedic. The other guy, Merv, is a former sapper.

'Thanks. If you go firm there, I'll get back to you in a moment.'

The aircrew begin stretchering in the badly bleeding and horribly disfigured casualties. Four of them are young children. The fifth is their father. The doc carries out the primary survey of each, before motioning them through to the operating rooms.

Airway – self-maintained. P3 . . .

'Breathing – O_2 supplementation. P2 . . .

'Next . . . circulation – no carotid pulse . . . begin immediate CPR . . .'

As the medics burst into action, trying to stem the bleeding, injecting morphine, attaching oxygen masks and applying the pads of the defibrillator, the doc asks us to start putting lines into them.

Each of us moves over to the nearest patient and begins tearing open saline and glucose drip sets. I try not to look into the face of the child I'm operating on. She can't be more than four years old; the same age as my daughter Ella. She's absolutely terrified. Her clothes have been torn to shreds in the blast. I glance across at her two sisters and older brother. All of them have lost at least one limb and blood seeps out of their bandaged stumps and lacerated bodies.

I take a deep breath to try to stop myself from losing it.

For more than an hour we fight to keep these kids alive. They drift in and out of consciousness. Those who are conscious sob silently, crying out occasionally to their father who's praying for a miracle. As I replace his bag of saline, I look into his troubled eyes. I promise myself never again to forget how incredibly privileged we are. These people have nothing.

We manage to stabilize four of them. But the six-year-old girl stops breathing again. The Godbox kicks immediately into alarm mode. 'Begin CPR . . . *begin CPR . . .*' The automated female voice sounds about as excited as a satnav warning of an approaching motorway exit.

'Begin CPR . . .' the doc echoes, as he moves swiftly to the little girl's side.

We spend the next thirty minutes trying to resuscitate her. Each of us takes it in turns to try to breathe life back into her. But it's no use. Her dark eyes stare sightlessly upwards. She's a bundle of rags on the operating table. Her father lets out a gut-wrenching howl that will follow me to the grave.

The three of us walk back to our compound in silence.

I find a quiet, dark corner and spark up a cigarette. As the tip glows in the darkness I think about the little girl lying on the table, robbed of her precious life.

Rob asks if we want a brew.

Merv and I shake our heads in mute unison. Neither of us much wants anything right now other than to be left alone. Rob carries on as if he's just returned from a trip to the NAAFI. It's not that he's immune from sorrow; it's just that he's seen this so many times before that he's learnt to build a different kind of wall around himself.

I wish I could do the same.

But I'm still standing by those petrified little kids and their poor father watching us fail to save his little girl's life. Then part of me isn't there at all. I'm back beside the lake in Bosnia . . .

Epilogue

*Men are not made for safe havens; the fullness of life is
in the hazards of life.*

Edith Hamilton

April 2010

Two weeks after Gaz died, I came back to the UK for his
funeral. The Roman Catholic church in Leamington
Spa was crammed with his friends, family and hundreds
of fellow soldiers. In the stairwells and corridors it was
standing-room only.

Six months later, he was awarded his second George
Medal *for repeated and sustained acts of immense bravery*
in Helmand. I imagine his wife and children responded
to the news with immense pride, but little comfort.

Those we leave behind are the unsung heroes. I just
wish I'd appreciated that rather earlier in my military
career. When I eventually got back from Afghanistan, it
was the first time I'd arrived at Heathrow without Lucy
and the girls being there to greet me.

I'd been a crap husband and an absent dad because I'd somehow convinced myself that my mission to save the world was more important. I'd selfishly thought life was at its best when shaken and stirred. I wanted to stay as close to the edge as I could without going over. What you risk reveals what you value, but by the time I realized that it was already too late.

After Gaz's funeral I met another quietly charismatic young ATO serving with Alpha Troop. I warmed to Staff Sergeant Olaf Schmid immediately. A former member of the Royal Marines' elite 3 Commando Brigade, he combined a sharp analytical mind with a calm and philosophical disposition – perfect qualities for a high-threat operator. He was killed neutralizing a device in the Sangin region on 31 October 2009, the day before he was due to return home. He was thirty years old.

When Captain Daniel Read lost his life in Helmand Province in January 2010, he was the 247th British soldier to do so since 2001 – and the fourth ATO in eighteen months. But we have yet to count the real cost of the conflict. More soldiers committed suicide after returning home from the Falklands than the 255 who were lost there in action. Twenty-four were killed in the first Gulf War – but seven times as many veterans have since taken their own lives. And there are more ex-military in prison, on parole or serving community sentences than are currently deployed in Afghanistan.

Post-traumatic stress disorder is a ticking bomb that requires more than a remote-controlled Wheelbarrow to neutralize it.

The success of Help for Heroes has resoundingly demonstrated the public's support for the families of the dead, and the many who have been scarred in body and mind by the continuing hostilities. It gives me hope that for them, at least, what began in anger need not inevitably end in shame.

When the CO first tasked us with the development of counter-suicide-bomber tactics, some dyed-in-the-wool Northern Ireland veterans believed we were wasting valuable time and resources. But it wasn't raining when Noah started work on the Ark. Few parts of our world have remained untouched by terrorism in the last two decades – but the fact that its champions appear, in most instances, to have failed to achieve their objectives should help us sleep at night. Bomb plots continue to surface at an alarming rate, but have been largely thwarted by the hard work and ceaseless dedication of our intelligence and security services.

Less reassuringly, on 28 July 2008 the Pentagon confirmed that Al Qaeda's senior bombmaker and chemical weapons expert, Abu Khabab al-Masri, was killed in a missile strike in Pakistan, and Rashid Rauf, the alleged ringleader of the airline bomb plot, mysteriously managed to escape from his Pakistani jail on 14 December 2007, only to be reported dead the following year. Which means that thus far the two of them appear to have been dispatched no less than five times.

And the sabres continue to rattle in Iran. In October 2009 the Revolutionary Guard vowed to take revenge on Britain and the US for the deaths of six of its commanders and thirty-seven others in a bombing they blamed on terrorists supported by 'the Great Satan and its ally'. As Northwest Airlines Flight 253 made its final descent into Detroit on Christmas Day 2009, a twenty-three-year-old Nigerian Muslim passenger attempted to detonate the plastic explosives sewn into his underwear. Umar Farouk Abdulmutallab studied in Britain and had been trained by Al Qaeda in the Yemen. Flight 253 had 289 people on board. It was only by sheer good fortune that his device failed to explode.

Did I manage to have any impact whatsoever in the war on drugs? I served in Colombia and Afghanistan, which between them continue to supply more than 90 per cent of the UK's cocaine and heroin, and more opium is being produced in Afghanistan now than when the Taliban were in charge – so I guess the answer's no. But we directly and indirectly disrupted numerous terrorist operations and stopped some very bad people from doing some very bad things.

As Major Hudson predicted, we sought out danger far

from the comforts and the well-lit avenues of life; we pitted our souls against the unknown and sought stimulation in the comfort of the brave; we experienced cold, hunger, heat and thirst and we survived to see another challenge and another dawn.

He said that it wouldn't be easy, but that it would be worth it. And he was right.

Glossary

Types of improvised explosive device (IED)

CWIED
Command-wire IED. An IED utilizing an electrical firing cable which affords the user complete control over the device right up to the moment of initiation.

DTMF
Duel Tone Multi Frequency (a type of radio-controlled) IED.

RCIED
Radio-controlled IED. The trigger for this IED is controlled by a radio link. The device is constructed so that the receiver is connected to an electrical firing circuit and the transmitter operated by the perpetrator at a

distance. A signal from the transmitter causes the receiver to trigger a firing pulse, which operates a switch. Usually the switch fires an initiator; however, the output may also be used to remotely arm an explosive circuit. Often the transmitter and receiver operate on a matched coding system which prevents the RCIED from being initiated by spurious radio frequency signals.

Cell phone RCIED — A radio-controlled IED incorporating a cell phone which is modified and connected to an electrical firing circuit. Cell phones operate in the UHF band in line of sight with base transceiver station (BTS) antennae sites. Commonly, receipt of a paging signal by the phone is sufficient to initiate the IED firing circuit.

Petrol bomb

A hand-thrown device containing a flammable composition (not necessarily petrol) that functions on impact. It is not considered an incendiary.

Pipe bomb

A crude IED containing either high or low explosive confined within a metal tube sealed at each end. The device is usually initiated by a crude timer such as a hand-lit fuse and delivered by throwing. In effect it is a crude hand-propelled time IED.

Secondary device

The underlying purpose of a secondary is to attack those involved in responding to an initial IED incident. Usually secondary IEDs are deliberately placed to target EOD teams, possible ICP locations, or predicted first-responders' cordon or monitoring positions. Successful secondary-device attacks are undertaken by

459

terrorists who are able to correctly predict first-responders' response procedures to a primary IED incident.

Suicide IED Explosive devices that are delivered to a target and initiated by a human being with the deliberate loss of life of the bomber. The logic behind such attacks is the belief that an IED delivered by a human has a greater chance of achieving success than any other method of attack. In addition, there is the psychological impact of terrorists prepared to deliberately sacrifice or martyr themselves for their cause. Commonly, suicide IEDs are worn by the bomber or carried in personal luggage. In addition, suicide devices have been incorporated into vehicles, bicycles and powerboats.

VBIED   Vehicle-borne IED. An IED
that incorporates a vehicle as an
integral element of its
construction. The vehicle
provides concealment for IED
components, and contributes to
the fragmentation hazard of an
explosion. Vehicles are usually
cars or SUVs but can be
anything from a bicycle or
handcart to a lorry. VBIEDs are
mobile, and thus afford the
terrorist a degree of tactical
flexibility. The quantity of
explosive within a VBIED may
vary depending on the type of
damage the perpetrator wishes
to achieve and the availability of
explosive. VBIEDs may be
activated by timer, remotely by
command initiation systems or
by suicide. In addition,
incidents have been recorded
where VBIEDs have been
driven to target areas by victims
of coercion, or in ignorance
(proxy).

VOIED	These are designed to function upon contact with a victim; also known as booby-traps. Victim-operated IED switches are often well hidden from the victim or disguised as innocuous everyday objects. They are operated by means of movement. Switching methods include: tripwire, pressure mats, spring-loaded release, push, pull or tilt. Common forms of VOIED include the under-vehicle IED (UVIED) and improvised landmines.

Types of explosive

ANFO	Ammonium nitrate fuel oil
C4	Composition 4 – military plastic explosive (US)
HMTD	Hexamethylenetriperoxidediamine
HMX	High-melt explosive
NG	Nitroglycerine
PE4	British plastic explosive
PE4-A:	Portuguese plastic explosive (used in massive quantities by Iraqi insurgents)

PETN	Pentaerythritol tetranitrate
RDX	Research developed explosive – cyclotromethylenetrinitramine
TNT	Trinitrotoluene (standard military high explosive)
TATP	Triacetone triperoxide

General

2i/c	Second-in-command
5.56	5.56×45mm round fired from SA80 A2 assault rifle
7.62 short	7.62×39mm round fired from AK-47, RPD and SKS
9 milly	9mm pistol
AC 130	'Spectre' aerial gun platform based on a Hercules C130 airframe
Actions-on	The term used to describe SOPs for a given scenario
AGC	Adjutant General's Corps
AK-47	Soviet Kalashnikov assault rifle; fires 7.62mm short ammunition
AOR	Area of responsibility
Apache	US and UK twin-engine attack helicopter (a.k.a. AH-64)
APC	Armoured personnel carrier
AQ	Al Qaeda

Asp	A telescopic truncheon
AT	Anti-tank (usually landmine)
ATO	Ammunition technical officer (the Army's counter-terrorist bomb disposal operators, all members of the Royal Logistic Corps)
AV	Anti-vehicle (usually landmine)
Beasting	Arduous physical training session
Bergen	Pack carried by British forces
BDO	Bomb disposal officer (specialists in de-mining and Second World War aircraft bombs; all members of the Royal Engineers)
Bleep	Royal Signals ECM expert
Blue	Friendlies/friendly forces
Bluey	British Forces airmail letter
Bravo	A known or suspected terrorist
CAM	Chemical agent monitor
Casevac	Casualty evacuation
CBA	Combat body armour
CBRN	Chemical, Biological, Radiological, Nuclear
CENTCOM	US Central Command overseeing security in the Middle East, Central Asia and Northern Africa. The command is headquartered at MacDill Airforce Base in Tampa, Florida.
CMT	Combat medical technician

CREW	Counter Radio-Controlled IED Electronic Warfare. Various jamming devices employed by US forces to combat radio-controlled IEDs.
CEXC	Combined Explosive Exploitation Cell
CF	US-led coalition forces
CID	Criminal Investigation Department
CO	Commanding officer (usually a lieutenant colonel)
Come-on	A technique used by terrorists to draw a victim or target into the vicinity of an unanticipated IED or other type of ambush. Successful come-on scenarios are usually executed by terrorists who are able to accurately predict the victim's reaction to a particular event or set of circumstances.
COP	Close observation platoon
CPA	Coalition Provisional Authority
CSM	Company sergeant major
CTR	Close target recce
DA	Defence attaché
Det, the	The EOD detachment
Dish-dasha	An ankle-length shirt, usually with long sleeves, similar to a robe
Div	Divisional HQ
DS	Directing staff

Duro	Bucher Duro high-mobility off-road EOD truck
DZ	Drop zone
ECM	Electronic counter-measures
EFP	Explosively formed projectile. An armour-piercing explosive
Endex	End of exercise
EOD	Explosive ordnance disposal
ERV	Emergency rendezvous
FARC	Revolutionary Armed Forces of Colombia
FOB	Forward operating base
GIGN	National Gendarmerie Intervention Group, commonly abbreviated GIGN: the French Gendarmerie's elite Special Operations counter-terrorism and hostage rescue unit
GPS	Global positioning system
Green Zone	The international zone in Baghdad
Gympie	GPMG (general-purpose machine-gun)
HE	High explosive
HME	Homemade explosive
Head-shed	A person in authority
Hesco	Sand-filled protective blast wall made by Hesco Bastion
HLS	Helicopter landing site
Hotrod	Water-filled IED disrupter
HQ	Headquarters

ICP	Incident control point
IED	Improvised explosive device
IEDD	Improvised explosive device disposal
Int	Intelligence
IPS	Iraqi Police Service
IR	Infrared
ISO	International Organization for Standardization: shipping container
JAM	Jaish al-Mahdi (Mahdi Army)
KES	Keyless entry system – radio-controlled automobile locking/unlocking system
LCD	Liquid crystal display
Mike	A minute (when used in the context of radio voice procedure)
Minimi	Light machine-gun firing 5.56mm ammunition
MO	Modus operandi
MWR	Morale, welfare and recreation
MSR	Main supply route
NAAFI	Navy, Army and Air Force Institute
NBC	Nuclear, biological and chemical warfare
NCO	Non-commissioned officer
Net	Communications network
NVG	Night-vision goggles
OC	Officer commanding
OP	Observation post
OSNAZ	*Osobogo naznacheniya* (or 'special

purpose'), a general term used for a variety of Russian special forces.

PATO	Principal ammunition technical officer
Pig stick	A water disrupter used to disrupt thin-cased IEDs
PIR	Passive infra-red sensor
PIRA	Provisional Irish Republican Army
PJI	RAF parachute jump instructor
PRR	Personal role radio
PTSD	Post-traumatic stress disorder
PWRR	Princess of Wales' Royal Regiment
QBO	Quick battle orders
QRF	Quick Reaction Force
RAF Regt	Royal Air Force Regiment (the RAF's infantry)
RAMC	Royal Army Medical Corps
RE	Royal Engineers
REME	Royal Electrical and Mechanical Engineers
RESA	Royal Engineers search adviser
RIB	Rigid inflatable boat
RF	Radio frequency
RLC	Royal Logistic Corps
RMP	Royal Military Police
RPG	Rocket-propelled grenade
RQMS	Regimental quartermaster sergeant
RSM	Regimental sergeant major

RSP	Render safe procedure
RV	Rendezvous
SA80	SA80-A2 5.56mm assault rifle
SAM	Surface-to-air missile
Sangar	Fortified bunker/sentry position
Security Service	MI5
Security Services	Collective term for the British intelligence, military and law enforcement organizations responsible for national security.
SF	Security forces, or Special Forces
Shack, the	Home of the WIS at Divisional HQ
Shemagh	An Arab headscarf
Shrike	A hand-held 'exploder' device used to initiate IED disrupter weapons
SIB	Special Investigation Branch
Sig	Sig Sauer 226 pistol
Simplex	Secure door entry system
Sitrep	Situation report
SKS	Russian semi-automatic rifle
Snatch	British armoured Land Rover
SO2	Staff Officer Grade II (usually a major or equivalent rank)
SOP	Standard operating procedure
Spectre	see AC 130
SR / S&R	Surveillance and reconnaissance
STT	Special-to-theatre (training course)

TA	Territorial Army
Thuraya	Satellite phone
TPU	Timing and power unit
UAV	Unmanned aerial vehicle
UXO	Unexploded ordnance (normally associated with conventional munitions)
WIS	Weapons Intelligence Section
WIT	Weapons Intelligence Teams, tasked to US military's counter-IED effort
WMIK	Weapons Mounted Installation Kit (refers to a heavily armed Land Rover variant)
WPNS	Weapons
YPA	Yugoslavian People's Army

Picture Acknowledgements

All photographs have been kindly supplied by the author or approved by the MoD except those listed below. Every effort has been made to trace copyright holders; those overlooked are invited to get in touch with the publishers.

First section
page 4: Army HQ, Thiepval, Lisburn, 7 October 1996: Brian Little/PA Archive/Press Association Images
page 8: detonator cord match, Metropolitan Police handout, 28 February 2005: Metropolitan Police/PA/PA Archive/Press Association Images; police firearms team prepare to enter a building: © Altered Images/Alamy

Second section
page 5: composite image: PA Archive/Press Association Images; vehicle detonating EFP: HL Studios

page 8: WO2 Gary O'Donnell, Iraq, May 2006: © Rex Features

Index

473

INDEX

INDEX